SOCIOLOGY AND THE WORLD'S RELIGIONS

Sociology and the World's Religions

Malcolm B. Hamilton

Senior Lecturer
Department of Sociology
University of Reading

St. Martin's Press
New York

St. Martin's Press, Scholarly and Reference Division,
175 Fifth Avenue, New York, N.Y. 10010

First published in the United States of America in 1998

This book is printed on paper suitable for recycling and
made from fully managed and sustained forest sources.

Printed in Great Britain

ISBN 0–312–21169–4 (clothbound)
ISBN 0–312–21170–8 (paperback)

Library of Congress Cataloging-in-Publication Data
Hamilton, Malcolm (Malcolm B.)
Sociology and the world's religions / Malcolm B. Hamilton.
p.   cm.
Includes bibliographical references and index.
ISBN 0–312–21169–4. — ISBN 0–312–21170–8 (paper)
1. Religions.   2. Religion and sociology.   I. Title.
BL80.2.H273 1997
306.6—dc21   97–40504
                                                  CIP

For my daughters
Kate, Emmalie and Sarah

Contents

Acknowledgements

I am grateful to those of my colleagues at the University of Reading who have helped me to clarify some of the ideas in this book and to bring it to fruition. I am particularly grateful to Christie Davies and Peter Waddington, who read and commented upon various versions of the manuscript. Thanks are also due to Bryan Wilson, Jim Beckford and Michael Hornsby-Smith who read an earlier manuscript out of which this books grew. I would like to thank, also, Stephen Sharot who read the chapter on Judaism, the concluding sections of which are much the clearer for his comments. None of these colleagues bear any responsibility for the many deficiencies which, no doubt, remain. Finally, I am indebted to Janet Binns for making the numerous corrections to the computer files after various stages of editing.

MALCOLM B. HAMILTON

1 Introduction

It is a strange contradiction that while sociological studies of religion are generally regarded as being towards the fringes of the discipline, those who are normally regarded as the founding fathers of sociology gave considerable prominence to religion in their work. Emile Durkheim devoted a lengthy volume to the analysis of religion and Max Weber's scholarship in this area produced no less than five volumes in English translation.[1] Marx, it is true, had much less to say about it although the little he did have to say was no less profound than the work of the other founding fathers, and has had no less influence. Also striking about the work of the founding fathers is their interest in, and appreciation of, the importance and relevance of the religious systems found in other cultures and civilisations, while much contemporary sociology of religion, in contrast, has confined itself to the study of religion in contemporary Western societies and even then rather narrowly to esoteric sects and cults, and to the study not of religion but of its absence, that is to say of secularisation. Durkheim's *Elementary Forms of the Religious Life* relies almost entirely upon data relating to the native peoples of Australia while Weber looked to China, India and to Ancient Palestine as much as to the Christian world.

Weber's interest in these other great traditions was, of course, stimulated by his work on the 'Protestant ethic'; was it the religious traditions of other great civilisations that promoted a very different economic ethos to that found in parts of the West? While the sociology of religion has shown rather slight interest in these other great traditions, despite its preoccupation with the work of Weber on the 'Protestant ethic', scholars from a variety of backgrounds have often turned to sociology for insights which might further their understanding of the origins and historical development of the particular religions that are the objects of their specialist interest. The impact of sociology on historians of religion, theologians and experts in comparative religion has been far from uniform, it is true, but in some areas, such as Biblical studies, it has been very extensive.

Along with the founding fathers of sociology the fathers, or perhaps one should say grandfathers, of anthropology were equally aware of the centrality and significance of religious belief and behaviour; they could hardly have failed to have been, given the type of societies they were concerned with. Herbert Spencer and Edmund Tylor devoted large sections of their major treatises to religion, while the work of Sir James Frazer was largely devoted to the subject. Freud, too, gave much attention to religion in his later work, albeit to celebrate its demise. The successors of 'armchair' anthropologists such as Tylor and Frazer established the subject as one based in empirical fieldwork and participant observation. Malinowski and Radcliffe-Brown devoted much time to the investigation, description and analysis of the religious systems of the cultures which they studied at first hand. Since their day, anthropologists have increasingly sought to carry out fieldwork in complex societies and have frequently focused upon the religious life of communities located within vastly more complex societies than those studied by Malinowski and Radcliffe-Brown and which espouse one or other of the great world religions.

Again, work of this kind in such societies is hardly likely to overlook the prominence of religion, but sociology, to its great detriment, has tended to adopt a stance of parochial indifference to the findings of anthropology, which it has tended to regard as the irrelevant study of obscure and imminently extinct curiosities. Its tendency to overlook the importance of religion or to be uninterested in it, as seemed to be the case with much twentieth century sociology, was the product of an ethos which saw secularisation as an ever more widespread and dominant process and religion as an increasingly anachronistic phenomenon in a world dominated by scientific and technological rationality. Developments in recent decades have substantially altered this view. For one thing, sociology, perhaps as a consequence of the process of globalisation with which it has much concerned itself of late, has at long last discovered other cultures and civilisations. For another, they have recently tended to force their attention upon the West quite vigorously and often most effectively as a consequence of religious developments and movements. It is Islamic rather than Middle Eastern society that the West now views with some alarm; it is Hindu rather than Indian nationalism which stirs its interest and concern. Secularisation has come to look like a rather localised affair. And secularisation has itself been questioned with the rise of fundamentalism, the charismatic movement and a host of sects, cults and religious movements in the heartlands of scientific and technological rationality.

The legacy of the founding fathers of sociology, anthropology and related disciplines is, then, one that is likely to be drawn upon increasingly if these disciplines turn their attention once again towards religion and to the variety of religious traditions that exist and have existed; one might predict they will do so if the secularisation thesis is as much outdated as it is often claimed to be. One purpose of this book is to encourage this, to survey sociologically inspired work on the world's religions whether by sociologists, historians or theologians, and to stimulate the comparative approach in the sociology of religion. Although there are many anthropological, sociological and sociologically-informed studies of various aspects of the world's religious traditions they tend to be compartmentalised and receive little attention from experts in other areas. Indologists speak infrequently to Sinologists, Biblical scholars infrequently to Islamicists, and so on. At the risk of being a jack of all trades and master of none, this book seeks to survey and bring this work together. It seeks to show, also, what sociology has contributed and can contribute to the understanding of the religious traditions of the world. In this it must inevitably look heavily to the work of Max Weber and in doing so seeks to emphasise the importance and intrinsic interest of his studies of the world religions and place them more prominently alongside the body of his work that has attracted so much more attention, almost in fact to the exclusion of his work on world religions. Weber's work provides to a major extent the organising principle of this book. Apart from the chapter on aspects of religion in tribal societies, most chapters on the major religious traditions begin with a discussion of Weber's work and its significance.

While there is a large and accumulating body of sociological work on the world's religions it is by no means systematic or even in its coverage. While Weber's investigations were informed by a very specific purpose and conducted from a very particular angle, namely the likely impact upon economic conduct of religious ideas and institutions, they sought to be as comprehensive as possible. No one since Weber has attempted anything remotely as ambitious and broad in scope. Scholars, in conformity with the late twentieth century ethos of specialism, have tended to stick to their niche. The result is an enormous variety of work covering specific areas, topics and periods in somewhat random and haphazard fashion since they have been chosen on the basis of individual inclination and interest rather than being informed by an overall strategy of enquiry. This makes the task of surveying them and bringing them together all the more difficult since it is harder to see how one relates to another. In no way then can this book be taken to be a sociology *of* the world's religions, an endeavour which, in any case, would be unrealisable. It must, then, of necessity reflect the rather random and patchy nature of the work that it seeks to survey. Even then it must be selective in its emphasis. Broadly it concentrates on work that bears upon the macro-sociological approach that was characteristic of Weber's work, though, of course, covering a wider range of themes than was the object of his focus. Descriptive ethnographic accounts of the minutiae of village religious life have, therefore, not been utilised unless they bear upon the broader picture. Many do not, but some relate the detail of the day-to-day religious life of the communities they have studied, to the broader issues.

The broader issues are those of the origins, main historical development and social impact of religious traditions. Origins in particular are of central significance in the case of the major world religions. As Turner (1976) argues in the case of Christianity and Islam, while in their historical development considerable diversity of interpretation arises at different times and in different places, such interpretation tends to be constrained by the possibilities allowed by the character of the origins of the religion which acquires enormous normative significance. On the other hand varied interpretations are possible and there is a degree of flexibility in religious ideas that is generally far greater than in other systems of ideas. Changing social conditions will tend to promote different selection of elements and understandings of doctrines.

Exponents of the sociological approach to the understanding of religion bring, of course, their own distinctive theoretical stance to their studies of religion which guide and inform their work on religious systems and traditions. Selection, emphasis and interpretation of data is always informed by some theoretical stance even though more or less consciously or explicitly. An excursion through this theoretical terrain is essential to an understanding of substantive treatments of aspects of the world's religious which are discussed in subsequent chapters.[2]

Evans-Pritchard (1965) distinguishes between psychological and sociological theoretical approaches to the understanding of religion, further subdividing the former into intellectualist and emotionalist theories. Psychological approaches locate the sources of religion in the individual, while sociological approaches locate them in the social and collective. Intellectualist approaches see religion as an attempt to understand and explain the world and emphasise reason, while emotionalist approaches see religion as a response to those circumstances of life that elicit an affective reaction, be it fear, anxiety, wonder or astonishment. Evans-Pritchard's categories, while somewhat crude, will serve usefully to organise our discussion of theoretical approaches.

These fit only approximately into the various pigeon holes Evans-Pritchard provides and, at times, have to be rather awkwardly thrust into them since none conform purely to the essence of the category, but embody to a varying extent features of each. For the most part, however, their fundamental features belong more to one rather than to the others and the schema does at least offer a means of orienting ourselves among the diversity of approaches.

Intellectualist approaches were characteristic of the nineteenth century and particularly of evolutionary theories of human society which tended to see religion as an outmoded set of beliefs and ideas. Characteristic of the work on religion of Comte, Tylor, Spencer and Frazer was their conviction that human society and belief systems undergo a process of evolutionary development in which better understandings of the world are developed and supplant previous, largely magical and religious, ideas.[3] For these writers religion stems from a human tendency, first identified by Hume in his *Natural History of Religion*, to model their view of the world upon their own experience of themselves and their own natures. Since they themselves seemed animated by something with purposes and intentions, so all things are similarly animated by a soul or spirit. In the course of dreams the normal constraints of time and space seem not to hold, so the spirit must be unconstrained by time and space. Through the human capacity to, and proclivity for, generalising from observation and experience, belief in a spiritual realm grew up. The animating spirit of the tree gave rise, in Comte's view, to the idea of the god of the forest; since one tree is much like another so all trees must be governed in their natures by a general spirit of trees. The great gods governing major aspects of nature and reality, such as the forest, the sun, the moon and so on, being vastly more powerful than human beings, had to be propitiated to avoid disaster and, on the other hand, could be persuaded and enjoined to provide benefits. Magical thought and practice, in contrast, rested upon a belief in impersonal forces. Central to the thinking of Tylor and Frazer on magic was the principle of association of ideas or homeopathy. Things which resembled one another or which had been in close contact with one another were believed to be somehow intimately connected with one another. What one did to one would take its effect upon the other. The essential ideas can be found in accounts, whether they be true or false, of European witchcraft practices. The witch might make an effigy of the victim, and the injuries inflicted upon the effigy accompanied by the spell would happen to the intended victim. Or the witch would procure some item that had been in intimate contact with the victim, nail clippings, hair trimmings or clothing and cast the spell upon them.

Much discredited for their speculative character as the specific ideas of these nineteenth-century evolutionary theories are, the broad assumptions of their approach continue to form the basis of a school of thought, neo-Tyloreanism, which has been prominent in anthropological circles and which has been particularly explicitly explicated in the work of Robin Horton.[4] This retains the essential idea that religion is fundamentally about explaining and understanding the world. Its central aims are explanation and prediction. A strong strand of this approach is also found in the current rational choice theory of Stark and Bainbridge (1987). For these theorists religion consists essentially of supernatural explanations of how desired rewards of a very general order of significance may be obtained in compensation for the failure to obtain them through more mundane means.

Quite distinct from intellectualist approaches, but still locating religion firmly within the individual, are the emotionalist approaches. In this category belong the works of Marett and Malinowski and also that of Freud, although the latter is very different from the others and must be treated separately.

Marett, writing early in the century,[5] prefigured some of the ideas of Malinowski who is the founding father of the fieldwork and participant observation tradition of British social anthropology. Malinowski's work, unlike that of Marett, was thus based upon sound and detailed first-hand observation of the religious, magical and ritual beliefs and practices of the society of the Trobriand Islands of Melanesia.[6] Oddly, his conclusions share much with Marett's more speculative work. For Marett religion has little to do with reason, at least as far as its roots are concerned, but everything to do with emotion. The emotions involved are those experienced in the face of that which inspires fear and wonder, anxiety and awe – a sense of the other, the divine – which the Polynesians call *mana*, the term Marett adopts to designate to it. Religion stems from experience and not from thought and reason. Ritual is the immediate response to such experience and is fundamental to religion. Beliefs and the cognitive dimension are merely secondary.

Marett's approach fails to account for the situations which generate the religious experience, the things which inspire awe and wonder, the things which have *mana*, extremely varied as they are across different societies. It is difficult to see how one could understand this diversity without recourse to the specific beliefs involved in each case.

Malinowski's views are more firmly founded in observation of concrete situations and the anxieties generated in and by them. Magical behaviour stems from the inability to ensure important outcomes or keep dangers at bay. It is the 'spontaneous enactment of the desired end in a practical impasse' (Malinowski, 1974, p. 80). It is 'founded on the belief that hope cannot fail nor desire deceive' (ibid., p. 87). This is graphically illustrated by Malinowski in his use of the example of Trobriand fishing techniques. Lagoon fishing uses a plant source of poison to stun fish which can then be easily retrieved from the water, yielding a fairly certain catch. Deep sea fishing is a dangerous enterprise using nets and has a very uncertain outcome. It is significant that deep sea fishing is steeped in magic while very little attaches to lagoon fishing. It is the danger and uncertainly that creates anxiety and tension in the individual which has to be reduced by a cathartic ritual which generally acts out the desired end and generates in the mind a conviction that it will thus be secured.

In more general terms, the dangers and uncertainties of life generate notions of Providence and Immortality. The former involves the belief in the existence of a power which is sympathetic to man and his problems in life, and can be harnessed to his aid. The latter belief is essential for mental stability and social order in the face of the inevitable bereavement and death that human existence entails.

It is such events as death and the other major life crises which for Malinowski underlie religion proper, as opposed to magic, and the type of rituals associated with religion. Such rituals serve to promote beliefs and responses which are stabilising and constructive in the face of the otherwise potentially highly destructive reactions that such events would tend to provoke.

While this type of approach adds enormously to the intellectualist position in emphasising those emotions clearly related to the religious view which intellectualism tended grossly to neglect, it suffers from an inability to account for specific religious beliefs and practices. Rituals are not the spontaneous reaction to anxieties, but the culturally determined, socially sanctioned, learned, and in many cases expected and often obligatory behaviours, deemed appropriate to the given circumstances. Emotionalist theories cannot dispense with cognitive variables without creating insuperable puzzles and difficulties for itself.

If Malinowski's views were based upon direct observation of the beliefs and practices of 'primitive' peoples, Freud's approach was based upon observation and analysis of the mental problems of his patients.[7] Freud perceived a parallel between the supposed mental development of the human individual and that of the species. Just as the individual goes through a sequence of stages in his or her mental and emotional life in infancy and childhood, Freud argued, so too the species has gone through a similar sequence in its development. Corresponding to the stages of narcissism, object selection and maturity in the development of the individual, so the species has passed through the stages of magic and religion and is reaching the stage of science. In both cases the mental and emotional life is essentially the life of the libido or sexual impulse or is inextricably bound up with it.

Narcissism is characterised by a focus upon the infant's own body and need for bodily gratification. The libido is not yet directed to an external object. At this stage the infant develops an ego and this becomes the object of its libidinal desires. When unable to satisfy desires in reality the infant tends to seek to satisfy them in fantasy and imagination. Corresponding to this stage, the stage of magic in the development of the species is characterised by a similar tendency to satisfy desires in the mind and to resort to fantasy, and specifically to rely upon the association of ideas that Tylor and Frazer spoke of. Thought is substituted for action. The patient who is suffering from neurosis is arrested in his or her emotional/libidinal development, according to Freud at this narcissistic stage and is given to ritualistic and superstitious behaviour, just as the practitioner of magic is.

Religion corresponds, in Freud's parallel of stages, to that of object selection. It is at this stage of the development of the individual that the Oedipus complex develops. The infant now finds an external object for its libidinal impulses, namely the parent of the opposite sex. For the infant male this libidinal desire for the mother results in the father being seen as a rival and threat. Deeply ambivalent emotions develop in relation to the, on the one hand protecting and caring but, on the other hand, punishing father. The father becomes an object of hatred as well as of affection resulting in a sense of anxiety and guilt. Anxiety concerning forbidden desires also intensifies in the process of socialisation.

In the corresponding religious phase of development the external world and nature in general takes on the characteristics of the father. Like a father it provides, but can also inflict privations. At this phase of development there is a tendency to attempt to deal with nature on the pattern of human relationships. That with the father provides the most immediately available, familiar and appropriate model. Nature is anthropomorphised, mollified and propitiated, persuaded and cajoled. An anthropomorphised nature takes on the guise of gods and spirits.

God is thus nothing other than an exalted father who is feared and revered.

Despite its faults the Freudian approach in one or other modified version has proved attractive to theorists of the world religions. Its deficiencies largely relate to its gross ethnocentricism and inapplicability to cultures in which the relations between parents and children, as well as conceptions of gods, are very different from those of late nineteenth- and early twentieth-century central European society. Its psychoanalytic base has equally, of course, been much challenged. In forms suitably modified to overcome its ethnocentrism, however, many theorists have found it can provide insights into aspects of religious belief and behaviour.

Intellectualist and emotionalist approaches focus upon the individual. For sociological theories proper religion stems from social sources not from individual needs or proclivities. Perhaps the earliest theorists who belong in this category are Marx and Engels. Marx nowhere in his work develops a general theoretical approach to religion; his views can be found in rather brief statements scattered throughout his writings.[8] There are broadly two strands to religion according to Marx; religion is at one and the same time the opium of the people, and an ideological support of an exploitative system and the position of its ruling class. In the alienated conditions of class society mystification of the real relations that its members have with society prevails. In such a condition, society, which is the people's own creation, is seen to be the creation of a power beyond themselves. Instead of seeing themselves as creators of their own conditions of existence, the quintessentially human characteristic, they see themselves as determined by an external force. In conditions of class-divided society this upside down view of things reflects the actual situation, since in such conditions they are not masters of their fate nor shapers of their own circumstances of life but victims of a system that they are forced to perpetuate by their own actions. This situation finds its expression in the form of notions of God who is said to have created man in his own image, whereas the truth is that God is the creation of man; a creation in which the characteristics of man appear in an exaggerated and exalted form.

The sufferings and privations of life for the exploited and oppressed lead them to turn to this God for succour and hope. Religion is the sigh of the oppressed creature, the opium of the people. This mystified form of thought can only impede real transformation of the conditions of exploitation and oppression. It promotes only resignation and the fantastic hope of something better in the next life or in some millennial expectation.

Such mystification serves the ruling classes well. It takes on the character of an ideology which justifies and legitimates an unjust social order in making it seem inevitable, preordained and unchangeable. More than this, it promises salvation in some other life or existence only on the condition of acceptance of the conditions of this life and existence. Ultimate deliverance from injustice and exploitation is made conditional upon acceptance of the prevailing social order and one's place in it, obedience to the law and social norms and conformity with values and expectations of the ruling class.

Religion can thus be both an expression of protest and a form of ideology despite the seeming contradiction between these claims, because not only does it not threaten the status quo in seeking to resolve problems only in fantasy but it actually serves to support the status quo. It is probably Marx's emphasis on religion as ideology that poses the greatest problem for his analysis. Religion undoubtedly may be and has often been put to ideological uses but it is difficult to see it as always ideological. The ideological aspect of religion seems parasitic on its more fundamental roots which, for Marx, lie in its opposition to oppression and its desire for a better condition of existence. But the injustices and sufferings that have to be endured in life cannot all be traced back to class division and exploitation. There would thus seem to be a role for religion, even in a Marxist perspective, in a social order from which all exploitation and injustice had been eliminated. Marx believed that once the proletarian revolution had instituted a new and just society there would be no further need for religion. But even if such a society were possible, suffering and misfortune would still occur, the major questions of the meaning of life in the face of inevitable death would not dissolve away, a sense of wonder and mystery in the world we see around us would remain. Marx remains rather silent on these matters.

Not dissimilar in some ways to Marx in his views on religion, Emile Durkheim saw religion as a projection of the relationship we have with society.[9] For Durkheim this is a relationship of dependence of the individual upon society. Society endures after we have perished, it makes us what we are through socialisation, it is the source of our moral sentiments, our conscience is its voice within us. Society requires the subordination and regulation of individual desires to its needs and purposes. For Durkheim, however, religion always expresses a truth, although not the truth that its devotees take it to be. In saying that the divine exists it expresses the truth that society exists as a reality *sui generis*, as a force external to, and master over the individual. The nature of our relationship with society is the same as our relationship with God. They are one and the same relationship. In worshipping God we express our dependence upon, and subordination to, the collectivity. In ritual we express and experience this subordination in intensified form. In collective rites we feel more intensely the external pressure of the collectivity. Social solidarity requires that we give periodic ritual expression to, and thereby reinforcement of, such feelings and sentiments. In this sense religion is functional for social cohesion.

Perhaps the most difficult thing to accept in Durkheim's account is the claim that our moral sense is merely the voice of society within us. We tend to think of moral heroism as involving the rejection of the voice of the majority or the crowd in situations where the majority seems concerned only to save its own skin, or where the crowd seems overcome by hysteria which obliterates restraint and the sense of fairness and justice. Religion has often been the inspiration and support for such moral heroism. Religion, also, seems often to divide society and to propel sections of it away from involvement and towards sectarian secession or isolation; and often towards violent conflict. Religion can thus be more universalistic and more particularistic than Durkheim's analysis allows for.

For Durkheim, religion, as with all social facts, has both causes and social functions. Religious notions stem from the experience of the social and also serve to ensure the cohesion of the social. Later theorists inspired in part by Durkheim's work equate cause and function. Religion is explained entirely in terms of the functions it performs for society. One of the earliest exponents of the functionalist view, Radcliffe-Brown, saw society as an organism with parts which functioned to stabilise and ensure the survival of the whole.[10] Religion, and in particular ritual, was seen as central to the maintenance of sentiments necessary for cohesion and solidarity.

If religion and ritual exist to sustain social cohesion why do participants believe that it is about ensuring prosperity, warding off dangers, achieving salvation or gaining mystical insight? For Radcliffe-Brown such beliefs are mere rationalisations and secondary to an understanding of the true roots of religion. But can we so easily dismiss participants' accounts of what they themselves believe themselves to be doing? Apart from the obvious dangers of misinterpretation and misunderstanding if we do so, there is a problem in functionalist

arguments that they rob the participant of any real reason for particip-
ating. How is it that participants in ritual manage to do what they do in
order to promote social solidarity when they have no idea that this is
what they are doing? How does it come about that they engage in
actions which promote social cohesion while believing that they are
achieving something quite different?

Later functionalist theories, perceiving such difficulties, sought to
bring back into view the individual and individual needs and motives.
Seeking a synthesis between the social and the individual they reintro-
duced elements of psychological approaches.[11] Religion served individual as well as social needs and largely achieved the latter through
the former. Religion satisfied the need for an ordered and meaningful
view of reality without which social stability was impossible. Without a
sense of ultimate justice in which good actions would receive appropriate reward and evil actions would receive adequate punishment, in
another life or existence if not in this, social order would break down.
It was acknowledged that religion, however, may not always perform
its function very well – or that it could actually be dysfunctional in
certain circumstances.

With such concessions the functionalist approach seemed rather
vacuous. Religion may promote solidarity but may equally promote
conflict. It all depends upon circumstances. This is not to offer much
by way of an explanation or theoretical account of religion. In incorporating the role of religion as provider of meaning, however, these
functionalist theorists reflected the views of Weber writing much earlier and laid the groundwork for subsequent perspectives which stressed
this meaning-generating and sustaining character of religion. This
approach is very much a synthesis of intellectualist, emotionalist and
sociological theories.

Weber did not formulate a general theoretical stance on religion in a
systematic way; he develops such a stance in various of his writings.[12]
While in essence his approach might be said to be broadly psychological, combining both intellectualist and emotionalist dimensions, the
social dimension of religion is never far out of sight for Weber,
although not in any functionalist sense. The roots of religion, for
Weber, lie in the necessity of accounting for the conditions of life in
which individuals find themselves, for their good or bad fortune.
Drawing upon the theological notion of a theodicy Weber speaks of
theodicies of good and bad fortune. Those who are fortunate in life
need to feel and to have others believe that their good fortune is
deserved or legitimate and not arbitrary. Those who suffer bad fortune

need to feel that in the longer term or wider context they will get their just desserts. It is impossible for human beings to accept that good and bad fortune in life are the product of mere chance and that existence is characterised, therefore, by a fundamental arbitrariness; they have an overwhelming impulse to find an underlying coherence, sense and meaning in the way things are. Religion is thus fundamentally about accounting for the apparent injustices and senseless aspects of existence and giving reassurance that they are only apparently so. Whatever the specific form that religion takes, Weber argues, it is always at root an attempt to make sense of the world. Speaking of the variety of forms of religion we observe in society and history, he says 'behind them all always lies a stand towards something in the actual world which is experienced as specifically "senseless". Thus, the demand has been implied that the world order in its totality is, could, and should somehow be a meaningful "cosmos"' (Weber, 1970c, p. 281).

Religious attempts to make sense of the world are always founded, Weber believed upon on ultimate values which are, in the last analysis, not amenable to argument or to validation by reason. Different religious outlooks are such ultimately irreconcilable orientations towards life, and the demonstration of this constitutes a central theme in his work.

Good and bad fortune in life, however, is generally determined by social location, that is to say by class, status or power. Good and bad fortune is to a very large extent social, structured and patterned. Consequently, religious views of the world will tend to be associated with different social groups having different life chances which are determined by social forces and patterning. To this extent solutions to the problem of theodicy will be collective and socially determined; major religious ideas will have social carriers, namely the social groups to which they speak most clearly and whose world and manner of life they make most sense of. The dominant religious ideas will be those whose social carrier is the dominant group in society. This group and its religious outlook will tend to shape the character of the society and even civilisation in which it is located. The Brahmin priests shaped Hindu civilisation, the Confucian literati Chinese civilisation and the Bedouin warriors Islamic civilisation. Also, as a consequence of the close association of religious traditions with specific social groups, the process by which certain ideas and orientations become predominant is also the process by which groups struggle to preserve and enhance their social position, emphasise social distance between themselves and others, monopolise opportunities, and so on.

On the other hand, although these religious orientations tend to fit, or at least not to clash, with the material interests of the groups which espouse them, they are only partly reflections of these interests. They are also in part products of innovators, prophets and thinkers – people with charisma who have special religious insight or inspiration and who act from genuine religious conviction. They are able to suggest solutions to problems concerning the meaning of life and the particular conditions which affect the social stratum concerned. These solutions, or theodicies of good and bad fortune,[13] address not just material interests but also ideal interests which have to do with the meaning of life, the justification of privilege and the explanation of suffering. Through this process, religious ideas emerge, develop and change but not as mere ideological weapons.

Theodicy also in the more traditional meaning of the reconciliation of a conception of God as transcendental and supremely powerful with a world under his control yet far from perfect gives rise to different types of religious outlook with different implications for conduct. Whether this reconciliation is found in messianic expectations of radical change in this world or some world to come, or whether in dualistic notions of struggle between good and evil, or in conceptions of karmic balance, will have a differential impact on practical conduct. Also, religious ideas have their own internal dynamic and tendency to lead in certain directions. For all these reasons a religious tradition can shape and influence the outlook of important groups in society and thus act as a real force upon the development of a society and culture.

More will be said on Weber's views as they relate to specific religious traditions in later chapters. Weber's general approach is reflected in a number of much more recent contributors to theoretical debates who have focused on the way in which religion generates meaningful pictures of reality. Probably most influential in this respect is Peter Berger.[14] Berger also emphasises the way religion constructs a meaningful picture of reality and the place of humanity within it. This meaningful picture he calls a *nomos*. We are, he argues, 'congenitally compelled to impose a meaningful order upon reality' (Berger, 1973, p. 31). Without it we would lose our footing in reality, become disoriented and suffer *anomia*. It is, of course, not individually but socially constructed and, therefore, acquired through socialisation.

Many aspects of life threaten this meaningful order, not least the fact of death. Such facts and experiences threaten to rob life and the world of its sense. Although humanly and socially constructed the *nomos* is seen as being in the nature of things and beyond human choice or will.

It is the role of religion to give it this character of being given and taken for granted. Religion sacralises the *nomos* turning it into a *cosmos* or sacred order. Religion, Berger states, 'is the audacious attempt to conceive the entire universe as humanly significant' (ibid., p. 37).

In constructing a *cosmos* religion, of course, must incorporate society into the picture and in doing so accounts for and legitimates social patterns. Religion thus develops various theodicies in accounting for apparent injustice and undeserved suffering. Religion is in turn upheld by social processes of support and maintenance, 'plausibility structures', without which it would easily lose its taken-for-granted yet precarious hold upon its followers. These social processes essentially uphold a mystified view of reality. While religion protects against the terrors of meaninglessness it cannot but present what is humanly produced as being divinely created. For Berger, however, this is not so much the consequence of alienation in conditions of class exploitation but of the human condition. This is perhaps the greatest question that might be posed in relation to Berger's approach; is the human condition really such that it needs such 'illusions'?

The diversity of theoretical approaches outlined above might best be viewed as an embarrassment of riches rather than as an embarrassment of disagreement and confusion. All of these approaches have added something to our understanding. Usually they have been too one sided and have neglected other dimensions in favour of one strand or other of the very complex phenomenon that religion is. The attempts at synthesis exemplified by Weber, Berger and others perhaps grasp this complexity rather better in incorporating these various strands that previous theories have identified and analysed. The test is whether they prove more or less useful, more or less enlightening in application in the empirical and substantive analysis of religions and religious traditions.

2 Religion in Tribal Societies

It is common to draw a dividing line between the 'world religions' and 'primitive religion' or the religion of 'primitive' societies, folk religion, 'primary' religion, and so on. It is often a misleading division since included in the world religions one usually finds Confucianism, Taoism, Hinduism, Jainism, and Sikhism all of which are confined to particular communities or parts of the world. One might argue that the only truly world religions are Buddhism, Christianity and Islam, while Judaism is in an ambiguous position.

If the distinction is expressed in terms of 'higher' versus 'primitive' or 'primary' religion, however, it does make some sense. The higher religions may be characterised as having a transcendental emphasis which primary religions lack. The transcendental religions are concerned with wider questions of the meaning of human existence while in the primary religions such concerns are largely absent. In them, the dominant concern is with immediate events in this world – pragmatic and concrete purposes – whereas the higher religions are oriented towards salvation.

It would be a mistake, however, to characterise the higher religions as *exclusively* concerned with the transcendental. They, too, share with primary religions a concern with the avoidance of pain and the promotion of wellbeing and prosperity. It is simply that this is often subordinated in them to the more transcendental aims. It would be a mistake, also, to think that all primary or primitive religions are exclusively concerned with the concrete and the practical, with this-worldly concerns. The Hopi belief that they existed as a people in order to perform religious rituals which ensured the daily rising of the sun and thereby the continuity of the world must surely be interpreted as a moving attempt to give their life in this world significance.

A second major difference between the transcendental and primary religions is that, in the former, systems of morality are always central whereas in the latter moral questions, at least in the universalistic sense, are absent. Primitive religions may involve ideas concerning the fulfilment of specific obligations to kin and so on but do not embody wider and more general moral conceptions.

If the distinction between higher or transcendental and primitive or primary religions is useful, it is still rather crude. There have been a number of attempts to classify religious systems in a more elaborate way. These schemes frequently assume an evolutionary aspect.

TYPES OF RELIGIOUS SYSTEM

A. F. C. Wallace proposes a fourfold classification of religious systems (1966). The four types are termed *shamanic, communal, olympian* and *monotheistic*.

Shamanic religion is the type found among such peoples as the Indians of North America, the Siberian tribes, the Eskimo, Andaman Islanders and many hunter–gatherer societies. Rituals are performed by non-specialists or part-time specialists. Divining the causes of misfortune and propitious times to undertake activities are prominent, as are curing and healing rituals. Mortuary and transition rituals are usually found and taboos and ritual avoidance beliefs are common.

In *communal* systems, found widely in Melanesia, Polynesia and Africa, the shaman is supplemented by belief in a pantheon of deities associated with aspects of nature, the seasons and events in the individual life cycle. These deities can be approached through rituals and there may be a greater degree of specialisation among those who mediate between men and the gods than in the shamanic type.

The *olympian* type is characterised by a pantheon of high gods who are worshipped and propitiated in temples through the mediation of full-time priests. Examples are the Inca, Aztec, Ashanti, and Dahomey.

Finally, *monotheism* covers the world and higher religions. It is characterised by a belief in a supreme deity or principle which controls all other supernatural beings or forces.

A second attempt to reduce the great variety of religious systems to an ordered classification is that of R. N. Bellah (1964). Bellah's classification contains five types which he terms *primitive, archaic, historic, early modern* and *modern*. While Bellah thinks of these as stages in the development of religion and thus adopts a clearly evolutionary approach he warns against any interpretation of his scheme as an actual, historically accurate description of the development of religion. The scheme is an admitted oversimplification.

Bellah discussed each of his five types in terms of three general aspects of religion, namely its symbol system which covers beliefs, the type of religious actions which predominate, that is the form of ritual, and finally the type of organisation.

In the *primitive* stage of development, best exemplified by societies like that of the Australian aborigines, we find a set of beliefs in a mythical world which is seen as being closely bound up with the natural environment and prominent features of it. Ritual is basically participatory involving all members of the group without specialists.

There is no distinct religious organisation. Bellah sees this type of religion as largely to do with the promotion of social integration and solidarity.

The *archaic* stage is characterised by the development of distinct deities with whom human beings interact. The religion takes the form of a cult involving worship of the deities and frequently involving sacrifice to them. The beginnings of a priesthood can be seen but which is not yet clearly differentiated from or subordinate to the political realm.

In the *historic* stage religion becomes increasingly transcendental. The gods and the sacred realm are now seen as separate and distant from the everyday world. World rejection and a concern with salvation become dominant themes. The priesthood acquires a degree of autonomy since the political and religious spheres are now distinct. Priests and religious functionaries become a distinct and separate elite. This allows religion to come into conflict with the political regime and it may provide, by this stage, ideological backing for reform movements and protests. Religion may now play a more dominant role in social change rather than merely legitimating the social order.

With *early modern* religion there is a swing away from world-rejection. Salvation remains the primary concern but is now seen as something to be attained not through withdrawal from the affairs of this life and world but through activity in the midst of it. Early modern religion begins with the Reformation and Protestantism. There is a greater emphasis upon personal conviction and the hierarchical character of the priesthood is weakened or abandoned. Early modern religion tends to promote social change through its emphasis on worldly activity.

By the *modern* period this de-emphasis of the transcendental, world-rejecting aspect of earlier traditions develops to the point where the notion of a superior sacred realm disappears. Social action and community work become the ideal and the organisation becomes fluid and impermanent, often taking the form of special purpose groups. The emphasis is upon individual responsibility for working out personal solutions which may take the form of 'secular' types of activity. Modern religion is ambivalent in its social impact, either tending to undermine social stability or, on the other hand, opening up opportunities for creative innovation.

Bellah sums up the development as one of increasing freedom of personality and society through religious ideas.

The range of terms used by Wallace and Bellah to classify types of religion, especially the religions of the less complex societies, suggests, then, that it is not useful merely to contrast primitive with transcendental religion. Also, many of the transcendental religions retain 'primitive' elements. Christianity could be argued to have its magical side; ancestor worship was as important in Confucian China as in West Africa. Nevertheless, it will be convenient to treat the pre-transcendental religions together since there are a number of common themes and similarities between them. The religions of primitive societies, described and analysed by anthropologists, also offer an opportunity to examine in detail the primary aspect of religion, shared by the 'higher' religions but difficult to examine clearly in that context because of its subordination to the transcendental dimension. Work on this aspect of the transcendental religions is, also, so much less abundant than that on primitive societies. Where possible, however, attention will be drawn to the similarities between primitive religions and the transcendental religions or at least to the primary aspects of belief in those societies in which the latter predominate. The lessons that anthropological studies have for the study of the transcendental religions are considerable.

The diversity of pre-transcendental religion is so great that it would be a foolish endeavour to attempt to summarise and discuss here the whole of the very extensive body of material written about it. Discussion, therefore, will be limited to three major themes or aspects, namely ancestor worship, witchcraft and spirit possession.[1] These themes are particularly revealing of the relationship between social structure and religious beliefs and practices which is a central purpose of this book to demonstrate.

ANCESTORS AND GHOSTS

The notion of a spiritual essence or aspect of the human being which 'survives' death as a soul, ghost, ancestor and so on, is a universal one. It is found in societies from the most simple to the most complex although with considerable variations of detail. The soul might, as in ancient Sumeria for example, enjoy nothing more than a shadowy subterranean existence, or it might in other cultures enjoy the delights of an everlasting paradise. Very often more than one non-material aspect of the human being is distinguished, each separating at death to go its way. The ancestor spirit may be distinguished from the personality and this from the breath, and so on. In ancestor worship it is only the first aspect that is the concern of ancestor cults. It is with these that we shall largely be concerned here.

As we have seen in Chapter 1 some early theorists in the sociology of religion believed that the origins of religion lay in the belief in the continued survival and importance of ancestral spirits for the living. Herbert Spencer in his *Principles of Sociology* traced the origins of beliefs in gods and spirits to a primal belief in a soul which survived the death of the individual. The existence of this non-material dimension of the human being was suggested to early man, he speculated, by their experience of dreams in which the dead might appear. The earliest forms of religious ritual took the form of propitiation of the dead. The notion of gods derived from prominent and heroic ancestral figures, founders of clans and lineages, and so on.

The study of ancestor worship, then, is not without a degree of general theoretical significance. Ancestor worship is (or was) prominent in China, Polynesia and West Africa. Most studies of it have been carried out in Africa where it is closely connected with the explanation of and reaction to *misfortune*. Among the most detailed studies are those of Meyer Fortes, carried out mainly among the Tallensi of Ghana (Fortes, 1959, 1965) who attribute nearly all events in a person's life, both good and bad, to the actions of ancestral spirits or to something similar, namely a Personal Destiny spirit, also associated with ancestral spirits.

Ancestor worship, Fortes claims (1965), is always rooted in domestic, kinship and descent-group relations and institutions. It is certainly not simply a cult of the dead. Not just anyone becomes an ancestor but only a person with living descendants of the right category. To become an ancestor establishes and expresses, therefore, the continued relevance of the dead person for his or her community and society. Ancestors are those who stood in a specific politico-jural relationship to their descendants and thus have nothing to do with attachments and affections which develop between one generation and the next nor even with the aspect of nurturance, protection and care between parents and children but rather with authority relationships. What becomes an ancestor is solely the aspect of authority that the deceased had over the descendant. Thus in matrilineal societies the father, who has the responsibility of bringing up and caring for his children and who often has a close, affectionate and easy relationship with them does not become an ancestor of any significance. Rather it is the mother's brother, a figure of authority who has legal responsibility for his sister's son, who becomes an ancestor and must be worshipped.

Ancestor worship, then, Fortes argues, is a representation or extension of the authority component in the jural relations of successive generations and not simply the expression in supernatural form of the total complex of affective, educative, and supportive relationships. It is not the whole person but only the jural status as someone vested with authority and responsibility that is transmitted into ancesterhood. This explains why beliefs about the mode of existence of ancestor spirits are usually very vague (see also Newell, 1976, pp. 22–3). Those who venerate ancestors are generally unable to say very much about what form they take, where they are or what kind of existence they lead. They are unconcerned, what is more, about such things since they are irrelevant from the point of view of the significance of ancestor worship in their lives.

Neither does veneration of ancestors depend at all upon what actual relations between the deceased and the descendant(s) were like when the former was alive. It has nothing at all to do with individual feelings. The relationship may have been characterised by tension and even dislike and hostility. The deceased may have been a paragon of virtue or the worst reprobate in life, but whatever the case becomes an ancestor and the object of veneration and cult worship. A senior descendant, an eldest son for example, whether virtuous or competent, wicked or inept, will have the responsibility of conducting the rituals of the cult.

In most cases, and particularly in West Africa, failure to conduct the appropriate rituals, make the necessary offerings, or to do whatever is required by the cult, will result in dire consequences and punishments being visited upon the living by their ancestors, once again quite regardless as to the degree of affection in which they were held or had for their descendants or of their character and personality in life. Proper veneration of the ancestors, on the other hand, will bring good fortune and prosperity.

This power of the ancestors and the attribution of misfortunes to their intervention in the lives and fates of the living is well described by Fortes in his study of ancestor worship among the Tallensi (1959). The Tallensi are organised into patrilineal kinship groups in which complete jural and ritual authority is vested in the father and the head of the household. Filial piety is considered to be of the utmost importance and as a result there is usually a high level of tension and suppressed hostility and antagonism as well as affection between father and son.

This repressed hostility can be seen in the taboos that first sons have to observe (Fortes, 1987). From the age of six a first son is forbidden to have direct or symbolic contact with his father. He cannot eat with him nor use any of his belongings.

When a father dies he becomes an ancestor and it is largely through the father's ancestral spirit that the son contacts all the various ancestral spirits which are important for him and which are thought to affect his life and fate. Misfortunes are commonly attributed to the action of such ancestors.

Very often, however, misfortune is attributed to a spirit which Fortes calls Prenatal Destiny. This spirit will usually be divined as the cause of a misfortune when the afflicted party is in some way out on a limb with respect to the social structure. Either the person is too young to be implicated in social relationships in a significant way, suffers from an incurable physical or psychological handicap or is in danger of being permanently forgotten because he or she has and is likely to have no offspring. Prenatal Destiny serves as an alibi for such 'failures' and handicaps, relieving kin of the responsibility and potential guilt as well as exonerating the individual concerned in his or her own mind.

Prenatal Destiny is likened by Fortes to Oedipal fate. This is more than simply an analogy used illustratively by Fortes. His whole analysis is heavily influenced by Freudian psychoanalytic theory. Prenatal Destiny symbolises those experiences which are characterised by an inability to become integrated into society and ultimately this amounts to a failure in the primary relationships between parents and children. Parenthood is the critical, irreducible determinant of the whole social structure. Prenatal Destiny is like the Oedipal idea because it recognises forces in social and personal development that cannot be changed or regulated by the social order. In Tallensi doctrine, Fortes tells us, those with bad or evil Prenatal Destiny are unconsciously rejecting society – the trouble lies in inescapable, inborn wishes.

Evil Prenatal Destiny, however, does not necessarily determine life-fate inexorably. There are ritual procedures for casting out evil Prenatal Destiny. Such rituals, Fortes argues, help to dispose of the emotional and moral tensions generated in structural contradictions and antagonisms and by this means the onus of rejection is shifted onto a supernatural plane. The feelings of helplessness and depression in the face of misfortune are made tolerable. Prenatal Destiny conceptualises that experience in which parental failure leads to the latent hostility towards parents getting the upper hand.

The opposite of Prenatal Destiny is Good Destiny. Every Tallensi man has a Good Destiny shrine associated with a particular configuration of ancestors. In return for submission and service these ancestors bring the owner of the shrine good fortune. The owner must sacrifice at his Good Destiny shrine and if he does so and carries out his kinship obligations to the living he will enjoy prosperity.

The powers of ancestors, Fortes points out, are the powers that a father has over his children but immeasurably magnified and sanctified. They are also removed from the normal controls that operate in everyday relations such as cooperation and reciprocity. Fortes likens the ancestors to Job in the Biblical story. The Tallensi can never be quite sure that they have fully satisfied the ancestors. Ill fortune does not, of course, follow anything but a fairly random pattern. Those who are scrupulous in performing their duties towards ancestors and kin are just as likely to suffer it as those who are lax. The Tallensi rationalise the apparent contradiction by saying that one can never be sure that some small thing has not been overlooked; in other words within the terms of the belief system. The reality, however, is that they experience the actions of ancestors as unpredictable and even capricious.

Good Destiny is the expression in religious symbols and sanctions of the ideal of parental care, success and the correct response by children and their growth into adulthood and maturity. Whereas Prenatal Destiny serves to identify the fact of irremediable failure in the development of the individual to full social capacity, Good Destiny recognises that the hostile component in parental–filial relationships has been overcome. Oedipal predisposition is transformed into Jobian fulfilment.

For Fortes this set of beliefs amounts to something like an official ideology. Ancestor worship, he says, is 'a body of religious beliefs and ritual practices, correlated with rules of conduct, which serves to entrench the principle of jural authority together with its corollary, legitimate right, and its reciprocal, designated accountability, as an indisputable and sacrosanct value-principle of the social system' (Fortes, 1965, p. 139).

Such a belief system is a powerful aid to authority since those who exercise it can claim that they are themselves bound by a superior authority which is beyond their control. Jural authority is placed upon a pedestal where it is inviolable and unchallengeable. The key ritual of sacrifice to the ancestors is a means of symbolising such subordination and also of making reparations to predecessors who have, in a sense, been ousted from their positions of authority.

Why should the Tallensi express these ideas in terms of ancestor beliefs? Fortes says little about this except that by projecting the whole thing onto a supernatural plane much anxiety inherent in the situation is avoided. Also, he says, the Tallensi cannot see the real nature of their beliefs because they do not have the cultural resources for analysing their religious symbolism in the way that is possible for the anthropologist. In any case, if they could analyse the belief system in this way they would have no need for it.

In this type of society jural authority is vested in persons by virtue of kinship and descent and so it is the deceased kinsmen – ancestors – who represent this authority and the continuity of the social structure. And it is the condition of filial dependence from childhood to adulthood which provides the model of subordination to authority in such societies and therefore the code of symbolism and ritual by means of which reverence for authority can be regularly affirmed and enacted. 'In their ancestor worship', Fortes says, 'Tallensi make clear to themselves the fact that, though parents depart, the authority and jurisdiction they wielded – and which enabled them also to be protective and benevolent – still goes on' (ibid.). The parents are seen to survive in transmuted form but what in fact survives is the web of kinship and descent relationships generated by the parents and the filial experiences standardised in the norms, values and beliefs inculcated by them.

Ancestors, Fortes suggests, are demanding, persecutory and interfering because parents are like this in the eyes of children. It is also an effective way of representing the sovereignty of authority. The absence of any connection between good fortune and good behaviour in reality serves to make the ancestors appear to be to be somewhat persecutory. Since misfortunes befall everyone to some degree regardless of their behaviour, the authority of the ancestors is always demonstrated, if only infrequently in some cases. The ancestors, nevertheless, however persecutory they may seem, always act justly and good behaviour, while it cannot in reality guarantee good fortune, does bind the ancestors to act justly. If misfortunes occur it can only be the fault of the descendants.

In concentrating heavily on the importance of ancestor worship in the maintenance and legitimation of jural authority, Fortes' work is inevitably focused upon descent group ancestors and their relationship with the living. If descent group ancestors are essentially punitive as a result of their authority role, McKnight (1967) has pointed out, then extra-descent group ancestors, as he calls them, should in theory be largely benevolent or at least not at all punitive. For example, the mother's brother in many patrilineal kinship systems has an easy and affectionate relationship with the sister's son. This ought to be reflected in the ancestor beliefs. Among the Tallensi, upon which Fortes' theory of ancestor worship is largely based, we should expect to find that maternal ancestors are tender and indulgent, as are maternal kin in life, and certainly not the cause of misfortune. Yet we find quite the opposite. Among the Tallensi and in many other patrilineal societies, maternal ancestors are even more punitive than paternal ancestors. Similarly, in matrilineal societies, patrilineal ancestors may well be punitive, contrary to the expectation that Fortes' approach would lead us to hold. Whatever its merits for understanding the cult of descent-group ancestors Fortes' approach seems not to be at all applicable to extra-descent-group ancestors.

The explanation for the punitive character of extra-descent-group ancestors lies, McKnight suggests, in the tensions generated between members of descent groups linked by marriage as must be the case where descent group exogamy is practised. One also fights with those one marries, as McKnight puts it. These conflicts concern such things as bride–wealth payment, affinal duties of sons-in-law and treatment of the wife. In a patrilineal society, the tensions and conflicts tend to centre on the mother's brother–sister's son relationship. The sister's son is caught between his own and his mother's descent group which makes him the target for revenge on the part of the latter group as a means of enforcing their rights. Resort to physical force is not possible between affinal groups so supernatural sanctions tend to be used. Hence the attribution of misfortunes to the action of maternal ancestors among the Tallensi and other patrilineal peoples. In matrilineal societies the paternal ancestors, as we have seen, may similarly be seen as the most punitive.

In drawing attention to the tensions and conflicts between affinally related groups and the role of ancestors in their expression and pursuance, McKnight presents Fortes' approach as being somewhat incomplete or partial, applying only to descent-group ancestors. It is tempting to go further than McKnight and reassess Fortes' approach in the light of McKnight's observations. The actions of ancestors in punishing descendants by bringing misfortune upon them might be seen in the more general light of the inevitability of tension in both descent and affinal relationships. Fortes, for example, describes the ambivalence and tension in the relationship between father and son among the Tallensi centred upon the authority role of the father and the desire for independence on the part of the son. He also shows how those responsible for exercising authority are able to legitimate it by appeal to a higher authority – that of the ancestors. Both in this relationship and that between a man and his mother's people there are close ties characterised nevertheless by conflicts of interest. In both cases ancestor beliefs are utilised in these relationships to control others. Seen in this way ancestor beliefs are less an ideological legitimation of authority structures, or not simply or primarily so, but also a means of managing conflict or even of pursuing it – a means of manipulation, control and the exercise of power as well as authority.

A second major challenge to Fortes analysis has focused upon the differences between ancestors and elders. Kopytoff (1971) has argued that the notion of ancestor cult carries with it extensive ethnocentric connotations which are misapplied in the case African belief and practice. It is not helpful, he contends, to speak of 'worship', 'sacrifice' and 'cult' in connection with the relationships that many African peoples have with their ancestors. In Africa ancestors should be seen as nothing more than deceased elders; the fact that they are not living elders does not mean that they belong to a different category of being. The relationships that the living have with them are the same in every significant respect that people have with living elders as far as the formal as opposed to the personal aspects of the relationship are concerned. Ancestors are not 'worshipped'; they are simply shown the same respect that elders are shown. People do not 'sacrifice' to ancestors they simply give them the gifts or tribute that are due to elders. It is just that people such as the Tallensi do not believe that the formal relationship they have with their elders ceases upon death although the personal and informal relationship does. Western observers of such cultures are inclined to apply, illegitimately, concepts such as worship, sacrifice and expiation where relationships with what are seen to be spirits of the dead are concerned.

This reformulation, Kopytoff argues, helps avoid many misunderstandings and remove puzzles that Fortes' account creates. Sacrifice to ancestors is seen by Fortes as expiation for the living having ousted the ancestor and a means of assuaging the guilt that is felt. But there is no evidence of guilt or of its relief in many African societies where belief in ancestors is prominent. Such notions are not necessary once we realise that ancestors have not been ousted at all but simply that the relationship that existed with them when alive continues to exist after their death. Similarly, the problem of explaining why some societies structured rather like the Tallensi along lines of unilineal descent do not, nevertheless, have strong beliefs in the importance of ancestors, is solved. In societies such as the Tiv and Nuer, although unilineal descent groups are important, elders are not. Ancestors have little importance for the living because when alive as elders they had little importance. Ancestors are not significant among the Songye even though elders have considerable authority because the Songye believe they are reincarnated in their grandchildren.

Thus ' "ancestorship" is but an aspect of the broader phenomenon of "eldership" '. Understanding it is not so much a question of uncovering deeply rooted psychological processes as of finding an adequate means of expressing African cultural categories in terms of Western concepts.

Kopytoff's challenging arguments have stimulated a lively debate, to no small extent because they raise some fundamental questions relating to the understanding of unfamiliar belief systems and the dangers of ethnocentricity in utilising concepts derived from Western traditions of belief. Brain (1973) and Calhoun (1980) question Kopytoff's equation of ancestors with elders. Brain points out that unlike elders ancestors know the thoughts of the living. The cult of the ancestors is also, in his view, far more than simply reverence for dead elders. Similarly, Calhoun considers that elders and ancestors are distinct categories. Ancestors, because they are dead, can be idealised and can represent collective as opposed to personal interests far more than elders can and as a result play a distinct role in the legitimation and maintenance of the social and moral order.

Clearly, there are similarities and differences between ancestors and elders in African societies. It is tempting to try to decide which are more important, the similarities or the differences. Janelli and Janelli (1982) come down in favour of the similarities in their study of ancestor worship in Korea. Mendonsa (1976), however, points out that this may well be a pointless exercise. Whether the similarities or the differences are crucial depends upon context. In the case of the Sisala of Northern Ghana the similarities are greater, for example, between office-holding jural elders and ancestors than between ancestors and elders who have no jural authority. Fortes' point that ancestor beliefs are a projection of the jural element onto a socio-religious plane is thus well made according to Mendonsa. On the other hand, it could be argued in defence of Kopytoff's position that in this particular society it is only certain elders with whom a significant relationship will continue after their death, those with jural authority.

A question one might ask at this point is why it is that only the formal and jural authority relationships with elders continues beyond death if Kopytoff is correct in his analysis. Why does the personal relationship not continue? Elders are also fathers, brothers and so on. Why do other relationships not continue beyond the grave? This observation tends to lead us to favour Fortes' as does the fact that ancestors often have shrines devoted to them with all the trappings of ritual and ritual objects associated with them. Ancestors are indeed dead elders but it is difficult not to acknowledge that death transforms them in some sense and makes them no longer purely, or at least much less, mundane.

So far we have considered only African material. Studies of ancestor worship in China and Japan have added new perspectives to the anthropological work on Africa. One issue that immediately arises when one compares African and Asian studies is that of the degree of punitiveness of ancestors in Asia. If ancestor worship is a means of exercising authority then we should expect to find that ancestors behave in a similar way in China and Japan where, as in Africa, unilineal descent groups have also been a central feature of traditional social organisation. It has often been claimed, however, that ancestors in China and Japan are primarily benevolent and rarely (Freedman, 1967; Jordan, 1972), or even never (Hsu, 1949, 1963) punitive. So dependent is the welfare of each generation upon its predecessors in this type of society, Hsu argues, that hostility between them is virtually unthinkable. This has been disputed by many who have carried out fieldwork in these countries (Ahern, 1973; Wolf, 1974a; Kerner, 1976; Smith, 1974; Yonemura, 1976; Janelli and Janelli, 1982) all of whom document cases of often quite punitive action attributed to ancestors.

Wolf suggests that the ideal in many Chinese communities is that ancestors will be benevolent and that there is reluctance to assent to the proposition that they might cause misfortune whereas the reality is that misfortunes may well be attributed to their intervention in specific cases, usually as punishment for neglect.

In their study of ancestor worship in Korea the Janellis explore this point further. There has also been a tendency on the part of researchers who are themselves from East Asia to overemphasise the benign aspects of ancestors, reflecting a general reluctance in the area to admit that ancestors can be punitive in popular belief. The Janellis reformulate Hsu's hypothesis arguing that intergenerational dependence explains why ancestors ought to be entirely benevolent in popular belief and why there is a reluctance to report that they are anything other than such but acknowledging that, at the same time, misfortunes are often attributed to them.

More than this, there is no uniformity of popular opinion or perception on this question, at least as far as Korea is concerned. Women, for example, are more likely to acknowledge the punitive character of ancestors than are men. This reflects, the Janellis argue, the different experience of men and women in typical social relationships and the varying degree of conflict entailed in them. A woman has two sets of relationships, those with her natal kin and those with her husband's kin whereas a man has only one set, those with his natal kin. The relationships a woman has with her husband's kin are frequently more conflictual than those men have with their natal kin. It is the lower dependence upon and greater strain with the affinal kin that makes women more inclined to see ancestors as punitive. Such differences find institutional reflection. Women's dealing with ancestors is largely in the context of shamanistic rites in which ancestors demand sacrifices, appear to be self-interested and are thought to have caused afflictions. In the ancestor rites conducted by men they appear much more passive, patient and benevolent.

However, in other parts of East Asia this difference between men and women in their perceptions of the punitive character of ancestors is less marked. This tends to be the case where men more often marry uxorilocally (post-marital residence in the home of the female partner), as in Japan, where the difference between the perception of men and women is slight, and in parts of Taiwan where a high rate of uxorilocal marriage combined with other factors seems to obliterate it altogether.

It does seem, however, that Chinese and Japanese ancestors are not thought to be as powerful and potentially harmful as many African ancestors are. Fortes himself admits that Chinese and Japanese ancestor beliefs do have a different character to those of Africa (1974, pp. 9–10). Whereas in Africa ancestor worship is largely concerned with expiating offences and atoning for ritual neglect, in China and Japan it is rather more concerned with keeping the ancestors content and at peace. In Africa it is geared to the protection of the living and in China and Japan to the consolation of the dead. This difference may well be explained by the fact, as Wolf points out (1974b, p. 168), that the African societies in which ancestor worship is prominent are for the most part stateless societies in which all authority is vested in senior kinsmen who dominate all aspects of lineage life and affairs whereas in China kin simply do not control many of the forces and agencies that shape an individual's life and fate. Here the state and local authorities are equally, if not more important. Wolf offers this as an explanation of why in China major disasters are not attributed to ancestors. They are, he argues, not seen as being that powerful. Great misfortunes were attributed to the actions of gods modelled on the imperial bureaucracy. His point could easily, however, be extended to account for the generally less punitive nature of ancestors in China and Japan.

Fortes (1961), on the basis of comparative African data, argues that where transfer of authority and property from father to son is relatively smooth and takes place step by step ancestors are seen to be less punitive, echoing the point made earlier by Freedman (1967) who suggests that in societies where corporate kinship groups larger than the family are important, ancestors are not so powerful or punitive. This is the case in China, where there is also a slow and more progressive transfer of authority from father to son.

Wolf (19746) also points out that in China misfortunes may be attributed to a category of dead persons who are not ancestors, namely ghosts. Ghosts include the neglected dead – neglected because they have left no descendants or who have died far away from home and have been forgotten – as well as murder victims, suicides and the unjustly executed. They are like homeless wandering bandits outside the accepted social structures and are wholly malevolent. Between ancestors proper and ghosts there are also other categories of dead – those who contributed to a persons line but were not members of it and those who were dependants of the line and have no one else to care for them. The ancestor tablets of the latter are placed on the right of the ancestor alter (the tablets of ancestors proper are placed on the left) while the tablets of the former are placed in a corner of the kitchen or in a hallway and they are thought of almost as ghosts. There is, then, a continuum of dead persons extending from full ancestors to malevolent ghosts.

Jordan (1972) also shows how in the South Western region of Taiwan that he studied family misfortunes such as illnesses are attributed to the ghosts of those who have no descendants or who are in some similar way social-structurally anomalous. The misfortune can be alleviated it is believed by altering this anomalous situation. For example, if an unmarried girl dies a spirit marriage may be arranged so that she will not be without descendants. The girl is married after her death to someone whose descendants will count as hers and who will commemorate her as an ancestor. Wolf (1974b) reports similar practises in the Taipei region.

Contrary to this view that kin without descendants can become malevolent ghosts, Weller (1987) argues that it is necessary to distinguish between two categories of ghost in Taiwanese belief, or at least two distinct ways of thinking about ghosts. In relation to ancestors the dead who are without descendants are regarded as pitiful. These 'marginal ancestors' are not feared for the misfortunes they might bring; people feel sorry for them. The gifts given to them are not so much to propitiate them as to express sympathy for them. Other categories of dead, such as those who have died in battle or who have no known kinship affiliations, are better seen as 'marginal gods' rather than marginal ancestors. These are propitiated because they are malevolent and feared. The key distinction, then, between ghosts and ancestors rests on the presence or absence of kinship links. As Weller puts it ghosts are strangers, ancestors are relatives. The dangerous ghosts are those who are no one's ancestors.

Despite reference to Jordan's data on ghost marriage as a means of removing the malevolence from those who are clearly marginal ancestors, Weller denies that marginal ancestors are seen as malevolent. Clearly there are uncertainties relating to the logic of Chinese beliefs pertaining to ancestors and ghosts stemming either from different interpretations of data or reflecting ambivalence and contradictions in the way they are conceptualised by the believers themselves. We have relatively little information about the circumstances in which misfortunes are attributed to ancestors or to ghosts in China and Japan. More information on this question might reveal a great deal relevant to the general understanding and interpretation of ancestor beliefs. There is clearly a great deal of work to be done in this field before theories such as that of Fortes or the modifications to it suggested above can be reliably evaluated and tested.

WITCHCRAFT

There are other reactions to misfortune than attributing it to the actions of ancestor spirits. It might be blamed upon the malevolence of a living fellow human being with mystical ability to cause harm – that is to witchcraft or sorcery. Witchcraft is generally the term used where the power is inherent in the individual and sorcery when it is learned knowledge of techniques using, for example, spells and substances or calling upon supernatural or mystical powers. The distinction, however, is not always as clear cut in practice.

Witchcraft has been extensively studied in primitive societies and there are also a number of studies from a sociological perspective of European forms of it. A common theme in such studies is that witchcraft accusations are related to the moral state of the group or of particular relationships within it. Through an examination of the pattern of accusations and the social relationships, tensions and divisions underlying this pattern, sociologists and anthropologists have shown how through witchcraft accusations individuals are made responsible or held liable for the welfare of their fellows. The association made between witchcraft and misfortune implies that if social relations were harmonious, misfortunes would not occur or would occur less often.

The classic study of witchcraft is Evans-Pritchard's *Witchcraft, Oracles and Magic Among the Azande*. This work was important for three main reasons. Firstly, it showed how conceptions of causation which go beyond the ordinary, everyday kind of causation that science is concerned with are central and crucial in understanding primitive beliefs, particularly witchcraft. The Azande usually attribute misfortunes such as sickness and death to witchcraft or sorcery not accepting that these things are matters of chance.

Most deaths are attributed by the Azande to witchcraft. In explaining a death as being due to witchcraft the Azande would not disagree about what for the Western observer would count as the 'facts' of the case. For example, if the deceased had been bitten by a poisonous snake and had died as a consequence, the Azande would not dispute this as a cause of the death but they will persist, nevertheless, in their attribution of the death to witchcraft. It is certainly not a question of them being ignorant of the fact that some snakes are poisonous and that their bite can cause death. They may not understand how the action of the snake toxin in the body brings about death but this is irrelevant to their belief that the death was caused by witchcraft. The questions they pose about the event go beyond a need for a 'normal' causal account to ask why the event should have happened at all. Why was the person bitten by the snake? Why was the snake in just that place at just that time? Why was it the deceased that was bitten and not someone else standing nearby? For the Azande these questions are answered by the attribution of the chain of events to the action of the power of witchcraft. It is because of the malevolent intentions of someone with witchcraft powers that the person stepped on the snake. It is because of witchcraft that the snake was there in the grass just at the time the person put their foot down in that particular place. This chain of events was brought about by an enemy of the deceased who out of hatred of them wished to cause harm to them.

The Azande do not dismiss the possibility of a purely natural or accidental death, but although all human beings must eventually die the time and manner of their death is explained in nearly every actual and particular case in terms of witchcraft.

Secondly, Evans-Pritchard's study showed how apparently bizarre and incomprehensible beliefs could be seen to have a kind of coherence when placed in their social context and also to have a degree of practical value for dealing with situations. Evans-Pritchard describes how he himself, for a period of time, used the Azande techniques of divination, employed for a variety of purposes such as determining propitious times to undertake journeys or economic ventures as well as for uncovering crimes including witchcraft activity, quite successfully. He also showed how the beliefs formed a closed, self-reinforcing system within which Azande thought was imprisoned so that it was unthinkable, almost literally, to challenge it as a system. There were, consequently, many ways in which beliefs false in our eyes could actually be upheld by experience. In fact, Evans-Pritchard lists 22 reasons that Azande can give to explain apparent contradiction of their beliefs by evidence. If an oracle,[2] for example, were to give contradictory responses to questions this might be attributed to the person consulting it not having observed all the required taboos beforehand or to counter-witchcraft acting against it, and so on.

Thirdly, the study showed how witchcraft beliefs are closely associated with strained personal relations, particularly where no institutional controls or means for resolving conflicts and antagonisms exist – where the relationships concerned are not governed by known and accepted procedures of regulation.

Evans-Pritchard found that among the Azande witchcraft accusations tended to occur in a patterned way between persons who stood in particular relationships to one another. Witchcraft tended to operate primarily among neighbours (the Azande believe, in fact that it is only effective over short distances) who were not kinsmen, superior in rank or of the opposite sex. In short, accusations of witchcraft were only made between persons who lived close to one another but whose relationship was not regulated by the rules and customs of kinship, rank and sex. And, of course, the oracles always produced names of people who were very plausible suspects since the Azande only ever put to the oracles the names of likely candidates, in other words those with whom they had recently quarrelled. To do otherwise would obviously, in their eyes, have been a waste of time.

All this suggested to Evans-Pritchard that witchcraft operated as a means of social control in areas where other institutionalised means were absent. Neighbours frequently came into conflict with one another but their conflicts were not regulated by the kind of conventions which regulate the relationship between kin, between commoners and chiefs or between the sexes. The notion of witchcraft, he argues, could be seen as a means of condemning vicious and hostile feelings generated by conflicts of interest, tensions and rivalries. Those who bore grudges or showed animosity to others would have to control their feelings lest their name be placed before one of the Azande divinatory oracles and ultimately be accused of being a witch. Witchcraft is thus bound up closely with morality and correct behaviour towards others. It is a means of expressing moral values and of condemning anti-social attitudes. The witch among the Azande, as in Europe, is seen as a reversal of everything that a good person should be.

The picture that Evans-Pritchard gives us is clearly a rather functionalist one and this is perhaps the chief weakness of the analysis. It probably overemphasised the positive role of witchcraft beliefs in promoting social order and harmony. Witchcraft beliefs might equally have tended to generate and intensify conflicts in the pre-colonial era when it was acceptable to take revenge upon a witch believed to have caused the death of a kinsman. It may be an effective means of showing someone that they are harbouring resentments which prevent good relations being maintained but it is not necessarily always the best means of preserving good relations to accuse someone of such a wicked and vile thing as using witchcraft, especially when the accused believes himself or herself innocent. In the past witchcraft accusations which were rejected by the accused may well have been followed by retaliation leading to blood feud. Witchcraft, as later studies showed, could be a means of pursuing conflicts as well as a means of resolving them – it can be a useful weapon for the furtherance of interests against others or in other words of exercising power.

Later studies of witchcraft and sorcery in primitive societies have brought out more clearly its role in power struggles and Gluckman, in a review of this work, has also shown that witchcraft is often an expression of deeply rooted conflicts and contradictions inherent in particular social structures (Gluckman, 1972). It is often an important factor in the breakup of communities and groups rather than a major force for social control and cohesion. These studies also led to a modification of the contention of Evans-Pritchard's Azande study that witchcraft accusations tend to occur in relationships not governed by structural norms and rules since in many other societies kin, and often close kin, accuse one another.

In the patrilineal societies of Southern Africa (for example Zulu, Swazi, Mpondo, Xhosa and so on) a group of men related through the male line and tracing common descent from a single ancestor four or five generations back occupy a group of homesteads each of which jointly owns land and cattle. On marriage these men bring wives into their own homesteads while their own kinswomen move away on marriage to their husbands' homesteads. Ideally a man will take several wives but in practice only a few senior men are able to do so.

The status of a woman who joins the homestead community as the wife of one of its members varies according to the status of her husband, the status of her father, and in the case of polygynous marriages her position in the order in which he acquired his wives. Because of this multiplicity of criteria it is not surprising that disputes and jealousies arise among the wives.

Also, each wife tries to further the interests of her own children against those of co-wives. Wives are in an ambiguous and contradictory position in this type of social structure. A wife has the duty of producing sons which strengthen the group of kin and ensure its continuity. On the other hand, a particular woman's sons compete for positions with the sons of other wives. In the very act of fulfilling her duty by producing sons a woman simultaneously weakens the group by undermining its solidarity. Furthermore, a man is closely identified with his brothers and half-brothers and with his patrilineal cousins but, on the other hand, he fulfils himself as an individual by marrying and having sons of his own. A wife thus stands at the centre of a conflicting set of values. She provides her husband with the means of creating his own autonomous household yet it is necessary for the group to produce new male members for any individual to achieve full adult status.

Polygyny thus inherently tends to produce tensions and conflicts which are not the consequence of clashes of personality or purely personal factors but of social structural arrangements which place people inevitably in conflict with one another. It is wives who are accused of witchcraft in these societies and usually by their mother-in-law, sister-in-law or brother-in-law. A daughter-in-law quickly comes into conflict with her husband's mother under whose supervision and authority she is. The mother-in-law represents the unity of all her sons, while the wife represents the independence of one particular son – her husband.

This pattern of tensions and conflicts, Gluckman argues, is common in patrilineal joint families and produces a variety of notions concerning the inherent evil of women and femininity whether they take the form of witchcraft beliefs or not. In China women were said to compromise male vigour. Hindus believe that a man gives up part of his life and virtue in intercourse. Many Bantu peoples believe in the mystically polluting and harmful powers of menstrual blood and the blood of birth.

Hence the characterisation among Southern Bantu peoples of women as witches. Zulus believe that a woman's desires attract familiars who demand from her the lives of her husband's kin in return for their favours. Wives are believed to be inherently evil and cause misfortunes. Yet they possess ritual powers for good as well.

When a misfortune occurs among the Zulu, a diviner is called. He calls out questions before the assembled community to try to discover what is troubling them. They will clap and shout as he does so and the closer he gets to the cause of the trouble the louder becomes the clapping. Ultimately he will specify the name of an individual who is causing the misfortunes, sickness or whatever through witchcraft. The named individual is likely to be a younger wife of one of the men of the community. The diviner knows very well the kind of tensions that will exist in the community and he is guided by the community in his divination of the causes of the trouble. The community, however, perceives the diviner's activities as entirely objective and the outcome is, in their eyes, due to the diviner's particular skills and special powers.

Divination procedures such as this take on a special significance in some societies. Witchcraft accusations often play a role in the course of fundamental rifts in a community that has grown large and is on the point of division. Fission of the group is a necessity in the economic and ecological conditions which prevail but is nevertheless a contentious and conflictual process which is experienced as destructive of a solidarity which ideally should always be preserved. It is, consequently, traumatic. Rival factions within such a group will attempt to control the divination procedure and produce an outcome which leaves the opposing faction responsible for the heinous act of witchcraft. This justifies a separation of the two factions, either the accused or the accusing faction leaving to establish an independent community, an action normally unthinkable in communities in which the maintenance of solidarity is of overriding importance but which becomes acceptable once one party can be labelled as beyond the pale through use of the evil powers of witchcraft.[3]

Again there is a fundamental conflict of principles of social organisation involved in such situations. Group solidarity should be maintained yet division is a necessary and normal part of the dynamics of such communities. The group is able to split only if some legitimating reason can be found for destroying its solidarity. In such societies radical changes in social arrangements are not contemplated lightly. Any break in continuity is seen as a threatening disturbance full of potential danger – likely in itself to bring about misfortunes. This is an expression of the essentially moral nature of the issue. It is a disturbance in the proper relations between people who are highly interdependent upon one another and responsible for one another's fate. If someone falls sick or dies in such a society it is because, in the minds of it members, the social order is not in a healthy condition. But when a group is on the point of inevitable division because of its size a misfortune will be interpreted as a sign of irreparable moral breakdown which warrants and even requires a breakup of the group.

The participants in this process are, of course, not fully aware that the disputes are actually unavoidable or that division is inevitable. Moral breakdown may have occurred but that it is due to deeply rooted contradictions in the very structure of the society is not readily evident to the members of the society. As Gluckman puts it:

> In short a belief of this kind has to be referred to a deep seated conflict of social rules, or principles of organisation, or processes of development, and not to superficial quarrels arising out of divergent interests... The essence of these situations is that the people concerned are not aware of these conflicts (1972, p. 18).

It is perhaps to some extent because of this lack of awareness of the deeply rooted nature of the conflicts that the forces at work are conceptualised as insidious, mysterious and intangible. In a sense they are exactly that. They are also difficult to control and to combat, working away in invisible but lethal ways.

Studies carried out in a wide range of societies seem to confirm Gluckman's claims. Among the Nupe of West Africa, for example, it is husbands who accuse wives of witchcraft (Nadel, 1954). Ideally, in this society a wife should be subservient to her husband, bear him children, raise them and look after the home. In reality wives often achieve a good deal of independence. Women frequently engage in trade and market activities which provides them with an independent source of income, often of a significant amount. Instead of the husband supporting his wife she often has to help him out financially.

It is often the wife who provides the money for a son's marriage payment to the bride's kin. This is considerably humiliating for men. It is not surprising that given a belief in witchcraft it is women who are said by Nupe men to have harmful witchcraft powers.

In another study Monica Wilson (1951) attempts to show why among the Mpondo of South Africa witches are believed to be motivated by sensual lust, while among the Nyakyusa of Tanzania witches are greedy for milk and meat. The significant factor in the Mpondo case is that because of kinship regulations men are surrounded by many women who are sexually taboo, and at the same time the rules of apartheid banned any sexual contact with white women. This leads to the idea that witches are motivated by sexual desire. In the Nyakyusa case there is a conflict between the obligations a man has to his lineage fellows with whom he holds and sacrifices cattle, on the one hand, and those he has to his age-mates with whom he lives in their own village but with whom he does not own cattle in common. This leads to the idea that witches are greedy for milk and meat.

Studies of witchcraft accusations in Europe have shown similar patterns. Macfarlane's study of witchcraft trials in Essex (1970) in the fifteenth and sixteenth centuries revealed that accusations were largely made against older women, often widows who were neighbours of and had a fairly close relationship, but not one of kinship, with the accuser. Accusations occurred as a result of quarrels between neighbours usually in circumstances where the accuser had failed to give help such as a gift, a loan of food or other things thus causing resentment on the part of the accused who was said to have turned to the use of witchcraft powers in revenge. The accusers were generally moderately well-off villagers and the accused their rather less well-off neighbours. Often the accusation was the final stage in the severing of a relationship. The contradictions involved here were those of the obligation on the part of the better off in small village communities to help the more needy against, on the other hand, the desire to devote resources to personal ends and plans, or in short, as Thomas puts it (1973, p. 662) a 'conflict between neighbourliness and individualism'. This is shown more clearly between 1560 and 1650 when there was a marked increase in the number of witch trials. Economic changes and growth of population had impoverished some villagers and this had placed a heavy burden of aid and assistance on their neighbours. The normal institutions of help to the old and poor – church relief, the manorial system, kin and neighbourly ties – became very strained. At the same time, the yeoman farmers were under increasing pressure to invest in and improve their land in order to maintain their prosperity. The tensions and conflicts, resentments and breakdown of relationships that resulted led to increasing accusations of witchcraft.

In situations like those outlined above a person has to steer a difficult course between conflicting obligations or between conflicting motivations. To go too far in one or other direction is to invite accusations of witchcraft.

Witchcraft is often associated with a person's actions to the degree that they fail to meet some ideal of moral behaviour or with the powers and capacities of a person as an individual as opposed to commitment to the collectivity. Someone who seems too successful, whose crops grow particularly well, for example, may be said to have witchcraft powers which could be used against others. Such people go too far in the direction of serving their own interests and in a sense may show a disregard of their moral obligations to others in using their talents too much for their own ends. On the other hand, someone whose crops grow very badly compared to others is equally failing in his or her duty to the community which depends to some extent on all contributing adequately to collective production. Individuals must attempt to achieve what Gluckman calls a 'golden mean of morality' (1972, p. 33).

This association of witchcraft power with individualism relates closely to the frequently ambivalent character that witchcraft powers are said to have in many societies. Very often men are believed to have powers of witchcraft which can be used for good ends, and especially to combat other evil witches at work in the community. But there is often a fine dividing line between a good and an evil witch. There is also a constant risk that the good witch will be seen to have used his or her powers for selfish ends and thus slide over into the evil category. Monica Wilson (1951) has described such processes among the Nyakyusa. Middleton (1960) has shown how among the Lugbara an elder can utilise the powers of the ancestors to punish recalcitrant subordinates as a legitimate part of his role in controlling group and community affairs but may, if he goes too far, attract an accusation of witchcraft. When a group is on the point of dividing, senior men of different factions who are competing for authority and control will vie with one another in claiming to have caused misfortunes in an attempt to demonstrate and validate their claim to have particularly privileged access to the powers of ancestors and, thereby, strengthen their leadership position. To claim too often to have brought a misfortune on someone, however, carries the danger that the elder will be accused of actually using witchcraft powers for his own selfish ends and not legitimate ancestral power.

This example illustrates the ambivalent character of witchcraft beliefs but it is noticeable that the pattern of accusations here is not like that among the southern Bantu peoples. Wives are not accused and neither are they in other patrilineally organised systems such as the Azande. What accounts for such differences in the pattern of accusations? Middleton and Winter (1963) have suggested, on the basis of a comparative examination of a wide range of cases, that witchcraft accusations are made against women where property interests are focused upon them. In the southern Bantu societies each wife in a polygynous household is allocated cattle and land which her own sons will inherit. It is because wives are at the focal point of a separate estate that inherent evil is thought to be mediated through women. In societies where a man's entire estate passes to a single heir who is responsible for administering it on behalf of the whole kinship group (among the Lugbara and Azande estates pass on death from brother to brother before going to the next generation) conflicts seem to be more directly between males and accusations of witchcraft are made directly by one man against another.

Where a society is organised matrilineally again we see a quite different pattern of accusation. Mitchell (1956) and Marwick (1965b) show that among the Yao and Cewa of Malawi it is often brothers who accuse one another. Since in such societies authority and property pass from mother's brother to sister's son, brothers tend to compete with one another for control of their sisters and their sisters' children in order to establish a basis of independence. Older brothers will try to deny this to their younger brothers who in turn struggle against the authority of the elder brothers. Again there is a conflict between legitimate aspirations and the demands of social solidarity here. Brothers, however, ought to maintain solidarity and these conflicts cannot be openly admitted or pursued. The reality of the situation cannot be seen, or in any case admitted, but is expressed in a disguised form in terms of accusations of sorcery.

A second frequent pattern of accusations in such societies is that where a man accuses his mother's brother. Maternal uncles wish to control this matrilineal kinswomen but so do these mens's sisters' sons, their nephews, since this will give them a position of authority and independence. Hence the accusations against uncles. The complexity of the ensuing arguments and quarrels may be such that sisters also end up by accusing one another or a brother or their mother's brother.

It is significant that in these instances it is not witchcraft that is the charge but *sorcery*. Attempts to explain why in some societies it is an accusation of witchcraft that is levelled against enemies while in others it is sorcery while in yet others both types of charge might be made have not been very successful. Middleton and Winter (1963) have claimed that where both occur witchcraft is associated with generalised misfortune – a long run of bad luck – while sorcery is associated with particular misfortunes. By their own admission, however, this association is only *sometimes* found. Where malevolent evil takes only the form of witchcraft, Middleton and Winter suggest, we find that the unilineal kinship principle is used in the constitution of local residential groups which are larger than the domestic household. Where it takes only the form of sorcery some other principle governs the formation of such groups. But as Turner (1964) points out, Middleton and Winter offer only two examples of the former situation and in one it seems that sorcery is in fact sometimes the charge. The root of the problem, according to Turner, is that there is no clear and consistent usage of the terms witchcraft and sorcery by anthropologists, nor is the distinction one which is clearly made in many systems of belief themselves. Traits assigned to witchcraft by one writer are assigned to sorcery by another. In such a situation it is impossible to uncover patterns and associations.

Insightful as many of the anthropological analyses mentioned so far are with regard to the role of witchcraft and sorcery beliefs in the management of tension and conflict, they do tend to suggest that such beliefs are generally positive in their effects and consequently retain a functionalist flavour. The beliefs and mechanisms of accusation facilitate the necessary division of groups which have expanded beyond a viable size but where this is nevertheless a painful and difficult process. While the result of conflicts and tensions the accusations play their part in the resolution of these tensions by breaking bonds which have become shackles and inhibitors of harmonious relations and good order. While acknowledging the important contribution such analyses have made to our understanding of witchcraft we should not be misled into thinking that witchcraft beliefs are always functional. As Mary Douglas (1963) and Vic Turner (1964) have pointed out, an accusation of witchcraft may intensify and magnify hostility and tension in situations which would otherwise remain relatively harmonious and which are not ones which are destined inevitably to result in division and separation. These beliefs generate tensions as often as reflecting them. The incidence of sickness and misfortune in any society is such that accusations are quite likely to occur even in the most harmonious of communities, potentially destroying that harmony. We should not forget that witchcraft is a socially available means of explaining and dealing emotionally with otherwise inexplicable misfortune and particularly death. It is not inevitable that as such it will have positive social consequences. Witchcraft accusations, as Douglas (1970) has pointed out, are attempts to exercise power over others; they are weapons used against enemies.

If witchcraft beliefs are to a large extent explanatory of misfortune, the question is raised as to why in certain societies this particular form of explanation occurs rather than some other. Why, for example, do they not occur in modern Western societies, in which people are just as prone to misfortune and where social tensions are just as endemic. One answer to this question might be that in our own type of society good fortune or misfortune can be explained by science and that there is therefore no temptation to link them to the moral state of social relations which prevail. The problem with this is, of course, that science cannot give an explanation for the kind of question the Azande, for example, ask in the face of misfortune and which we also are inclined to ask, namely why did it have to happen at all.

In any case, as Douglas (1970) points out, the approach which sees witchcraft as simply providing an explanation of misfortune in the absence of better ways of doing so ignores the fact that in many primitive societies belief in witchcraft does not exist nor is there any resort to supernatural explanations of misfortune. The pygmies of the Congo, for example, are content to do without such explanations. The reason for this, she suggests, is that they are able very easily to move away from one another as soon as undue strain in relations appears. Witchcraft beliefs do not occur where social contacts are sparse and diffuse or where roles are fully ascribed. Where people press close in upon one another, where social interaction is intense but ill-defined, then we should expect to find witchcraft beliefs.

Turning to the absence of beliefs like witchcraft in modern societies Max Gluckman (1972) believes that we cannot explain this non-occurrence in terms of the advance of science and knowledge. He believes it is due to the fact that in modern societies we are not so inextricably bound up in complex cross-cutting networks of relationships and interdependencies as people are in primitive societies. We do not ascribe moral responsibility for misfortune to one another because our relationships are not intense and interdependent. They are, to use Gluckman's terms, simplex whereas in primitive societies they are multiplex.

In modern societies we deal, to a very large extent, with different individuals in different aspects of our lives. Our spouse, grocer, teacher, colleague, vicar, brother, friend, neighbour, local policeman, tax official, chemist, builder, solicitor, chess opponent, are likely to be all different persons. In a primitive society the roles of kinsman, leader, spiritual guide, friend, neighbour, fellow hunter, are likely to be combined in the same person or persons. Where relationships are close, complex and multi-layered in this way an exaggerated emphasis tends to be placed upon the importance of others and their responsibility for one another.

Gluckman agues that this difference between modern and primitive societies has led to a situation where in the former, far from blaming one another for sickness and misfortunes which we have not brought on one another, we are increasingly reluctant to blame one another for the harm we do actually cause. A view has grown to prominence which seeks to treat the criminal as an unfortunate victim of social and personal circumstance. The problem lies in psychology, upbringing, social, physical and mental deprivation, and so on – all factors beyond the control and responsibility of the individual who is less to be punished but rather to receive treatment.

This tendency, Gluckman suggests, may be one which has ultimately resulted from a process of change in which people are separated from dependence on kin and progressively from dependence on any social group – a dependence which in pre-modern social systems places a high moral evaluation upon all actions and all feelings.

SPIRIT POSSESSION

Religion is more than a set of beliefs and practices. It also involves *experience*. Religious experience may take many different forms – faith, inner peace, ecstasy, and so on. One of the most dramatic forms of religious experience is that associated with and attributed to invasion or possession of a human body by a spirit, demon or deity. Signs of possession are such things as trance-like states, odd behaviour, fits, speaking in tongues, wild ecstatic dancing, change of personality, and so on.

When interpreted in religious terms this kind of behaviour may be seen in two ways – either as an infliction brought about through possession by a molesting spirit or demon, or as a sign of divine recognition and selection – a special visitation on those who are to fulfil the purposes of or act as intermediaries with the spirit world. In actual practice, however, this distinction may be blurred. Anthropological research has shown that the possessed person may make a transition from the category of the strangely afflicted to that of the specially blessed or endowed. The ethnographic data on this has been very usefully reviewed by Lewis (1971), who also discerns certain significant patterns in the data pertaining to spirit possession.

In fact, Lewis is primarily concerned with something which is both narrower and wider than 'spirit possession'. Trance-like states are not always attributed to the invasion of some spirit into a human body. Some cultures attribute trance-like behaviour to the loss of the person's soul. On the other hand, many peoples consider a person to be possessed by a spirit without any trance-like behaviour being manifested. Lewis is primarily concerned with trance states which are attributed to possession by some external spirit or agent.

He distinguishes between two types of possession and two types of cult or set of practices and rituals centring on these types. The first he calls *peripheral cults* since they play no part in upholding the central moral code of the society. They generally involve women or men who are in a largely subordinate and inferior social position. The spirits concerned are seen as largely malicious, capricious and amoral. They are commonly believed to originate from outside the society – the deities of other tribes or peoples.

The second type of possession and associated cult is called by Lewis the *central possession religion*. The spirits involved in this type are concerned with morals – they intervene in human affairs when misdemeanours have occurred and they uphold and sustain public morality.

Lewis examines a wide range of instances of both of these types and is able to derive some significant generalisations and interpretations.

The first type of cult is extremely common among women and he argues that it is to a large extent a disguised protest on the part of women directed against the dominant sex. It takes the form it does because in the societies in which it occurs women do not have more direct means of furthering their aims.

One of the best examples of this type of cult and situation is that which occurs among the Somali of East Africa, data on which was collected by Lewis while engaged in fieldwork among them. In this largely Muslim society men are very dominant and women highly subordinate to them. Marriage is often precarious and divorce is easy for men. Women cannot enter mosques and are regarded as weak and submissive creatures. In this society women are often afflicted with possession by spirits which make certain demands through the woman in an authoritative manner and speaking in a special language which has to be interpreted by another woman who is a shaman skilled in such matters.

Typically, Lewis tells us, the afflicted woman is a hard pressed, somewhat neglected wife struggling to bring up a family. Her husband is typically away for long periods. She may have rivals if the husband is polygynous which creates tensions, conflicts and jealousies. The precariousness of the marriage tie makes her life insecure.

The spirits which possess such women are believed to be consumed by greed and envy. They hunger after dainty food, fine clothing, jewelry, perfume and all sorts of luxuries – in short all those sorts of things that women typically crave. They voice their demands for such things through the woman and will leave her alone only when these very costly demands have been met by the woman's husband who also has to pay for a special ritual dance attended by many other women.

In Lewis' opinion this is a strategy employed by women to obtain benefits that they cannot obtain more directly. Somali men are not entirely unaware of this deviousness. Their attitude is somewhat ambivalent. They believe in spirits and in the possibility of possession but when their own wives are possessed they are more inclined to see it as malingering. As Lewis puts it:

> they interpret this affliction as yet another device in the repertoire of deceitful tricks which they consider women regularly employ against men ... they regard the opposite sex as possessing a unique endowment of guile and treachery. (1971, p. 76)

But possession of this kind is not entirely confined to women. Downtrodden categories of men are also liable to possession. In this case the cult associated with it can be seen as a kind of protest on the part of these groups against the dominant group in society.

How are women who resort to such devices able to get away with it? It is, in fact, very difficult for a husband, whatever he may believe, to do anything other than comply with the demands. He accepts the existence of spirits and of spirit possession in the case of other women and, of course others, men and women, will believe that in the case of his own wife it is real and genuine and that he has an obligation to do whatever is necessary to free her from the affliction.

He cannot really ignore these pressures. If the wife insists that the possession is genuine he cannot completely reject it as malingering because the symptoms are real enough. It is certainly not just an act or performance. The woman clearly suffers as a result of it and has, apparently, little control over it. She can successfully *claim* to be blameless in the matter.

In any case, Lewis points out, although the demands are expensive, they do not pose any real challenge to the system and to the principle of male authority and superiority. Possession is a way of making demands and expressing dissatisfaction without actually challenging the authority structure and without being personally responsible for one's behaviour. Men, on the other hand, in meeting the demands of the *spirit* can claim that they are not giving way to their wives and are, therefore, not jeopardising their dominant position. The principle of male superiority is preserved.

On the whole, then, a husband will tolerate one or two instances of this spirit possession if they are not too frequent. Otherwise he may beat his wife and if this does not work he may threaten divorce. It is often a matter of a fine balance between the demands made by women and the patience of men.

The fact that men tolerate it all, Lewis suggests, perhaps testifies to a sense of guilt – a feeling that perhaps there is some injustice in the way women are treated and that they do have some cause for complaint.

Getting possessed by a spirit has a marked tendency to become habit forming with some women. Recurrent bouts may occur. Ideally the spirit is exorcised by a female shaman once and for all through ritual procedures, but in some cases the 'cure' turns out to be only temporary and the spirit returns. In time the woman learns to live with the spirit and to 'tame' it. This usually involves more ceremonies, dancing, and so on. Often the woman ends up by becoming a member of a regular circle of women liable to possession under the general direction of a female shaman. Such possession societies hold regular meetings, dances, feasts and ritual performances. Ostensibly for therapeutic purposes these activities really constitute a regular cult which may exclude men from its proceedings. What begins and presents itself as a healing activity becomes a religion. Men accept it as a healing activity while in reality it is a form of religious drama and the basis of a female subculture. What begins as suffering ends up as religious ecstasy.

Women who join such groups may themselves become shamans able to diagnose possession in other women and to understand the dictates of the possessing spirits. Whereas in the early stages of their possession history their symptoms are uncontrolled and involuntary, by this stage they develop into a controlled and regulated pattern. The afflicting spirits have been mastered and can be used for general good, for diagnosis and for healing.

This pattern of development is very typical in spirit possession according to Lewis It is usually in this way that a shaman, male or female, acquires his or her skills and position in the society. A shaman, once in control of powerful spirits can exercise considerable influence. Just as in the case of the Lugbara elder discussed above in the section on witchcraft, a successful shaman can cross the dividing line between legitimate use of ritual sanctions and illegitimate use. A shaman risks being accused of using his or her power over spirits to cause sickness rather than curing it if he or she goes too far in the use of this power. Such an accusation may be a strategy used by opponents to curb the power of shamans if it is thought to be a challenge to other sources of authority. This is especially likely in cases such as the Somali when subordinate men become shamans and if it seems that they may use this alternative basis of power to acquire a position of influence and authority in the community. In a sense they are condemned by their own standards and in their own terms. The powers that enabled them to protest and struggle against the authority structure are turned against them and used to engineer their downfall.

Turning now to the central possession religions, in these, typically, shamans, while in a state of trance and possession by a spirit that they have mastered, are able to diagnose the causes of sickness and misfortune and suggest appropriate cures and remedies, communicate with the spirit world, exercise a degree of control over it by ritual performances thereby ensuring prosperity, punish misdemeanours through their control of spirits, and so on.

The possessing spirits may vary considerably from one instance to another. Where ancestor worship is important the possessing spirit will generally be an ancestor. In such cultures there is frequently a belief in a variety of different spirits which can possess a human being but true shamans are only possessed by genuine ancestor spirits. Only well established shamans will be able to tell whether someone newly possessed is so by an ancestor spirit or by a malicious demon. In this way the established shamans can control recruitment to the position of shaman for which there may be considerable competition. Possession of the socially relevant and significant kind is thus confined to a particular circle, faction or elite. Only persons belonging to the appropriate social group or category will be accepted as novice shamans.

The novice shaman will tend to suffer from spirit possession which is as much an affliction in the early stages as it is for members of peripheral cults. Initially there will be attempts to exorcise the spirit. Failure to do so will lead to gradual acceptance that the possession is a permanent thing and that the possessed person, if considered suitable, is a shaman in the making. In time he will learn to live with and master the spirits.

Central possession religions and peripheral cults may coexist alongside one another. Frequently, the central religion involves largely men and the peripheral cult largely women.

Lewis concludes his study with a discussion of the relationship between spirit possession and psychological disorders. Many writers on the subject have sought to explain spirit possession in terms of psychological disorder or abnormality. Lewis disagrees with this interpretation. While many individual shamans may be mildly neurotic or mentally disturbed most are not or at least not seriously so. 'We cannot', Lewis says, 'meaningfully reduce shamanism and spirit possession as total cultural phenomena to expressions of private fantasies of psychotic individuals' (1971, p. 186).

Lewis prefers to see spirit possession as a culturally defined initiation ritual for those who feel called to the vocation or profession of shaman – an initiation ritual which testifies to the candidate's ability to contact and deal successfully with dangerous and powerful forces. The crucial thing is that a successful shaman must control his spirits and his behaviour. He is not usually a person whose behaviour is beyond his own control in the way that a mentally disturbed person's is.

It has been argued that individuals in traditional societies subject to mental disturbance can, through adopting the role of shaman, control and channel their eccentricities in culturally acceptable and indeed socially useful directions. Rather than becoming a problem for others, as is the case in Western industrial societies, they find a creative and constructive role in which they can be of service to others. Lewis, however, emphasises again that spirit possession and shamanism conform to a culturally defined pattern and are not the idiosyncratic actions of individuals.

Finally, comparison of spirit possession and psychiatric disorder might suggest the further possibility that the shaman is in some sense a psychiatrist or psychoanalyst. He cures sicknesses which have their roots in the mind. Lewis points out in this regard that shamanism does not confine itself to disorders which are or could be mental in origin but is generally equally concerned with illnesses that clearly have a physiological basis. He considers that it would be more accurate to say that psychiatry and especially psychoanalysis are, in fact, rather limited and imperfect forms of shamanism. It could be argued that the 'truths' of psychoanalysis are as dubious as the interpretations that tribal peoples give of abnormal behaviour and that the latter are, consequently, as good as the interpretations of the psychoanalysts. At least both are equally hypothetical. We have to recognise that the idea of spirits of the kind that possess people has much in common with concepts in psychiatry and psychoanalysis such as that of the unconscious. Perhaps they do serve to some extent as concepts which explain abnormal behaviour in a way which allows it to be understood in terms of and related to social tensions and power relationships.

Many studies of spirit possession subsequent to Lewis's book have borne out his main points. A survey of a sample of 114 societies carried out by Greenbaum (1973) found that possession trance was more likely to occur in societies with fixed internal status distinctions and differences of role as occurs, for example, in highly stratified societies and those in which slavery exists. It is the rigidity of social structure, a common feature of such societies, which seems to account for the frequency of spirit possession. Where individuals are denied by the social structure freedom to achieve their aims and where close control over daily activities is imposed, possession trance is likely to be common. In such societies, Greenbaum reasons, social controls make decision making for the individual a risky and dangerous affair. Possession relieves the individual of responsibility for actions by changing the identity of the agent concerned from the human individual to that of the possessing spirit.

A number of studies may be cited in support of this interpretation and which show that possession may be an aid in coping with stressful situations (see Bourguignon, 1976 (Haiti); Macklin, 1977 (New England); Obeyesekere, 1977 (Sri Lanka); Pressel, 1973 (Brazil); Saunders, 1977 (Egypt); Spiro, 1978 (Burma)). Bourguignon, for example, argues that the role playing in spirit possession acts as a form of compensation for those who experience neglect in daily life and whose self respect needs bolstering. Reviewing the range of other studies she claims that possession acts as a safety valve in situations of stress. Possession also allows a degree of power over others to be exercised by those who would never otherwise be in a position to do so. Walker (1972), in another extensive review of the literature, takes a similar view.

Not all recent work, however, supports Lewis. Some have taken issue with other aspects of his analysis. Gomm (1975) questions the

extent to which possession can be seen as a challenge to the authority
of dominant individuals and groups. The concessions won by the
afflicted women, for example, serve only to reinforce their subordination because they are won at the price of accepting it. Morton (1977)
shows that those who become regular cult devotees in Ethiopia are
often cut off, as a result, from their kin, their friends and their spouses
who may divorce them. They become wholly dependent upon the cult
leader and often to a greater extent than they were upon husband and
kin prior to their career of possession. Wilson (1967) questions whether
spirit possession should be seen at all in terms of male–female conflict.
Possession, Wilson argues, whether it is of the peripheral cult form or
of the central religious form, is rather the result of conflict and tension
between members of the *same* sex. In the case of peripheral possession
which predominantly affects women it is competition between women
that is involved. Possession frequently occurs when a man takes an
additional wife. This is a threat to the position and status of the first or
earlier wives. Possession may be a means of affirming status and of
receiving reassurance from the husband of the wife's continuing importance to him. It is a strategy in the face of a threat from another
woman. Also, a woman's status varies according to her competence
and adequacy as a wife and mother in relation to culturally expected
standards and it fluctuates through the life cycle according to whether,
for example, she is still capable of bearing children, and so on. These
are matters of comparisons and competition between women and not
matters of conflict and tension between men and women. Possession of
the peripheral type, Wilson argues, just as in the case of central
possession religion, may be seen as a form of *rite de passage* whereby
a new status or social identity is defined and affirmed.

As for central possession religion and the process by which shamans
are recruited Wilson argues, rather less convincingly than in the case of
peripheral possession, that the epidemiology is, in fact, much the same.
However, his empirical evidence on this is sparse. Also, he goes too far,
perhaps, in characterising peripheral possession as a rite de passage. In
fact one might criticise Lewis's interpretation from the opposite position to that of Wilson and question whether central possession constitutes a rite de passage. The history of affliction and ultimate control
and mastery of spirits is hardly a type of ritual as rites de passage
undoubtedly are. It is more a process of personal crisis and development involving stress and psychological difficulty, not unlike peripheral possession, but where the individual concerned, for personal
and social reasons, is able to turn the experience into a means of

finding a central social role and a position of status in the society, in contrast to those who become involved in peripheral cults. While it might be somewhat extreme to say that shamans are those who would otherwise be classified as clinically mad but are saved from this fate by the socially approved role of shaman, it may well be the case that shamans are people who have suffered mental stress and disturbance which they have come to terms with and overcome in such a way as to give themselves an acknowledged social role – one which utilises the insights and capacities that are often gained through traumatic experience. In the same way, those involved in peripheral cults may have found ways of living with their difficulties through the cult, although perhaps, as Wilson suggests, at a cost. It certainly seems odd to liken the acquisition of the centrally significant social role of shaman to the ritual or ceremonial induction of the individual into such a role. It would seem rather more accurate to understand it as the discovery or even creation by the individual of such a role through a process of inner struggle, tension and ultimate catharsis.

Clearly, spirit possession is a varied and complex phenomenon and no single approach, as Walker points out (1972, p. 1) is adequate to explain it. Even Lewis's distinction between central and peripheral types seems to break down in the context of more complex social structures such as that of Brazil and Haiti.[4] Bourguignon (1976) questions Lewis's characterisation of voudou in Haiti as an amoral peripheral protest cult. It may once have embodied an element of protest, she argues, but no longer does so. It is now more like a central morality religion embodying elements of Catholicism and upholding central moral values. However, it differs markedly from the central cults described by Lewis. It does not involve a long period of illness and affliction prior to mediumship. There is no mastering of an originally afflicting spirit and transformation of it into a helpful agent. Much the same is true of the Brazilian cults such as Candomble and Umbanda. In the latter case, Pressel (1973) argues that it has elements of both the central and peripheral types and that this is generally true of possession in more complex social systems.

In some respects Lewis' distinction between central and peripheral possession seems too simple to encompass the complexity that the phenomenon manifests. Jones (1976) has suggested a more elaborate classification based on the work of various fieldworkers in Nepal where alone a considerable diversity of forms is found. Jones distinguishes four types according to whether the possession occurs at designated or undesignated times or in designated or undesignated places. *Reincarnate possession* is for life and therefore undesignated from the point of view of time. In this form an individual reincarnates the spirit of a deceased individual and takes up residence in a monastery or religious centre where he becomes a full-time religious practitioner of divination, curing and apotropaic and other rituals. *Tutelary possession* is the opposite of reincarnate possession. It occurs at designated times but in no particular place. The person possessed calls up a spirit during a seance held wherever circumstances demand and becomes possessed by it for the duration of the ceremony. *Oracular possession* occurs in some sacred place such as a temple, church or monastery (designated in space) and on a designated occasion such as a village festival. Finally, *peripheral possession*, like Lewis' type of this name, is spontaneous and undesignated as to time or place.

These four types, all of which can be found in Nepal, can be related, Jones argues, to features and variations in Nepalese social structure. Initial possession is generally 'peripheral' in type; that is to say it is spontaneous and occurs at no special time and in no special space. Nepalese society, divided as it is by caste and ethnically plural, is such as to deny many people opportunities for self-respect and prestige. Low castes often provide the religious specialists who combat disease and misfortune through control of spirits though their possession is at first involuntary. Women too are more likely to experience possession than men and unmarried women, widows and servants are more likely to than married women with children.

Possession is likely, in many cases, to develop into one of the other three forms. The type of social situation seems crucial in determining which. Reincarnate possession seems particularly appropriate to Tibetan Bhuddist communities where the landless typically either turn to trade or enter the monastery. Spirit possession here takes the reincarnate form and is incorporated into the monastic setting.

In the isolated villages of tribal areas of Nepal which lack the complex institutions of temple and monastery and where the influence of Hinduism and Buddhism is superficial, tutelary possession dominates. In these circumstances it is the shaman who plays the primary role.

Oracular possession is found in the Brahmanical communities of western Nepal. In this caste-divided society it provides a means by which socially and economically deprived individuals can achieve some status as an oracular medium in a hierarchical and rigidly divided system in which positions of status are determined hereditarily. It thus resembles, Jones argues, the oracles of the classical slave societies of Greece and Rome.

Whether Jones' typology can fruitfully be applied to other societies remains to be seen. A further complication of the pattern of spirit possession is that possession takes different forms in different societies. The main variation is that it may or may not involve trance (Bourguignon, 1966; 1976). Possession is the invasion of the person by some external spirit. Trance is a change in normal behaviour, personality, perception and so on. These may occur independently in different cultures or even in the same culture. Possession trance occurs when trance states are attributed in the culture to possession. As yet we have little understanding of the reasons for the pattern of variation between societies in this respect. Bourguignon (1976), surveying a wide range of societies, claims that those which have only possession without possession trance tend to be smaller and less complex than those which have possession trance but the relationship is statistical and by no means one to one.

If much, however, remains puzzling and unclear on the question of spirit possession one thing perhaps does emerge from work on the question. Most researchers seem agreed that it is not random in its occurrence but affects individuals who stand in definite structural relationships to others. While it may be related, in many ways, to personality, and quite clearly involves personal difficulties and psychological problems, it is also both socially patterned in its epidemiology, and socially determined in its character.

3 Hinduism

MAX WEBER ON THE WORLD RELIGIONS

The sociology of the world religions is still to a very large extent the sociology of religion of Max Weber. Until very recently there were few studies of non-Christian religions from a sociological perspective. A certain amount of fieldwork in the more complex non-Western societies has been carried out by anthropologists but has been patchy in coverage, while studies of whole religious traditions in their historical setting remain relatively rare. The world religions remain a seriously neglected field in the sociology of religion which has concentrated almost entirely on a narrow range of issues within the sphere of the Christian tradition such as the nature of sectarianism, secularisation and so on.

This part of this book will, therefore, be closely concerned with Weber's remarkable contribution to the comparative sociological study of the world religions. Each of his major studies will be discussed before discussing subsequent sociological and anthropological contributions. In discussing Weber's work we must remain aware, however, that very particular interests and purposes led him to look at the religions of India, China and Ancient Judaism, namely the question of their impact upon economic life and attitudes, a concern which stemmed from his first study in the field of religion, his famous *The Protestant Ethic and the Spirit of Capitalism*. It is often claimed that what he intended to do in this project was to address the question of why capitalism did not develop in other parts of the world where conditions might well have been as favourable, if not even more so, as they were in the West. Weber tried to show, this argument continues, that while the conditions necessary for the development of rational capitalism were for the most part present in the East, one crucial factor present in the West was absent in the East, namely a religious ethic which could have the impact that ascetic Protestantism had in Europe (Parsons, 1949, 1965; Yang, 1961). Others have rejected this interpretation of Weber (Buchignani, 1976; Molloy, 1980) and later it will be argued that the 'orthodox' interpretation of Weber's strategy in his studies of the world religions cannot be supported. Nevertheless, the economic impact of the world religions is an important theme in them.

His work on the world religions, then, cannot be taken as a general treatise since as Weber himself acknowledged it set out to look at them from a very particular perspective and angle. Yet it is, nevertheless, extremely rich and insightful. Weber's work goes well beyond its limited intended objectives to provide an immensely ambitious, complex and wide-ranging examination of many aspects of the major religious traditions in their historical and cultural setting.

Another major theme in Weber's work is that of *rationalisation*. Weber believed that Western civilisation was characterised by what he called the progressive 'disenchantment' of the world and its replacement with an increasingly rational attitude in all spheres of activity. Disenchantment here is used in its original and literal sense implying the waning of the magical and supernatural conception of reality which prevailed in traditional pre-industrial societies. Rationalisation is not used by Weber in a normative sense. He intends it to refer simply to an objective process which is not judged in itself to be either good or bad, desirable or undesirable.

In the sphere of religious life this trend towards rationalisation, engendered by Judaism and taken up by Christianity, culminated in an ethical rationalism of the purest form represented by Calvinism which played its part in turn in promoting the thoroughgoing rationalisation of all life conduct including economic activity.

Broadly then, Weber's studies of religion can be divided into two. On the one hand there are the studies of Confucianism, Taoism, Hinduism, Buddhism and Jainism – the religions of the East. On the other, there are the studies of Judaism and Protestantism – religions of the 'West'. Weber had also intended to carry out a study of Islam and of Catholicism but did not manage to complete this task. There are, however, many observations on them throughout his writings.

It is clear that Weber believed that there were fundamental differences between Eastern and Western religion. In the East the tendency was towards mysticism which usually took an otherworldly form. The dominant tendency in the West was towards asceticism and often of an inner-worldly kind. In the East mysticism tended to make higher religious concerns rather elitist. Prophecy was largely exemplary in type and salvation denied to the masses. Popular demand often forced religious leaders to make accommodations to popular needs but this generally resulted in ritualism and the fostering of a magical outlook. In the West, in contrast, prophecy was ethical and promoted ascetic religious attitudes. More often in the West the ordinary person was able to seek salvation in and through his or her daily activities. By a thorough ethical rationalisation of life conduct some forms of Western religion had definite consequences for the character of the societies in which they occurred. The attempt to reorganise the world in accordance with God's commandments, the constant tension between the world as it is and as it ought to be, provided a stimulus for social change and ultimately for the development of rational capitalism.

WEBER ON HINDUISM[1]

Weber begins his study of Hinduism in *The Religions of India* (1958) by characterising the distinctive features of the social structure of Indian society and, in particular, caste organisation. Then he looks at the orthodox Hindu tradition, its development and outlook upon life and the world. He goes on to examine Buddhism and Jainism both of which developed from Hinduism and which he contrasts as heterodox movements against Hindu orthodoxy. He describes how Buddhism spread beyond India. He discusses how all of these doctrines, which were in his view essentially elitist, made accommodations with popular religious needs. Finally, he assesses the influence of dominant religious attitudes upon society in India and upon practical conduct. In this chapter we shall be concerned only with his analysis of Hinduism and briefly with his treatment of Jainism. His observations on Buddhism will be discussed in the next chapter.

Any discussion of the structure of Indian society has, at the very start, to deal with the question of caste organisation. Weber begins his account of Indian civilisation and society with an examination of Hinduism, caste and their relationship. At the outset Weber notes how Indian legal institutions, the autonomy of the merchant classes, occupational specialisation, attitudes to wealth and acquisitiveness were all factors conducive to the development of capitalism, which nevertheless did not appear in India until imported under the British domination. Does this mean that in the case of India Weber did think that the crucial missing factor was the religious one? Not at all. For example, he says, 'here we shall inquire as to the manner in which Indian religion, *as one factor among many*, may have prevented capitalistic development' (ibid, p. 4). Again we see that Weber is not able to test the Protestant ethic thesis in the case of India since there are so many factors besides religion which would have hindered the development of rational capitalism in this society (see Buchignani, 1976).

Caste organisation is one such factor. In discussing the spread of Hinduism, and with it caste organisation, throughout India, Weber is concerned not with the religious factor *per se*, which he tackles more directly later in the study, but with caste as an aspect of social organisation – a material rather than an ideal factor.

Hinduism spread caste organisation since it tended to absorb local and tribal groups wholesale as castes with a position in the caste hierarchy. Tribal groups would emulate, as far as possible, the customs, taboos and avoidances of Hinduism in order to claim as high a status position in the system as they were able. Hinduism proved an irresistible force in India – so much so that its two great rivals, Buddhism and Jainism failed hopelessly to win over many followers for any length of time. Buddhism practically disappeared in India and the Jains are only a tiny minority of the population. One thing Weber aims to do in the study is to show why this was so and why the two salvation religions, Buddhism and Jainism, could not provide legitimating support to ruling strata and therefore lost out to Hinduism.

The success of Hinduism and the spread of caste in India was associated with this ability to legitimate rank and status and this in turn was associated with economic advantages and privileges. The assimilative capacities of Hinduism were also related to its undogmatic character concerning religious ideas.

The concept of *dogma* hardly exists within Hinduism, Weber tells us. Within the broad limits of Hinduism each caste or sect follows its own way of life, even to the extent of venerating different gods. Unlike Christianity, within Hinduism a teaching may be orthodox without being bindingly valid. This is because Hinduism is primarily ritualism, according to Weber. The idea of caste duty or *dharma* is the central notion. Above all things a person must live by his caste *dharma* and this is different for each caste, each social position.

There are also, Weber points out, a variety of religious aims or goals which Hindus may hope to achieve. Broadly there are three types of religious goal though each has a number of variations. They are (i) rebirth after death into a new earthly existence as good as, or better than the present one, or rebirth in a paradise, (ii) immortality in some form of existence in a paradise, (iii) the cessation of individual existence and complete incorporation into the whole, or in other words, the attainment of a state of *nirvana*, a blissful state of non-existence of the separate self which defies description.

The paths to these goals can vary immensely and may involve very different ways of life, forms of conduct, religious practices and ritual observances.

There is, of course, a close relationship between religious and ritual observances and status distinctions. One important consequence of this is the setting up of all kinds of barriers between the castes – barriers which are reinforced by ideas of pollution. Caste, then, is the fundamental institution of Hinduism in Weber's view and caste entails the existence of a special ritually pure and superior group, the Brahmins – the priestly group. In the last analysis, Weber argues, rank position is determined by the nature of its positive or negative relation to the Brahmin. In this light Weber discusses the status position of the major groups or *varnas* – the Kshatriya military, noble, governing group, the Vaishya merchant group and the Sudra peasant, labouring, artisan, servant group. These major divisions, are of course, not the real effective and operative caste groups of Indian society. Weber points out that castes have a tendency to proliferation and fragmentation into sub-castes or *jati,* each with its occupational specialisation and each socially segregated from the others by rules of purity and pollution and endogamous marriage.

The implications of all this are clear. Caste organisation led to a conservatism and dread of innovation that was inimical to economic development. Weber says:

> A ritual law in which every change of occupation, every change in work technique, may result in ritual degradation is certainly not capable of giving birth to economic and technical revolutions from within itself, or even of facilitating the first germination of capitalism in its midst. (1958, p. 112)

This, then, has to be seen as a *social* factor which would have inhibited the growth of capitalism and economic innovation. Despite the close interrelationship between the caste system and the religious ideas of Hinduism, the caste organisation is a form of social organisation.

The religious ethos of Hinduism, however, was not itself likely to have provided a motivating force for such a development, in Weber's view. Hinduism, apart from its traditionalist and conservative impact, also supported and legitimated caste organisation in a significant way. There are two basic principles common to all Hindus which are closely bound up with caste; *samsara* – the belief in the transmigration of souls or reincarnation, and *karma* – the idea of compensation for actions or retribution for actions which determines the nature of one's reincarnation. Of them Weber commented 'these alone are the truly "dogmatic" doctrines of all Hinduism, and in their very interrelatedness they represent the unique Hindu theodicy of the existing social, that is to say, caste system' (1958, p. 118).

This works in the following way. According to how a person has acted in this life he will be reincarnated in an appropriate form in the next. A life of correct behaviour, that is behaviour strictly in accordance with one's caste dharma, will result in reincarnation as a member of a higher caste. For bad behaviour the penalty is reincarnation as a lower form of life. One of the worst fates the Hindu could conceive was that of reincarnation as a worm in the intestine of a dog.

Every ethically relevant action in life has some consequence for the chance of a better or a worse social position in a later life. It also follows that every person is born into a given caste and social position as a result of conduct in a previous life. The Hindus, then, believe that they can rise to the highest positions or sink to the lowest according to the nature of their actions. This cycle of existences goes on for eternity, at least for most people. There is, then, no end to the world and no day of judgement. The caste order is eternal.

The extreme traditionalistic implications of such doctrines are easy to see. These ideas justify and legitimate the caste ranking. They make social position seem to be both the product of an individual's own behaviour and yet unavoidable and unchangeable. If someone is in a low position it is their own fault and there is nothing that can be done about it. The only hope is to accept the current position and live by the rules of the caste so that a better position in a future life may be achieved. This clearly generated a vested interest in maintaining and upholding the caste system even for those occupying low positions in it. It is remarkable how in India lower caste groups have accepted their position and the discrimination and invidious distinctions associated with it.

Of course, we have to qualify this with the observation that castes, that is sub-castes, will try to move up the hierarchy and claim a higher position as a whole group. This they may be able to do if they have the wealth and influence and can claim descent from a higher ranking ancestor and have this claim acknowledged and validated by the Brahmins. Individuals cannot do this but a whole sub-caste might be able to. This, nevertheless, implies acceptance of the system as a whole; it is a strategy parasitic upon the system. It usually involves, also, acceptance of an inferior position in it in relation to other groups that still remain above the sub-caste that has climbed up a little way.

The caste system, then, and the basic ideas of Hindu belief, inter-relate in this highly conservative manner. Such ideas were to a large extent developed and promoted by the Brahmin intellectual stratum. It is clear that they had a vested interest in doing so.

Weber goes on to examine, in the second part of *The Religions of India*, the character of Brahmin thought, education and religiosity to see why it developed in the way it did and to assess its implications for Indian civilisation and development. He also looks at the rival hetero-doxies of Buddhism and Jainism.

Orthodox Hindu thought, as it developed from the basic doctrines of samsara and karma, became concerned with the implications of an eternal cycle of rebirths and with the question of how there could be escape from this everlasting cycle, from the wheel of rebirths, as the Brahmins expressed it. If men went through an endless succession of lives, then any particular life, including the present one, is meaningless and a matter of indifference. For someone concerned about the mean-ing and significance of life, this was not a comfortable state of affairs. It meant, also, that not just an infinity of new existences had to be experienced but an infinity of deaths had to be faced.

Thus a concern with ultimate salvation grew up, centred on escape from the cycle of rebirths. The Brahmin intellectuals developed a whole variety of responses to this predicament. Heterodox solutions were developed by anti-Brahmin groups, including Buddhism and Jainism. Weber was primarily interested in the implications of these doctrines for everyday conduct and way of life. He begins his discussion of them with a general characterisation of the Brahmin outlook comparing it with that of the Confucian literati of China. There are many simil-arities between the two groups, he points out. Both were an educated minority or elite that prized knowledge and learning. Their intellectual and educational qualifications gave both a kind of magical charisma. Both were steeped in ancient literature and versed in the ancient language in which these texts were written. Both were, on the whole, opposed to ecstatic or orgiastic expression of religiosity or any form involving a high degree of emotion. Despite an emphasis in the early Vedic writings on the drunkenness and dancing of the Gods intoxic-ated by the sacred drink, *soma*, the official ritual of the Vedas is comprised of hymns and formulae, sacrificial procedures and prayers.

If there were striking similarities between the Brahmin priests and the Confucian literati the differences between the two strata were more significant. In China the literati were appointed officials subject to recall. In India the Brahmins had permanent, hereditary rights to land and, therefore, independent, regular and dependable means of support.

The Brahmins were, also, ritual specialists with a monopoly of such knowledge and quite distinct form the political and administrative stratum. There was no fusion in India of ritual and political functions as there was in China.

The difference between India and China in this respect is associated, Weber thought, with a very different political history in each case. Unlike China, India was never unified for any great length of time under a centralised administration. More often than not it was divided into numerous warring principalities and states. Warfare was frequent as was conquest. Dynasties rose and fell, ruling groups were defeated and replaced. Instability and flux characterised much of India's history. This situation tended to favour the Brahmins, Weber argued, since rulers and princes became highly dependent upon them for legitimation of their regimes, magical protection against defeat and procurement of success in war. The ritual services of the Brahmins became indispensable. Their independence that stemmed from land ownership was the consequence, Weber argues, of the fact that to secure their loyalty and support the Kshatriya princes had to grant them land in outright ownership. On the other hand, the Brahmins tended to promote disunity as it was in their interests to do so. The outcome was the subordination of political or secular authorities to the religious domination of the Brahmin stratum.

The consequence of the situation of the Brahmin priestly caste in India was that although opposed to magical ideas in principle they were not able to throw them off. They were not able to leave magical practices to the specialists as the Confucians had been able to leave them largely to the Taoists. Being a high ranking priestly caste the Brahmins' power, authority and position came to depend upon belief in the efficacy of magic and ritual.

If the magical charisma of the Brahmins depended upon knowledge of esoteric scriptures it depended to an equal extent upon ascetic practices. In China asceticism was rejected by the dominant literati, at least in its more extreme forms. In India the Brahmins promoted asceticism but being a dignified intellectual elite they adopted what Weber calls *apathetic* forms of asceticism, rather than orgiastic or ecstatic forms.

The Brahmins also developed a strong tradition of mysticism. In fact, while asceticism was thought to be essential for the chance to be reincarnated into a higher caste, true salvation, that is escape from the cycle of rebirths, could only be achieved, according to Brahmin teaching, through mystical contemplation which they claimed was a prerogative of their own caste group. In effect, then, only a Brahmin could hope to achieve real salvation while all others could only hope for eventual reincarnation as a Brahmin.

Brahmin mysticism frequently took an otherworldly form. The ideal for the Brahmins was to withdraw from worldly activity into contemplation and meditation. This he should do once he had seen the son of his son. In other words the ideal was to become a holy man in old age. Associated with this meditative way of life a whole variety of practices and techniques grew up. Yoga, for example, of many different varieties, assumes an indifference to the world and demonstrates a desire for mystical experiences.

A great variety of philosophical holy teachings were developed in India over a very long period of time during which a multiplicity of schools and rival doctrines competed with one another as a result of the thought and contemplation of Brahmin holy men. Fundamental to all of them is the notion of gnosis or deep understanding of the truth of the world, and the underlying nature of reality achieved through meditation. This leads in two basic directions, according to Weber. One conception accepts a fundamental distinction between the knowing self and the known material reality; this is the dualistic solution associated with the Samkhya school. The other rejects this dualism and holds that reality is made up of only one monistic principle – an impersonal divine being which is the only true reality, the only real thing. The world which appears to us was thought to be an illusion. The world as we see it is ephemeral. What is real and lasting is the being which manifests itself as the variety of individual objects, entities, persons and so on. All of these things are one in reality and each and every one of them is at one and the same time the whole, or *Brahman* as it is called. In this Vedanta school of thought it is held that in reality there is no separateness – no individuated 'things' or parts. Reality is a seamless whole and there is no point at which one thing begins and another ends. It only seems that way to us who have to apprehend that reality through conceptual thought which inevitably gives a distorted picture of it. When this conceptual apprehension of reality is overcome by direct apprehension through meditative techniques it becomes clear that the individual self likewise has no separate existence but is simply Brahman along with everything else. Realisation of this is to achieve union with Brahman in which salvation consists. Salvation is thus achieved primarily through knowledge and the removal of ignorance.

Despite these differences between the various rival schools of thought, fundamental to them all was a belief in the essentially illusory nature of reality and that salvation could be attained only by mystical union of the soul, which becomes individuated as a result of a false conception of reality, with the divine whole or Brahman.

In Hindu thought, however, there are many roads to salvation. Apart from Samkhya and Vedanta there are four other recognised schools of orthodox philosophy. What makes all of these schools orthodox is their acceptance of the Vedic scriptures as authoritative – the fact that they do not dispute the binding character of ritual duties or attack the position of the Brahmin caste.

Such ideas had little appeal for non-Brahmins, Weber points out. Members of the educated laity and particularly the Kshatriya often felt the need of a path to salvation more rewarding than that offered by Brahmin thought and found the rarefied, highly philosophical and elitist creeds and practices of the Brahmin religious specialists, or virtuosi as Weber calls them, unattractive. The Kshatriya in particular were not well disposed to the otherworldliness of Brahmin thought, immersed as they were in very worldly concerns and responsibilities. There tended to occur, therefore, a number of accommodations and modifications of these Brahmin ideas some of which remained within a broadly orthodox framework and some of which did not.

One of the most important of these developments, according to Weber, found its expression in the great epic of the Mahabharata or more specifically in that section of it known as the Bhagavad Gita. This takes the form of a dialogue on the eve of a great battle between the warrior Arjuna and his charioteer who is actually the God Krishna. The debate concerns the attitudes and behaviour appropriate for a Kshatriya warrior to warfare, death and the taking of life in the face of Hindu teaching against the taking of life, even animal life – the doctrine of *ahimsa*. The battle to come is one which occurs during a civil war. Arjuna shrinks from the thought of great bloodshed, of having to take the lives of his own people, even his own relatives. Krishna puts forward a series of arguments which show him that he should not be so concerned about it. Arjuna is simply an instrument of God. The material world and everything that happens in it is only illusion in any case. He is a Kshatriya and cannot avoid his fate or deny his nature.

The basic theme in Krishna's arguments is that everyone should behave in accordance with their caste dharma whatever that leads to.

Worldly activity, even warfare and bloodshed if one is a Kshatriya, as long as it performed in accordance with caste dharma, is no obstacle to salvation provided certain conditions are fulfilled. The main condition is that even when engaged in worldly activity one must remain indifferent and detached. One must renounce all concern for the outcome or with the fruits of the activity and simply carry out one's caste duty because it is one's duty. As long as all emotional attachment to the outcome is eradicated the action will be without karmic consequence and will not drag the actor back towards material existence. To be concerned with the fruits of one's actions means being tied up with karma or retribution and compensation. As long as action is performed with intent for and concern with its consequences one builds up karma which will result in a new incarnation. The devout person must become an indifferent observer of his or her own actions.

Weber argues that this great work of Hindu scripture can be seen as an intellectual synthesis of Brahmin thought and Kshatriya attitudes to life. The Brahmin ideal of indifference to the transitory nature of the world is fused with a ritualistic element. Brahmin mysticism takes an inner-worldly direction and at the same time reinforces caste differences.

The implications of such a doctrine, Weber argues, were considerable. The most important was that an 'absolute relativising of all ethical and soteriological commandments' (1958, p. 190) was promoted. In other words there could be no universally applicable ethical standards. Ethical behaviour was made entirely relative to caste position.

This accommodation to the religious needs of laymen, that is non-Brahmin priests, was not successful in abolishing the gap between those who could and those who could not follow an other-worldly religious way of life. Although inner-worldly in orientation, this new outlook remained an elitist doctrine of intellectuals with little appeal for the masses. It emphasised faith and wisdom. One had to trust that one's behaviour led one to salvation. Salvation could not be earned by actions since to try to earn salvation would inevitably build up karma and push salvation further away. It was a doctrine which entailed the necessity to see and to understand the nature of reality, of Brahman – an intellectual and philosophical enterprise beyond the capacities of ordinary people.

Such doctrines failed to satisfy the religious needs of the masses who tended to be oriented towards more orgiastic and ecstatic religion, a personalised conception of God and a personal saviour figure. Because of this a number of Hindu sects and heterodox teachings grew up which were able to integrate quite well into the main stream of Hinduism. A number of rival, heretical systems also developed outside the Hindu tradition since they rejected the Vedic scriptures and were strongly opposed to Brahmin religious domination. The two most important were Jainism and Buddhism.

Jainism

Jainism developed, according to Weber, among the Kshatriyas and in particular among Vaishya merchants and traders. It was, therefore, of particular interest to Weber given his concern with the relationship between religious ideas and economic development.

In Weber's opinion Jainism was largely a reaction to the Brahmin view that only someone born a Brahmin could achieve salvation. It was opposed to the teachings of the Vedas. Nevaskar (1971) points out that it took root in areas where the Brahmin monopolisation of intellectual life and domination of education was less pronounced than in other parts of India. It was also in such areas that Buddhism flourished, according to Nevaskar.

Although by tradition Jainism is said to go back into the very distant past, its real historical founder appears to be Mahavira (c 560–468 BC). Mahavira was a Kshatriya. The story of his birth that has become traditional, as Nevaskar points out, was intended to show that it is a greater honour to be born a Kshatriya than a Brahmin.

Jainism teaches that salvation, that is freedom from the cycle of rebirths, could be attained only by an ascetic way of life and detachment from this world which is considered to be fundamentally imperfect. Jains believe the body to be evil. Those who are exponents of asceticism are greatly honoured by Jains. Knowledge, while essential, cannot be attained except through other-worldly asceticism. The Jains also emphasise right conduct as the means of salvation, unlike Hindu thought which traditionally emphasised correct thinking and that human suffering is due to a wrong conception of the nature of the world.

For the Jain religious virtuoso, the monk, conduct should ideally conform to five basic principles – ahimsa, absolute truthfulness and honesty, chastity, and renunciation of all pleasure in external objects or of too great a love for anyone or anything. Monks take these religious duties extremely seriously. In order not to become entangled in personal relationships they were required to spend their lives wandering from place to place rejecting any permanent home or dwelling place, even the idea of a monastery. Their only means of subsistence should be the food freely given as a gift by the lay followers. They must abandon all personal property, even to the extent in one sect, the Digambaras, of going entirely naked. The majority Swetambaras wore only a simple white robe. Monks must be careful not to take any life, including that of the humblest insect, even inadvertently. They will sweep every step of the ground in front of them with a soft brush before placing their foot upon it lest an insect be crushed and may wear a face cloth to prevent insects being taken in with the breath.

Even for the laity all occupations which may involve the taking of life, even inadvertently, are forbidden. Agriculture and industrial activity or any occupation requiring the use of sharp tools, fire and so on were banned to them. The safest activity was that of trade in which many Jains earn their livelihood. Since the laity, in contrast to the monks, are not permitted to travel without the permission of their religious leaders, the favoured form of trade is that of middle men. Scrupulous honesty is also expected of the laity in all aspects of life including trading activities.

A Jain layman could acquire wealth through trade but was taught that he must not strive to become wealthy or seek pleasure or joy in owning possessions. Ideally he should limit his possessions and give any surplus to the temple.

In this emphasis on honesty and tolerance of wealth, but not its consumption, Jainism is rather similar to certain forms of Protestantism, Weber notes – a comparison that Nevaskar (1971) has more recently examined in some detail. The consequences, however, were not the same in each case. Like Protestants, Jains were excluded from 'political capitalism', such as tax farming and so on. Like some Protestants their reputation for honesty earned them much business and made them wealthy. The prohibition on unnecessary consumption stimulated them to reinvest profit. They remained, nevertheless, confined to commercial capitalism and did not engage in manufacture because of adherence to the doctrine of ahimsa.

Weber considers the possibility that Jainism was the product of a bourgeois class of traders. The sect is, he notes, associated with rise of the city in India. But he goes on to argue that these religious ideas stemmed mainly from Kshatriya thought and lay asceticism. They imposed, in fact, a considerable measure of restriction on mercantile activity and could hardly be seen as a reflection of mercantile interests. Jainism enjoyed its greatest flowering not at a time when the bourgeoisie was developing but when city politics and guild power were in decline.

The other great heterodox tradition that developed in India was Buddhism. This we shall examine in the next chapter. Here we shall consider the work that has been done on Hinduism since Weber.

THE SOCIOLOGY OF HINDUISM SINCE WEBER

To date, no scholar in the field of sociology has matched Weber in breadth of knowledge of and insight into the world religions and their relationship to the societies in which they have been dominant. Not even within particular specialist areas of sociological study of particular religious traditions has there been anyone to rival Weber's historical scope and grasp. The sociology of the world religions remains a poorly developed and neglected field. Most of the work that has been done since Weber has concentrated on detailed and largely ethnographic studies of religious belief and practice within small communities, usually carried out by anthropologists. Even these remain limited in number, scope and often in quality.

Much of this work has addressed issues raised by Weber's studies but much of it has been concerned with problems of its own. Particularly prominent has been the relationship between popular interpretations of religious doctrine and popular practice in relation to orthodox, canonical and priestly or monkish interpretations. This bears upon Weber's concerns since a criticism often made of him is that he tended to assume that the religion in question could be taken to be that expressed in scriptures and texts. What is important for his claims, however, is the actual popular understanding of the religion which often deviates considerably from scriptural and canonical forms. Hinduism is no exception.

The sheer diversity of belief and practice encompassed by the term Hinduism in India has posed severe problems for the sociologist of religion. Not only is there the difficulty of understanding popular religiosity in relation to that of the canonical tradition but in India popular religion shows a diversity which almost defies generalisation whilst at the same time it is difficult to claim that any canonical form of Hinduism exists. It might be thought, for example, that belief in karmic determination of fate would be central throughout India but even here there is room for considerable local variation. Kolenda's (1964) study of a sweeper caste in Uttar Pradesh shows that they do not explain their low caste position in terms of karma. Only the broad distinction between castes who serve others and those who are served by others is explained by them in this way. They believe themselves to be descended from a high caste ancestor, their own low position being explained in terms of them being cheated out of their true status. This attitude is compatible with a view that the misfortunes of life can be alleviated by magical means. Gough (1960) found low-caste villagers in Tanjore similarly sceptical while Maloney (1975) reports much the same thing for villagers in Tamilnadu. Wadley and Derr's (1989) work in Karimpur, Uttar Pradesh found little linkage between karma and rebirth in popular belief. Karma had much more to do with explaining misfortune in terms of retribution for sins committed in this life. In some regions, among certain groups there may even be complete ignorance of the notion altogether as is the case with the Chamars of Uttar Pradesh (Cohn, 1959).

Nevertheless, a central theme running through most studies of religion in India, is that of the relationship between popular belief and practice on the one hand and Brahmin orthodoxy on the other. We usually find, contemporary studies have shown, two closely interconnected and overlapping systems of religious ideas – one relating to the 'official' and canonical and the other to popular adaptations of this. Anthropologists have suggested that each of these relates to rather different functions or needs and concerns. The canonical forms are particularly the concern of religious specialists such as priests and monks but also of laymen in certain circumstances and for specific purposes. Popular interpretations are the concern of laymen in the more mundane aspects of their daily existence.

Mandelbaum (1966) has introduced a useful pair of terms to refer to these two aspects of a religious tradition, namely the *transcendental* and the *pragmatic* dimensions. The transcendental complex relates to such things as the long-term welfare of society, the explanation of social institutions and the legitimation of the passage of individuals in and out of these institutions through rites de passage. The transcendental complex is concerned with the ultimate purposes of man, with salvation and with the fate of the soul after death. The pragmatic complex relates to more limited concerns, personal matters and individual welfare. It may be concerned, for example, with curing sickness, blessing an enterprise, warding off bad luck, and so on.

The degree of segregation between these two complexes, the degree to which they are independent and distinct, Mandelbaum notices, varies considerably from one religion to another and also within particular religious traditions from one community to another. He examines the reasons for this in the context of communities in South Asia.

Generally the typical Hindu village in India treats the two complexes as on the whole separate and distinct but complementary. Each has somewhat different rites and utilises somewhat different symbols. Different religious specialists are involved in each – Brahmin priests in the transcendental complex and various diagnosticians, exorcists and shamans, usually of low caste, in the pragmatic complex. Much the same situation exists in Muslim communities, he points out.

Among tribal peoples in India this degree of segregation is not found. There are two distinct categories of officiant in religious rituals and ceremonies, the priest and the shaman, but they address themselves to the same deities and both participate at the same time in the same rituals.

In Buddhist communities in Sri Lanka there is an even more pronounced separation of the two spheres than in village India. Only the transcendental complex is considered to be Buddhist. The pragmatic complex is not considered wrong or a deviation from Buddhism but simply a different and distinct affair even if an inferior one.

Finally, Mandelbaum mentions a number of reform movements within Hinduism and Buddhism which are either opposed to the pragmatic complex or despise it and consider it to be worthless and irrelevant.

We can order, then, these situations on a scale. At one extreme we have the tribal Hindu case in which the separation is minimal, followed by the Hindu village where the distinction is weak and then the Sri Lankan Buddhist village where it is strong with the reform Hindu position which rejects one side of it entirely located at the opposite extreme. Corresponding to each of these cases there are four types of situation which Mandelbaum terms undifferentiated, partly differentiated, fully differentiated and reform respectively. Mandelbaum believes it is possible to place all religious systems and variations within religious systems along this scale. Each type is related, he argues, to Bellah's stages in the evolution of religion, namely primitive, archaic, historic and early modern.

The reason for this very widespread phenomenon is attributed, by Mandelbaum, to the fact that there are two sets of needs or motives underlying religiosity. One centres on explaining the world and giving significance to life while the other centres on the relief of suffering. The two dimensions are in many ways opposite. One concerns what is general and timeless while the other relates to the specific, personal and immediate.

Mandelbaum's distinction is very useful and helps us to understand some of the diversity of interpretation and practice that we find when we look empirically at religious communities. Work in the ethnography of the world religions, however, has shown that the actual situation may be rather more complex than Mandelbaum allows for.

A number of writers have questioned Mandelbaum's distinction between transcendental and pragmatic aspects of religion in its application to the differences between Brahmin and popular religion. Many fieldworkers have found the situation to be rather more complex. Babb (1975), for example, working in Madhya Pradesh state, found Brahmin priestly religion to be as much bound up with pragmatic concerns as Mandelbaum's tribal priests. Wadley (1975) reports for Karimpur in Uttar Pradesh that it is often difficult to distinguish between transcendental and pragmatic concerns in everyday belief and practice. Gold's (1988) study of pilgrimage in Rajasthan broadly supports this view. Others have focused on the tradition of renunciation as the true expression of transcendentalism as opposed to the priestly function (Dumont, 1970b). Babb (1975) also reports that renunciation is seen as a source of spiritual power.

Despite the diversity of belief and practice in India several writers have attempted to come to terms with it. Marriott (1955), following Redfield, distinguishes a general 'great tradition' in contrast to popular 'little traditions' and Srinivas (1952), speaks of much the same dichotomy in terms of all-India 'Sanskritic' forms versus non-Sanskritic local forms. Marriott's work in Uttar Pradesh shows that both great and little traditions can remain in equilibrium in the village community, neither excluding the other. He identifies a process of universalisation whereby elements of the local tradition may be universalised to become part of the great tradition (for example the thread worn by the twice born may have been a local custom which was absorbed into the general Sanskritic tradition) and parochialisation whereby elements of the great tradition are transformed and localised in popular practice. The two traditions thus constantly interact and change one another. Srinivas describes a process of Sanskritisation in which more prestigious Sanskritic elements associated with Brahmins and high caste practice replace local non-Sanskritic elements among groups who aspire to a higher social standing.

More recent work has tended to find this model unhelpful in that it tends to oversimplify a complex reality and to impose an over-dichotomous picture of this reality. Fuller (1992) points out, also, that it represents the Brahmin and, therefore, an ideological view of Hinduism. Sanskritic Hinduism tends to be presented by Brahmin groups as the paradigmatic form so elevating their interpretation of the tradition to a superior position relative to other interpretations favoured by lower status castes.

Against this rather dichotomising approach to the understanding of religious diversity in India, Harper (1959) has argued that the two complexes identified by writers such as Marriott and Srinivas should be understood in relation to one another as parts of the same system. Harper points out that gods worshipped in a South Indian village can be placed in three categories; vegetarian, Sanskritic *devaru*, meat-eating, local *devata;* and blood-thirsty, demonic *devva*. The first type are worshipped primarily by Brahmins and higher castes and the latter two by lower castes. The devaru might be said to fit Mandelbaum's transcendental complex since they are worshipped for largely spiritual ends whereas the others are worshipped largely for pragmatic this-worldly ends. These gods form a hierarchy (Harper, 1964) which includes human beings. The vegetarian deities stand in much the same relationship to the meat-eating deities as high castes with their purer lifestyle stand in relation to impure low castes. Just as higher castes require the services of low caste members in order to remain pure, that is to perform those tasks that would be polluting for them to perform themselves, so the gods require the priestly services of human beings in order to remain pure themselves. These services are performed by the Brahmin priests who absorb the impurities of the gods and must, consequently, be in a relatively pure state to do so. The notions of purity and pollution provide, then, the unifying theme of Hindu religion. Dumont (1970a) similarly places the purity–impurity distinction at the centre of his analysis of Hinduism as the overriding principle. Sharma (1970) also supports this view on the basis of data pertaining to Kangara district in Northern India where, she shows, there is an underlying consistency of idiom, namely that of purity–pollution, in all aspects of ritual whether Sanskritic or purely local, transcendental or pragmatic. Also, as with Harper's data, Sharma's supports the view that the Hindu pantheon can be interpreted as an upward extension of the caste system. Moffatt (1979), describing Harijan beliefs in Tamilnadu, concurs to a large extent with this view but shows that it would be very misleading in this case to present the various levels of gods as being exclusively gods of the different strata of society. In this region, it is not the case that Brahmins worship only the high, vegetarian gods while Harijans worship gods representing the whole spectrum of deities which are either identical to or replicatory of the gods worshipped by groups much higher in the system.

Against this view that the purity–pollution divide is at the heart of and is the organising principle of Hinduism, Maloney (1975) argues, on the basis of data relating to Tamilnadu, that a picture of a hierarchy of gods distinguished by their degree of purity is really not so much the reality but an ideological device by which the orthodox seek to enhance their own status position. Again it seems, at least according to Maloney's view, attempts to find a coherence and unity in Hinduism end up by presenting a largely Brahmin and sectional view of things as the actual and objective state of affairs, a point that Van der Veer (1988) makes in his study of monks and priest in the pilgrim centre of Ayodhya in Northern India.

A similar view has been argued even more cogently by Fuller (1992). Harper's analysis of removal of ritual impurity of the gods through the way they are worshipped (*puja*) is faulty according to Fuller. Puja essentially honours the gods rather than purifying them. The procedures which worshippers go through to remove their own impurity are necessary because to worship the gods in an impure state is to dishonour them. There is no sense of any danger of worshippers transfering pollution to the gods as a low caste person or untouchable might transfer pollution to a Brahmin.

Other scholars are equally sceptical of the emphasis placed upon purity as *the* central theme of Hinduism by writers such as Dumont, Harper and Sharma. Wadley (1975), for example, would place just as much emphasis upon spiritual power. Purity and power, she argues, are inseparable. Power depends upon the spiritual state of the person and therefore their condition in terms of purity.

The view which emphasises a division between Sanskritic and other forms of Hinduism, as we have seen, stresses that the religious system is very much an expression of the social system of caste organisation. The view that purity lies at the heart of it might well be compatible with this but in the eyes of some, and most notably Dumont (1970a), the social system is in fact considered to be essentially determined by religion and in particular by this central principle of opposition between pure and impure. This opposition is fundamentally bound up with the notion of the impurity of organic life, a Brahmin obsession according to Dumont. Anything which is closely related to the body and bodily functions is inherently impure in Brahmin thought. The caste system is thus for Dumont essentially a system in the intellectual sense. It is a system of ideas and values or an ideological system as he would put it. In this system we should not see the varnas as categories in a linear order but as a series of successive dichotomies, oppositions or exclusions. Brahmin, Kshatriya and Vaishya are opposed to the Sudra as the twice born castes. Brahmin and Kshatriya are further opposed to the Vaishya and Sudra as exercising authority which the others do not. Finally, the Brahmins are opposed to the other three as ritual specialists.

The society is organised in status terms on the basis of pure hierarchy in the original sense of the term, namely in terms of religious and ritual superiority. In the case of Hinduism this means ritual purity which is jealously protected from contacts which would diminish it. From this springs the rules governing social interaction, intermarriage and so on.

Dumont is aware, however, that relatively high caste groups – Kshatriya castes – often do not maintain a lifestyle commensurate with their high status in the system. They are frequently not vegetarian and their traditional caste dharma involved the taking of life.

The ambivalent position of the Kshatriya castes with respect to religious values can be seen very clearly in Carstairs' (1957) study of a Rajput community. Being a Kshatriya caste the Rajputs are inevitably bound up with worldly affairs and concerns. As a military caste their dharma, furthermore, involves the taking of life. They are also meat eaters, drink alcohol and keep concubines. Yet they accept the renunciatory values and goals of Hinduism. Although the religious goals of Hinduism were desired and pursued to very varying degrees by different individuals, most Rajput men in the village gave at least lip service to them and some attempted to pursue them seriously. The primary aim was the pursuit of *moksh* through the purging of everything worldly, sensual and carnal. Abstinence, celibacy and disengagement from sensual and emotional gratification were upheld as essential to achieve liberation from the cycle of rebirths and the freeing of the soul so that it could merge with the divine. This was a goal that might take many incarnations to achieve but in order to progress upon the road it was necessary to engage in devotional exercises, prayer, meditation and to observe ritually correct behaviour. Unlike Brahmins, whose caste dharma made it far more possible to pursue the religious life, the Kshatriya Rajputs were mostly doomed to fight a losing battle in this religious endeavour.

Dumont attempts to overcome the apparent problem that the contradiction of Kshatriya status and impure lifestyle implies for his approach by treating power, as opposed to ideology, as an intrusive and distorting factor. The Kshatriyas were the rulers who exercised power and authority in secular affairs. They were landowners and commanded military power. This power gave them a higher status than they would otherwise have enjoyed according to the purity/pollution rules. Power can offset pollution.

> power exists in the society, and the Brahman who thinks in terms of hierarchy knows this perfectly well; yet hierarchy cannot give a place to power as such, without contradicting its own principle. Therefore it must give a place to power without saying so, and it is obliged to close its eyes to this point on pain of destroying itself. In other words, once the King is made subordinate to the priest, as the very existence of hierarchy presupposes, it must give him a place after the priest, and before the other, unless it is absolutely to deny his dignity and thus the usefulness of his function. (Dumont, 1970a, p. 77)

Dumont, then, does not deny that the relatively privileged material position of the Kshatriya – one might say their class position is the product of their power just as it is for any group. Their status is also influenced by their power but the real and fundamental determinant of status is ritual purity.[2]

It is difficult to see why Dumont should wish to give priority to ritual purity in the determination of status in Indian society rather than recognising that in fact both power and ritual values are important. One might equally, for example, consider power to be fundamental and religion to be a disturbing factor which explains the anomalous position of Brahmins. Even then, one might explain their position not so much in terms of ideology but in terms of the power they enjoyed as indispensable ritual specialists and practitioners who legitimated and ritually protected the rule of princes, as Weber does. Their high status position would thus be the outcome of their monopolisation of crucial and scarce services and the fact that this enabled them to acquire land and thereby economic autonomy. Berreman (1966, 1967) sees the Brahmin emphasis on ritual purity as ideological in a rather different sense of the word from Dumont's use of it. For Berreman it has manipulative utility in dividing in order to rule and in justifying caste division. Each caste is so concerned to protect its relatively higher position from encroachment from those below that unity of purpose in opposing Brahmin and Kshatriya domination is undermined. Low caste status and relatively less privileged social situations are legitimated in terms of karmic retribution for misdeeds in past existences.

Conformity with and acceptance of the present order of things is promoted since it will bring a better rebirth in the next existence and rebellion a worse one.

It is important, however, to see how power and ritual values interact and to analyse the complex relationship between them. Both Dumont and Berreman are right up to a point. It is a mistake to interpret Hinduism as merely or even predominantly an ideological tool as it is to treat power as a secondary and distorting factor in the traditional Indian status system. Weber's view was more sophisticated if not so clearly spelled out. Brahmins in Weber's analysis, while they had a vested interest in the ritualisation of all aspects life, were also predisposed to see the world as something to be ritually controlled and life as something requiring constant purificatory attention as a result of their social location and function. Caste status may be seen as the joint product of power and ritual values.

In many ways reflecting this Weberian subtlety whilst boldly grasping the nettle of attempting explanation which roots cultural aspects firmly in material processes of struggle between groups for resources, power and status, is the highly original recent study of Milner (1994). Milner considers that many of the features of Hinduism can best be understood by focusing clearly upon the fact that status in Indian caste-based society plays a role the centrality of which is greater than in any other known to us. For Milner, status must be seen as a resource and a particular form of power. It does not make sense, if this is true, to separate rigidly, as Dumont does, power and status. Status is a peculiar sort of resource, however, in that it is inalienable and 'inexpansible', that is to say there are severe limits to the extent to which it can be increased or expanded. High status presupposes that few enjoy it. To give greater status or prestige to those low in a status hierarchy is to devalue the status position of those at the top.

It is a feature of status systems, as Weber (1968) showed in his classic analysis of them, that the members of the groups that comprise them are required to conform to a particular and often quite distinctive lifestyle and pattern of conduct including consumption patterns. There are typically restrictions on occupational choice, mode of earning a living as well as a code governing speech, dress, manners and so on, particularly in the case of high status groups. Association with members of other status groups may be restricted and a test of status is often acceptance of association, especially intimate and private association, on the part of acknowledged members of the group. Thus there may be barriers to intermarriage, socialisation and commensality with members of other groups. High status groups will typically attempt to restrict mobility into them. Their lifestyles and codes of behaviour are in large part ways of achieving this, of keeping out the *parvenu*. In order to restrict mobility boundaries must be carefully defined and maintained.

It is not difficult to see how this might be applied to Indian society. Weber, of course, saw caste organisation as a paradigmatic form of status stratification. What Milner adds is the insight that status is closely related to sacredness and through this realisation he is able to offer an interpretation of many of the features of Hinduism as a religion. Indian society exhibits an extreme case of status stratification and, therefore, an intense preoccupation with the definition and maintenance of boundaries through restrictions on social intercourse, commensality, intermarriage and so on, and through the adoption of distinctive codes of practice and lifestyles on the part of the various caste groups. All this is conceptualised, managed and legitimated through concepts of purity and pollution, or in other words, through the religious values and principles of Hinduism. Milner applies this approach to certain other central features of Hinduism, namely its typical pattern of worship, its soteriology and its eschatology.

In Hinduism, worship of the gods can be seen, according to Milner, as a process of status enhancement based upon status deference. In a status system the status of an individual or group can be enhanced by interaction with those of acknowledged high status. The closer and more intimate the interaction the greater the status enhancement. In order to establish and maintain such a relationship with higher status groups those lower in status must show deference. For those higher in status, displays of deference help to confirm their high status. Also those who wish to enhance their status must attempt to set themselves apart from those who are lower than themselves in status and demand in turn deferential treatment from them.

Such relationships and processes are characteristic of worship of the gods in Hinduism. The gods, of course, have high status. Worship of them involves the worshippers making themselves worthy of attention in the presence of the gods, praising and showing deference to them and establishing intimate association with them.

In worship, the worshipper must be in as pure a state as possible. Worship should not begin without rituals of purification having been carried out. Purity figures as a metaphor for status here, according to Milner, but is interpreted in literal fashion by most Hindus. It expresses, however, the sacral status of the worshipper in relation to the deities and establishes their worthiness in the eyes of the gods through the fact that it is a way honouring them. As metaphors rituals of purification set worshippers apart from that which is impure and through the use of purifying substances, such as water or cow dung, increasingly brings them into closer association with that which is pure. This mirrors the process of status enhancement in which there is a setting apart from those lower in status and an attempt to establish close association with those higher in status.

Secondly, the deity is given praise and shown deference just as a higher status person would be flattered and shown deference. Again, this involves honouring the god. Finally, close association or communion with a god usually takes the form of offering food which is then consumed by the worshipper. Interpretations of the meaning of this practice vary considerably but in all cases an intimacy is established between worshipper and the gods which results in a blessing upon the worshipper. It is significant that the giving and sharing of food is fundamental in most cultures to the establishment and maintenance of intimacy and close association.

Similarly, the Hindu concept of salvation can be understood to reflect status concerns. Salvation in Hindu thought, Milner argues, can be seen as a form or analogue of social mobility or status transformation. Our understanding of processes of status transformation can thus enlighten us on the meaning of notions of salvation. Milner identifies two primary sources of status, conformity to norms and association. The latter we have examined in discussing worship. The former involves processes of securing the approval of others by demonstrating conformity with the behavioural patterns and the lifestyle expected by the status group concerned. In the religious context, these two sources of status find their expression in alternative conceptions of paths to salvation, namely whether it is achieved by works or by grace, that is to say good works and conformity to divine law or simply through a gift of God.

In Hinduism this debate can be seen most clearly in the Bhagavad Gita where three major paths to salvation are discussed, namely *jnana yoga, karma yoga* and *bhakti yoga*. The first two emphasise conformity; to causal laws in the first case and to norms in the second, while the last emphasises intimate association with the deity. Thus Smarta orthodoxy, given its formal acceptance of jnana yoga but practical emphasis on conformity to dharma, is interpreted by Milner as representing the status strategy of conformity, particularly to norms and

moral standards, while sectarian bhakti devotional cults are interpreted as representing the status strategy of association.

Turning to eschatology, Milner points out that the realm of beliefs
and practices pertaining to the sacred, while they may be projections of
social relationships, frequently reverse these relationships rather than
simply being copies of them. This is because religious beliefs usually
offer compensations for the injustices and privations of this life. Thus
Christian teaching states that the last shall be first and so on.

Applying this to Hinduism we might expect that its eschatology will
express reversals of social patterns. In its doctrines of samsara, karma
and moksh, Milner argues, this is precisely what it does. Thus the
notion of an endless cycle of rebirths is a reversal of the social pattern
of little or no mobility. The idea of samsara is one of endless mobility.
The law of karma states essentially that status in the next life is an
entirely achieved one, depending upon conduct in this life. The actual
social pattern, however, is one of rigidly ascribed status. The social
pattern of Indian traditional society places a heavy emphasis on differentiation of status and maintenance of boundaries. It is significant that
true salvation, escape from the cycle of rebirths, at least through the
most prestigious route of renunciation and acceptance of the insights
of Advaita Vendanta, involves a rejection of dualism and separateness,
relinquishing social identity and the recognition of the unity of self
(*atman*) and the ultimate reality (Brahman).

Other traditions, such as Vaishnavism and bhakti devotionalism,
interpret things somewhat differently, of course, but these can be
seen as on the one hand conservative and on the other radical variations of the mainstream view.

Milner's analysis is bold, provocative and thought provoking. There
are, of course, numerous objections that could be made either in
respect of its general theoretical foundations or the specific interpretations of aspects of Hinduism. The richness and breadth of his analysis
means that it will not be possible here to take up many of these points.
One general question can be raised, however, namely that while it is
ingenious in its interpretations it may be somewhat selective in choos-
ing aspects of Hinduism which best fit the theoretical model and in
selecting the evidence which most supports it. But few original and
innovative analyses of something as complex and intractable to understanding as Hinduism are free of such faults, and it does not follow
that Milner's analysis need not be given close thought and examination
on the part of those who wish to achieve a better understanding of
Hinduism.

One specific omission from Milner's analysis that might be mentioned is the way in which karma is used ideologocally in Hinduism. Milner is aware that the doctrine is not only concerned with the determination of future fate but has other dimensions. He mentions how in its implication that current social position has been determined by actions in past lives, it takes on the role of presenting the world as embodying a system of perfect justice. Strangely, he does not refer to the way this can be interpreted as a legitimating and, therefore, perhaps ideological device used to uphold the stratification system.

Also his analysis neglects the common use of the notion of karma to explain misfortune in popular Hinduism. While Milner is aware of this he does little more than to acknowledge that there are a diversity of interpretations and uses of doctrines such as that of karma and others in Hinduism. What is striking, however, is the way in which karma is used to make sense of eventualities in life and to give meaning to them in popular Hinduism rather than to explain current social position or to provide hope for a future improvement. As we have seen, it is not uncommon in parts of India that such ideas are actually rejected. Use of the doctrine of karma to make sense of contingencies and to explain misfortunes cannot be easily related to the status system central to traditional Indian society, however, and would seem to require a broader interpretation such as that of Babb (1983).

Babb points out that the doctrine of karma always stands alongside a set of other ideas used to explain misfortune which tend, in fact, to be more readily resorted to than the notion of karma. Wadley and Derr's (1989) findings in Karimpur support this. There karma was used as an explanation for misfortune relatively infrequently, especially with regard to everyday misfortunes. Illness, for example, is most often explained in terms of the malice of another person, spirit or agency in the Chhattisgarh region of Central India which Babb studied as is also the case for Himachal Pradesh as reported by Sharma (1973). On the other hand, despite much variation in the interpretation and use of the idea and occasional ignorance of it, as we have seen above, it is on the whole widely understood and accepted. It seems that it is important in popular thought yet rarely resorted to in concrete circumstances. Why this should be so might be answered in terms of Mandelbaum's pragmatic and transcental complex with karma belonging to the more transcendental dimension concerned with ultimate fate and destiny with little application to everyday pragmatic concerns. This, however, is patently not the case Babb points out. Everywhere karma is used to explain certain kinds of specific misfortune that befalls people from time to time.

Babb's answer to this rests upon the observation, drawing on Sharma (1973) and Daniel (1983), that different ways of explaining misfortune are linked to notions of varying degrees of responsibility and the allocation of blame. Some explanations imply the victim or others carry responsibility while others imply that it is simply fate or chance and there are a variety of midway positions between these poles.

The idea of karma, of course, implies that the sufferer of misfortune carries responsibility for it whereas many of the other ways of accounting for misfortune in India imply mere fate or destiny beyond the control of the individual. Attribution of misfortune to malevolent others, however, unlike in the case of fate, allows ameliorative or therapeutic action. So does the idea of karma, at least for the longer term. Yet there is an element of fate or destiny in the notion. It seems, as Babb (1983) puts it, to affirm and deny human responsibility at the same time. An individual cannot know their karmic balance. Misfortunes in this life could occur as a result of actions in past lives which they cannot know about and in a sense are not responsible for. Karmic theory rests upon the 'hypothesis of amnesia', to use Babb's turn of phrase. On the other hand, the karmic idea upholds the notion of personal responsibility for fate. It is significant, Babb points out, that karmic theory places human problems in a deeper temporal setting. Other ways of accounting for misfortune, such as attributing it to witchcraft, the wrath of ancestors and so on, while similar in many respects to the idea of karma, have an immediacy which karmic theory does not. Karma can thus account for the injustices of this life and promise retribution or compensation in the next while at the same time being used to account for specific misfortunes. It can act as a theodicy and an explanation of specific and immediate troubles simultaneously. As Babb puts it 'present experiences become the product of the entire moral career of the transmigrating self...specific misfortunes...are less the consequences of specific discoverable, and thus correctable omissions or errors, and more the symptoms of the general moral condition of the experiencing self' (1983, p. 177). But in doing this it pays the price of not being able to offer much practical help in a concrete and immediate situation. Here reference to witchcraft, ancestors or deities allows action to be taken. Such explanations, however, cannot relate the occurrences to a wider moral reference and order of meaning. Karma tells people that the moral life is in some way consequential. It links moral responsibility and destiny but in such a way as to acknowledge the unpredictability of life in the short run. It can be used to explain misfortune but in a way that affirms a meaningful understanding of the place of men and women in a meaningful reality.

This analysis, whether correct or otherwise, thus takes us a long way from status concerns and shows the limitations of Milner's approach in this regard both in addressing the other and more popular use of the notion of karma to that of the determination of social position and in terms of an understanding of its broader significance for the mainten-ance of a meaningful understanding of life. Where status does come into the picture, as Fuller (1992) points out, is in the differential tendency to attribute misfortune to karmic versus non-karmic causes by caste. Higher castes tend to regard the popular attribution of misfortune to personified agencies as superstition and so fill the void by resort to the idea of karma. Given that the lower castes are less inclined to accept karmic ideas, one tends to find, therefore, that the probability that misfortune will be ascribed to karma varies inversely with the probability that it will be blamed on other sources.

The other aspect of Hinduism that seems to be lacking from Milner's analysis about which a good deal has been written and which we shall examine here concerns the prevalence and centrality of female deities in Hinduism. What Milner says about this occurs within the context of his discussion of the Brahmin ideal of sexual restraint. Sexual abstin-ence, or at least strict control and limitation of sexual activity, is always a symbol of self-discipline and control, crucial to Brahmins since in the renunciatiory ideal lies the source of Brahmin power and status rather than in political or economic position. Such self-restraint is not easy and there is always the anxiety that it will not be main-tained; there is always the fear of seduction and temptation. This becomes expressed in the image of the aggressive female symbolised by the devouring goddess such as Durga or Kali.

This hardly does justice to the often remarked upon prominence of female deities and the importance of the feminine principle in Hinduism. As Kakar (1978) puts it, 'Hindu cosmology is feminine to an extent rarely found in other major civilisations' (p. 110). Milner's reference to fear of the devouring goddess is, however, a theme that has frequently been commented upon by writers who have generally taken a psycho-analytic approach rather than a sociological one. These writers have seen in goddesses such as Kali symbols of the mother, a figure around which there is much ambivalence in Indian culture due to practices of child rearing (Carstairs, 1957; Kakar, 1978; Obeyeskere, 1984).

Carstairs (1957) interprets the renunciatory ideal of Hinduism in terms of a neo-Freudian human personality formation theory, along similar lines to Spiro's analysis of Buddhism examined in the next chapter. In India, he points out, the infant child is indulged to the extreme until about the age of one and a half to two years. At this age the mother's attention becomes less reliable, the infant now sleeps away from the mother and weaning begins. The child's confidence is shattered and mistrust of the world comes to dominate its outlook. This is commensurate with the doctrine of *maya* – that the material world is illusory. This contrasts markedly with the upbringing of children in the West where in infancy frustration at delayed satisfaction is frequently experienced and, consequently, the child often indulges in moderate aggressive fantasies but finds that they do not to lead to the withdrawal of maternal affection and care. The Indian child experiences the desertion of the mother as final and the frustration is, therefore, much more intense. It receives expression in religious fantasy in which the mother becomes a terrible, revengeful, bloodthirsty and horrifying goddess, Kali, who decapitates men and drinks their blood. Obeyesekere (1984) takes a similar view dubbing Kali as the 'castrating mother'. She must be propitiated and given total submission. In other words she becomes the protective mother once again only when men submit and make themselves helpless infants in relation to her. Similarly, the ideal of suppression of carnality and sexuality, the renunciatory ideal of Hinduism, is interpreted by Carstairs as symbolically expressing a return to infancy – a state in which it was possible to exercise complete power to compel maternal compliance with one's wishes.

The Indian ascetic, the total renouncer, Carstairs observes, achieves three things: firstly, omnipotence, against which even the gods, the ultimate father figures, are powerless; secondly, a sense of bliss which corresponds to sexual satisfaction; and finally release from separate selfhood and union with the divine which corresponds to the overcoming of separation from the mother. He points out that the ascetic who attains the very highest peak of religious endeavour is believed to acquire supernatural powers including foreknowledge of the time of his attainment of moksh. There are celebrated occasions when such a saint takes *samadhi*. He is lowered, alive and cross-legged into a pit and covered with earth. The saint has attained, Carstairs claims, through the complete annihilation of all desire and distracting stimuli from the external world, the feat of regression to the prenatal state and is symbolically returned to the womb and to eternal bliss at one with the creator.

Carstairs applies this approach to a number of other features of Hindu belief and practice including aspects of pollution ideas, the sacredness of the cow, Shiva and Vishnu worship, the taboo on taking life and on eating meat. The latter, for example, is claimed to be the conscious reaction formation against repressed oedipal feelings of hostility against the father which are never allowed direct expression.

Kakar's analysis (1978), although also inspired by psychoanalytic ideas, is rather different. The relationship between mother and son in India is indeed a highly emotionally charged one, he agrees. The ideal of the good mother finds its expression in protective goddesses such as Lakshmi, Sarasvati and Parvati. The Indian male does indeed harbour a deep fear of abandonment by the mother. This fear is overcome in the fantasy of the nurturing and reassuring character of such goddesses. In the ideal of moksh, also, we see the goal of transcendance of isolation and separation through union of self and the totality, again a denial in fantasy of abandonment.

Other female deities express in fantasy the idea of the bad and threatening mother, but rather than this being the consequence of the sudden withdrawal of maternal affection in the child rearing pattern it must be attributed more to the intensity of maternal affection that is characteristic of child rearing in India in the early years of life. In India the birth of a son is an event of enormous importance for a woman. It establishes her worth and identity. A son is a kind of saviour given her position in the Indian family structure. She lavishes, as a consequence, care and affection upon her son. At the same time the son can become an object not simply of gratitude and affection, but of the mother's unfulfilled erotic desires and wishes as a result of a socially enforced progressive renunciation of sexuality for Indian women. Women thus turn the full force of their eroticism towards their infant sons who feel overwhelmed and threatened by this. The other side of the Indian view of women as nurturing and protective is the semi-unacknowledged conviction of their lustful, insatiable and life-sapping sexuality. Men are thought to lose strength and vitality through sexual intercourse and loss of semen.

The appeal of Krishna in Hindu culture is attributed by Kakar to the fact that for women he is a surrogate and perfect son with all the delightful, even if somewhat immoral and reprehensible attributes, of the beloved son. This is very different from the male relationship to Krishna which takes the form of personal devotion, often likened to the ideal of the feminine passive and receptive devotion to a lover. Obeyesekere (1984), on the other hand, considers that women's fascination with the Krishna figure suggests the idea of a surrogate lover.

Much of the psychoanalytic interpretations outlined above will seem rather far-fetched. Also, they do not always agree too closely with one another. As with any Freudian approach there is always the problem that one can read into the practices whatever symbolism fits the theory and the danger of selecting only that which does. There is also the problem raised below in connection with the similar analysis of Buddhism that there are only a limited number of possible child rearing patterns yet there is enormous diversity in religious belief and practice. The fact that Carstairs explains Hindu asceticism and devotionalism while Spiro explains the quite different anti-saviour figure aspects of Theravada Buddhism – which has been characterised as the middle way and which specifically rejected extreme asceticism – in terms of much the same child rearing patterns, cast considerable doubt upon this approach. It is an approach which continues, nevertheless, to appear fruitful in the view of a number of authors.

4 Buddhism

WEBER ON BUDDHISM

Buddhism offered a rather different route to salvation than Jainism. The path of the Jains was that of other-worldly asceticism; that of the Buddhists was other-worldly mysticism.

Ancient Buddhism, Weber remarks, postulated no deity or god. It had no cult practices. In fact the Buddha and his disciples were completely indifferent to the question of whether there was a god or gods, spirits or demons. Buddhism has never denied the possible existence of such things. It simply considers the matter irrelevant to Buddhism. The Buddha taught that salvation could be achieved only by the personal actions of the individual and not by recourse to personal saviours or redeemers.

Buddhism accepted that salvation was to be found in escape from the cycle of rebirths and the attainment of nirvana and it accepted the doctrine of karma. Salvation is achieved by avoiding action behind which there is some intent. The Buddhist ideal is, then, to free the self from all worldly desires. It is desire which gives rise to worldly activity; desire means attachment to life. For the Buddhist all attachment entails suffering. Salvation is the escape from suffering.

Unlike Christianity which emphasises sin, Weber points out, Buddhism emphasises suffering and escape from it. It teaches that all passion must be avoided because passion represents the fight against the inherent transitoriness of all existence – the refusal to accept the futility of worldly action, a refusal which is doomed to failure. All desire and all passion stem from the will – the will for life. Salvation is achieved by extinguishing the desire and the will in order to escape the consequences of karma which leads inevitably to a new incarnation. Good action leads to a better incarnation but an endless cycle even of good incarnations means an endless cycle of suffering since they inevitably involve loss, fear of loss, illness and ultimate death. Bad action leads to a worse incarnation with even more suffering. Actions which are carried out with indifference for the outcome do not lead to the acquisition of karma. Only good actions can be detached in this way. Bad action cannot be detached and will inevitably lead to bad karma.

In seeking to achieve these aims Buddhism, according to Weber, takes a direction which is devoid of any practical consequences for society.

Assurance of one's state of grace, that is, certain knowledge of one's own salvation is not sought through proving one's self by any inner-worldly or extra-worldly action, by 'work' of any kind, but in contrast to this, it is sought in a psychic state remote from activity. (1958, p. 213)

Of course, these ideals could only be realised by full-time monks. In fact, the monkish way of life, particularly that of the wandering mendicant monk, was idealised. The early disciples of the Buddha took up this way of life.

Weber concludes that 'a rational economic ethic could hardly have developed in this sort of religious order' (ibid., p. 216). The teachings of the Buddha were not likely to promote social change or any kind of reform. Buddhism, Weber, said, was essentially apolitical and asocial. Unlike Western monasticism the Buddhist monastic ideal did not promote any rational methods of ordering life conduct in all its aspects. All that happened, in fact, was that when permanent communities of monks grew up they acquired land, and the monk in effect became a landlord living on income derived from the productive labour of lay workers attached to the monastery. Buddhist monks were primarily concerned with meditation and contemplation, supported by rents from land or the produce of slaves or bondsmen, or simply by gifts from the laity. Buddhism, then, represents a 'complete elimination of any form of inner-worldly motivation to conduct or rational purpose in nature' (ibid., p. 222).

The following of ancient Buddhism was drawn largely, Weber argues, from the great noble families and rich burghers, that is the secular strata of nobles. It was not, therefore, a religion of the under-privileged but of the higher non-Brahmin groups. Its anti-Brahmin attitudes gave it appeal to such strata. The socially oppressed were not attracted by it at all. Its methods had nothing to offer them and it was indifferent to social change. It was yet another elitist development. It became, however, one of the great missionary religions in history. Weber accounts for this partly in terms of the desire of the monks to increase the number of supporters and therefore providers of sustenance.

In Part III of *The Religions of India* Weber traces the development of Buddhism and its eventual division into the two great branches or schools of Mahayana and Hinayana, its adoption as the official state religion under Ashoka, its spread beyond the Indian subcontinent, its ultimate disappearance from India itself, the restoration of orthodox

Hinduism and the emergence of various sectarian forms of the latter such as Shivaism and Vaishnavism.

The dominant theme in all this is the contradiction or conflict between the extreme elitism of Buddhism and many other Indian religious systems and the needs of the masses. The major split that occurred within Buddhism relates to this lack of appeal in its original form. In order to maintain a following in the face of competition from other doctrines it had to accommodate its teachings to such needs.

Under King Ashoka, who unified most of India under his rule, Buddhism became the official religion. Ashoka even set out to make it a world religion by sending out missionaries in all directions. In order to play this role, Buddhism had to undergo a considerable transformation, according to Weber. It had to allow the laity, through education and a period of monastic life, a chance of an improved reincarnation. Its salvation techniques were bent in the direction of faith in magic and in reliance on saviours.

The actual division into Mahayana and Hinayana forms began with a dispute over matters of monastic discipline and specifically over the question of the acceptability of donations in the form of money from the laity to monks. But it was not long before a number of purely doctrinal differences appeared within the *sangha*. The outcome was that Mahayana, a more lax form of Buddhism in Weber's view, separated from the more traditionalistic form of Hinayana or as it is more usually known by its followers, Theravada. The two schools eventually became geographically based with Mahayana dominating the North (China, Tibet and Japan) and Hinayana the South (South East Asia and Sri Lanka).

Weber interprets the essential difference between the two branches, centred on the belief in a saviour figure as an aid to the religious aspirations of the laity by Mahayana Buddhism, and which the traditional form opposed, in terms of this need to appeal to a wider following. This saviour took the form of a *bodhisattva* or saint – one who had attained enlightenment but who chose to forgo entry into nirvana in order to help others come closer to the goal. This highly meritorious act enabled the bodhisattva to transfer a surplus of good karma to the faithful following in a virtually magical way, ensuring a better incarnation, possibly in a paradise. In some forms of Mahayana merely chanting the name of the saint could result in a better karmic balance.

These modifications failed to have any significant implications for the development of a rational inner-worldly form of life conduct. In fact their magical and ritualistic character was even less conducive to rational economic development. 'Mahayana Buddhism', Weber states, 'has combined only an ascetic and essentially Brahmanical intellectual mysticism with coarse magic, idolatry and hagiolatry or edifying prayer formulas for the laity' (ibid., p. 256).

Buddhism within India itself, however, could not ultimately compete against Brahmin thought for the allegiance of the mass of ordinary people, even in its modified Mahayana form. The Brahmins were able to develop forms of Hinduism which made even greater accommodation to the religious proclivities of the masses. This it did by absorbing the popular and folk cults and their deities within the Hindu pantheon. A distinctly popular and plebeian character appears in orthodox teaching at this time and a markedly sectarian trend can be observed to emerge within Hinduism. Shivaism, Vaishnavism, the cults of Rama and Krishna all became widespread and fused within Brahmanical ideas.

The re-establishment of Brahmin influence and teaching was also associated with the support it tended to give to patrimonial[1] rule and bureaucratic administration which Buddhism had been less able to give. Brahmin priest were able to fulfil the ritualistic functions demanded by both rulers and the masses which neither the Buddhist nor the Jain monk could easily do.

This retreat into magic and ritualism again meant that no religious ethic of any significance for change and development was likely to emerge in India. Weber concludes his study with a general character-isation of the nature of oriental religion form this perspective. He makes the following observations: (i) Asiatic salvation doctrines were always exemplary, that is for full-time monks or religious virtuosi, (ii) they emphasised knowledge, wisdom, and were largely mystical, (iii) this made them elitist, (iv) they frequently took an other-worldly path to salvation and (v) when they did adopt an inner-worldly outlook it was still largely mystical in character.

The implications of this for Weber's main concern are clear. In Asia, Weber comments, there was no lack of lust for gain and profit but:

> It was lacking in precisely that which was decisive for the economics of the Occident: the refraction and rational immersion of the drive character of economic striving and its accompaniments in a system of rational, inner-worldly ethic of behaviour, e.g. the 'inner-worldly' asceticism. (ibid., p. 337)

If the religious factor was not conducive to the kind of economic development that occurred in the West we must not forget that

Weber shows very clearly in his studies of oriental religions that many other necessary conditions for such a development were also lacking. The explanation for the different history of the East does not lie solely in its dominant forms of religious ethos. Weber's studies in the world religions cannot be interpreted as merely an attempt to assess the validity of his Protestant Ethic thesis (Tenbruck, 1980). Weber also shows that, to a great extent, the prominence of many of the oriental religious outlooks was itself promoted by social, political and economic factors even if these religious orientations can in no way be reduced to the interests of particular social strata (see Molloy, 1980; Warner, 1970). Fulbrook (1978) goes so far as to say that the *ultimate* level of explanation in Weber's work is that of structural conditions underlying forms of idea systems and associated meanings and motivations and which determine the extent to which the latter can arise and achieve historical efficacy.

THE SOCIOLOGY OF BUDDHISM SINCE WEBER

We saw in the last chapter that contemporary studies of Hinduism have led some to question Mandelbaum's schema of a transcendental and pragmatic complex. Recent work in Buddhist communities suggests again that a substantial modification of it is required. The transcendental and pragmatic distinction, respectively associated in the Buddhist context with specifically Buddhist versus pagan religious beliefs and practices, overlooks the fact that there is a division within Buddhism itself between a canonical and more popular version, the latter existing alongside various pagan spirit cults representing a pre-Buddhist tradition. Many studies of village Buddhism (Obeyesekere, 1968; Tambiah, 1968, 1970; Spiro, 1971) have shown how Buddhist ideas are interpreted and adapted in such a way as to meet the religious needs of a peasant population or at least deviate from orthodox teaching in actual practice (Gombrich, 1971). Some have drawn the implication from this that Buddhism is not simply an otherworldly religion as Weber characterised it, accusing him, as many others have, of relying too much on scriptural sources (Spiro, 1971). The consequence of these findings is that ordinary people may not be compelled to resort to magical forms of belief and practice but can find an appeal in Buddhism which, in suitably modified form, is able to provide a satisfactory religious and spiritual life for them.

A second point that arises from these studies relevant to Mandelbaum's thesis is that the two complexes are not simply complementary but mutually dependent upon one another. Both of these points are particularly clearly seen in Tambiah's work in North East Thailand (1968, 1970). Tambiah shows that Theravada Buddhism, in peasant interpretations, is capable of being related to mundane empirical objectives and practical goals. In lay belief the otherworldliness said to be characteristic of Buddhism is not so apparent. The idea of rebirth, which is what most villagers desire and hope for rather than the abstract and difficult notion of nirvana is essentially, he points out, a practical and worldly goal. Even the popular belief in the existence of various heavens and similar forms of existence after death is conceived as a transitional period prior to further rebirths. They are all stages on the road to a return to life in this world. Also, at the village level monkhood does not necessarily imply a life-long vocation. It is usual in this part of the Buddhist world for young men to become novice monks for a period of time before embarking upon the responsibilities of adult life. This raises questions whether Buddhism is as elitist as Weber claimed it to be.

This sojourn in the monastery that most Thai youths experience can be seen, Tambiah (1968) argues, as a form of rite de passage which marks the passage form childhood to adulthood. Those who take up the ascetic regime of the novice monk acquire merit by doing so, thereby producing good karma and increased chances of a better rebirth. Not only do they acquire merit for themselves but also for their families, since it is their families which enable them to enter the monastery by releasing them from their worldly obligations.

Tambiah sees this in terms of a relationship of reciprocity between the generations and between monk and layman. The younger generation gives up worldly pleasures and pursuits in undertaking the life of the novice. The rule for the novices is an ascetic one requiring celibacy, renunciation of personal possessions and observance of the rules of the *vinaya* code governing the life in the monastery. Youth is asked to give up these things, a kind of sacrifice of sexual vitality and potency, according to Tambiah, in order to follow this ascetic way of life. This renunciation of sexual vitality produces instead ethical vitality which counters and combats the effects of bad karma and thereby suffering.

The young, of course, are able to make this sacrifice because they are not yet householders and family heads with responsibilities to others. In other words, those who are about to embark upon adult life make the sacrifices for those whose lives are well advanced and who may be approaching or who are, at least, closer to death. In return the younger generation receives benefits in the form of certain ceremonies and rituals performed for them by their parents and kin. It is also the care and provision that their families have given them through child-hood that ensures that they will one day become independent house-holders. It is only because the older generation transfers its powers, capacities and authority to the young that they are able to enjoy the benefits of adult life.

Reciprocity can also be seen in terms of an exchange between lay-men on the one hand and both novices and full monks on the other. The ascetic lifestyle of the novice and the monk builds up a surplus of merit which benefits the layman; in return novices will enjoy the benefits of adulthood when they return to lay life. Novice and layman are thus bound up together. The otherworldly asceticism of the monk is made possible because of the layman's support. The laity feed and clothe monks and novices and provide for their shelter. Under the rules of the vinaya monks must not work to support themselves but rely only upon that which is freely given to them. Feeding and supporting monks are highly meritorious acts and earn the layman good karma and a better rebirth – inner-worldly rewards.

Fortes (1987) goes further than Tambiah in proffering a clearly more Freudian interpretation, echoing Spiro (1965), discussed below. Fortes sees the reciprocity between monk and layman as a symbolic, ritually legitimated working out of repressed rivalry and mutual hostility. The renunciation of sexuality is seen by him as an expression of filial sub-mission and a form of symbolic castration before regression to a state of infantile-like 'back-to-the-womb' dependence on parents and sexual innocence as a member of the monastery. Filial piety, expressed through the institution of monkhood, is thus a customary legitimate device for converting repressed hostility into socially respectable humility.

A further dimension of this relationship between layman and monk is noted by Keyes (1983). The belief in transfer of merit from sons who enter the monastery to their parents, although unorthodox according to Buddhist teaching, is something that facilitates and makes possible the abandonment of worldly responsibilities and the loss of labour and procreativity to the family. Without it, a period within the monastery could only benefit the individual undertaking it and this would be unlikely to be tolerated by his family. The idea of merit transference ensures compatibility between the pursuit of merit by the individual for his own benefit, on the one hand, and the social imperative of acting in the collective interest, on the other.

The same relationships and patterns of reciprocity have been discerned in Burmese village Buddhism by Spiro (1971). Also, Spiro found popular interpretations of Buddhism in this country to be in many ways similar to those of Thai villagers. Spiro distinguishes between what he calls *nibbanic* Buddhism which is the canonical or 'normative soteriological' form and *kammatic* Buddhism which is the popular adaptation of the former.

While nibbanic Buddhism, Spiro argues, was the religion of a world-weary privileged stratum, kammatic Buddhism (from the Pali *kamma*), or as Spiro characterises it, 'non-normative soteriological' Buddhism, is the religion of relatively less privileged strata. It is a selection and modification of normative Buddhism but still Buddhist, according to Spiro.

Kammatic Buddhism has modified considerably the doctrines of nibbanic Buddhism. Nibbanic Buddhism considers that life entails suffering (*dukkha* in Pali, the language of the Buddhist scriptures – a term which means, more accurately, the opposite of wellbeing. The closest word in English that anyone has so far been able to suggest is 'unsatisfactoriness'). In kammatic Buddhism suffering is not considered to be inherent in life but only temporary. It can be overcome by achieving a better rebirth.

While nibbanic Buddhism holds that the source of suffering is desire and craving and that suffering can consequently be ended by extinguishing desire, kammatic Buddhism does not seek to renounce desire but seeks satisfaction of it in a future worldly existence, a worldly aim.

The fundamental goal of nibbanic Buddhism, escape from the cycle of rebirths and the achievement of nibbana, is not something which most Burmese villagers seek. Kammatic Buddhism seeks a good rebirth and not nibbanic salvation. Gombrich (1971) reports also that in Sri Lanka the aim of nirvana is not sought by most villagers at least in the near future. Like St Augustine who prayed that God would make him chaste and continent – but not just yet, village Buddhists were happy to have nirvana deferred almost indefinitely.

Nibbanic Buddhism teaches that there is no self or soul which endures – the doctrine of *anatta*. Rebirth is not the rebirth of the soul in a new body since there is no enduring soul to be reborn. It is simply an effect in the future of karmic causation or consequence – of actions performed in the past. In popular Buddhism in Burma, if nirvana is sought it is not conceived of as extinction of the self. The doctrine of anatta, however, is not clearly understood by most villagers in Burma who, even if they did understand it, would for the most part be psychologically incapable of accepting it. Their ideal is a form of salvation in which the self endures.

Kammatic Buddhism holds that a better rebirth is achieved by good karma. Deliverance from suffering, therefore, is achieved not by the extinction of desire and karma, as nibbanic Buddhism maintains, but by increase in good karma. Suffering is due to bad karma. Immorality must be avoided because it brings bad karma. Good karma comes from meritorious actions. Salvation is achieved by the accumulation of merit not extinction of karma.

Meditation in nibbanic Buddhism is desirable because it is necessary for attainment of wisdom leading to ultimate salvation – nibbana. The wisdom that is attained through mediation is the wisdom that the self or soul is really only an impermanent flux. The Buddha taught that nothing is permanent and that all is transitory. Meditation reveals the truth of this and enables the extinction of desire which falls away when the illusory nature of the soul is realised. Even meditation will now be done without desire, even for salvation, and will be without karmic consequence. In kammatic Buddhism, on the other hand, if it is desirable to meditate it is because it is meritorious not because it brings wisdom.

But merit mostly comes from giving in a religious context – feeding monks, donations towards the building and upkeep of monasteries and pagodas, and so on. Quite contrary to orthodox teaching, in kammatic Buddhism merit can be transferred form one person to another. It can, for example, be transferred to a dead relative during the days immediately after death through the performance of meritorious acts by the living to increase the good karma of the deceased and earn him or her a better rebirth. The fact that such an idea is strictly contrary to the orthodox doctrine of karma, is simply not perceived or is ignored by most villagers. Others rationalise it within the principles of karmic causation by claiming that the rituals performed give the deceased an opportunity to applaud the living for their desire to share merit. The act of applauding is itself meritorious, so merit is not actually transferred but earned by both parties. Such rationalisations of what appear to be practices contrary to orthodox Buddhist doctrine are common.[2]

On the grounds that the Buddhism that is practised by the vast majority of people in Buddhist societies takes this kammatic form, Spiro questions Weber's interpretation of Buddhism. Weber's view was based, he claims, on the canonical forms of scriptural Buddhism rather than on an appreciation of the beliefs and understandings of the everyday practitioners of the religion. The 'dominant motive among

Burmese for believing in karma is not so much to discover the "mean-ing" of suffering as to do something about their own suffering' (Spiro, 1971, p. 128). It provides them with a means for attaining future pleasure.

These beliefs, Spiro argues, fit the experience of the Burmese of how things in reality actually are. They are consistent with the perceptual and cognitive structure of the Burmese mentality. Our perception of the way the world is fundamentally structured is laid down in child-hood, according to Spiro. He draws upon a theoretical position asso-ciated with Kardiner and Whiting which holds that religious conceptions reflect fundamental childhood experience and childrearing patterns.

The doctrine of karma, Spiro points out, states that one can rely on oneself and one's own actions for salvation, and secondly that there is, in fact, no saviour one can rely on – one *has* to rely on oneself. The belief that one can be saved by the efforts of a compassionate saviour, a divine figure, Spiro claims, can only carry conviction if it is congruent with experience in the formative stage of life, namely in infancy, when perceptions of what the world is fundamentally like become deeply rooted. The early experience that is congruent with the idea of a saviour figure is one of persistent and enduring love and emotional nurturance. The child is assured that he or she is not alone and a cognitive structure is created isomorphic with belief in saviour gods.

It is extremely unlikely that such a cognitive structure would be acquired in Burma, Spiro claims. It is true that infants in this culture are indeed treated with the greatest nurturance. Their need for affec-tion is constantly satisfied and dependency indulged. But this indul-gence is rather abruptly and unpredictably withdrawn at the end of infancy. In childhood, beyond the stage of infancy, physical expression of affection is rare and verbal praise and expression of affection slight. This is thought to be necessary once children are able to understand in order not to spoil them. It is not unusual for children to become victims of teasing and they are compelled to carry out many small chores. Strict obedience is expected of them and punishment is often severe. 'Burmese socialisation', then, 'is characterised by an important discontinuity between the indulgent nurturance of infancy and its rather serious withdrawal in childhood' (ibid., p. 133).

Thus no experiential model exists in Burmese culture for the devel-opment of the notion of a divine saviour. The only view which could carry any degree of credibility and conviction is that one can and must attain salvation by one's own efforts.

Salvation is attained for the ordinary Burman, as we have seen, by giving in a religious context, that is largely by feeding and providing for monks. The relationship between laymen and monks, according to Spiro, parallels that between parent and infants – dependent, provided for and in a state of blissful irresponsibility. There is a suggestion of a kind of magical reciprocity whereby feeding monks places the layman himself eventually in the blissful position of infancy once again.

The notion of karma has been said to embody a 'psychological indeterminacy' (Obeyesekere, 1968) in that it entails an inevitable uncertainty. One can never be sure what fate may bring because one never knows how past actions have affected one's karmic balance. Misfortunes can be explained in terms of bad karma acquired in past lives but the price is that the future is always uncertain. This also fits the Burmese experience, Spiro agues. Since affection is unpredictably withdrawn in childhood the world is experienced as a fundamentally unpredictable place.

Spiro's theory, then, is not one of origins of belief systems but of why certain beliefs carry conviction and take root while others do not. Mahayana Buddhism reached Burma as early as Theravada but did not take root. Christianity has been notably unsuccessful in the Theravada countries of South East Asia while it has had considerably greater success in other part of Asia. Religions that emphasise saviour figures lack conviction for the Burmese given their cognitive structure. Theravada Buddhism emerged when and where it did for reasons which Spiro does not go into. Exposure of Burma to it is largely an accident of geography but once exposed a significant factor in its acceptance was that its general principles carried conviction. It is the generic notion, then, that salvation must be attained by one's own efforts that is promoted by this particular cognitive structure. The particular form and detail of the doctrine is accidental. In short, the cognitive structure which is favourable to such a belief is a necessary but not a sufficient condition for the prevalence of the belief.

The character of Theravada Buddhism can be clearly seen in examining its monastic institutions, the sangha. The Burmese hold the way of life of the monk in the highest esteem. The monastic life reveals, therefore, much about the nature of the Burmese attachment to Buddhism. Monks are predominantly concerned with seeking salvation for themselves. They are unlike priests, they do not serve a congregation, they are not intermediaries with the divine and they do not administer sacraments. The relationship between monk and layman, Spiro argues, is in some respects the reverse of that which exists in Christianity between priest and layman. In the case of Buddhism the layman supports the monk and by doing so assists him in attaining his primary aim of salvation. In Christianity it is the priest who enables the layman to achieve salvation by his sacramental function.

The ideal for monks is to meditate regularly and frequently in the quest for wisdom and enlightenment. Their life free from toil and responsibility is supposed to facilitate spending time in meditation. In fact, Spiro reports, most monks do not do so. Gombrich (1971) similarly observes in the case of Sri Lankan Buddhism that monks consider frequent meditation to be impractical and uncongenial. The routine of Burmese monks consists largely of the daily round of alms begging and teaching the village children the fundamentals of Buddhism. Alms begging was carried out largely so that villagers could acquire merit and good karma. Monks rarely ate the food given to them by villagers during the daily begging round. Much better food was provided for them by better off members of the community which was cooked at the monastery. Ryan (1958) reports much the same for Sri Lanka where monks had, in fact, largely given up the daily round, the food being provided by organised rotation of donors. Monks in the Burmese village where Spiro carried out his fieldwork seemed to suffer much boredom and slept a great deal. The majority had come from poor rural families. In the monastery they enjoyed a much higher status and standard of living than they could expect otherwise. Tambiah (1976, pp. 356–7) reports that in Thailand entry into the sangha is an important route for upward mobility and the acquisition of education for those of relatively humble origins.

Those who choose to become monks have, Spiro argues, a certain personality. It is the general type of the Burmese personality but in an exaggerated form. Monks manifest a strong 'need for dependence', according to Spiro. The monk–layman relationship places the monk in the structural position of the child and the layman in the position of the parent. It is significant, Spiro points out, that in Christianity the priest is called 'father' by the layman whereas in Burma the monk calls the layman 'father'.

Because of childhood experience, the Burmese, Spiro claims, exhibit a strong unconscious desire to return to a blissful state of infancy. The monastery is an institutionalised means for realising this fantasy. Entering the monastery is interpreted by Spiro as a form of regression symbolised by the physical appearance of the monk. Monks shave their head which gives them a foetalised appearance. Celibacy is interpreted by Spiro as an institutionalised and symbolic resolution of the

Oedipus complex. The benefits of infancy can only be enjoyed through renunciation of women and sexual relations.

Often a man will abandon wife, children and other dependants leaving them with no support in order to enter the monastery. This demonstrates a lack of sensitivity to the needs of others and a pre-occupation with self which monks in general manifest, according to Spiro. They are characterised by narcissism. The monastic life provides a legitimate means for indulging this narcissistic abdication of respons-ibility. In everyday life, Spiro speculates, monks would tend to be misfits, neurotics, and failures. In the monastery they can achieve an honoured status in the society. They can escape the stigma of abnormality because as monks their behavioural pattern confirms to culturally prescribed norms and values The monastic order acts as a sort of collective saviour in Theravada Buddhism.

Far from being judged abnormal, the ascetic way of life of monks brings them the highest esteem and veneration. While they are gener-ally of a low intellectual level, in Spiro's opinion, and manifest a tendency to narcissism and vanity, their esteem is enhanced by their generally very high moral standards. The precepts of the vinaya are for the most part strictly kept. Laymen regard their asceticism as extra-ordinarily difficult and greatly admire it. It is believed to give them extraordinary powers – in Weber's terms magical charisma. Without monks, also, laymen cannot acquire merit and improve their karmic balance and their rebirth.

Spiro's neo-Freudian interpretation of Theravada Buddhism has been challenged by Gombrich (1971) and Southwold (1983) who criti-cise Spiro for basing his findings relating to monks on a very small sample (21) who are not typical of the sangha in general. The monks of Spiro's study, according to Southwold, are typical only of those who practice Spiro's 'normative' Buddhism and should not be generalised to all monks.

Gombrich takes issues with the claim that child-rearing practices promote Theravada beliefs on the grounds that Spiro fails to present adequate evidence for the alleged character traits of the Burmese which are postulated to be the reason for their commitment to Theravada beliefs. Spiro actually deduces these character traits from the beliefs themselves. 'Spiro seems to ... have built up a picture of what Burmese personality ought to be like, given their religious systems.' (Gombrich, 1972, p. 485). It does not in any case seem plausible, he argues, that differences in religious conceptions could be explained in terms of differences in child-rearing practices. In all cultures babies are given unconditional nurturance. Are we to believe that belief in saviour figures is only possible when this is maintained through childhood or at least only gradually withdrawn? If Spiro's theory were correct we would expect to find the basic elements of Theravada belief, if in different form, in many other cultures. There is a lack of solid evidence that this is the case. Also, it would be difficult to account for religious change in terms of Spiro's theory. An example is the rise of bhakti devotionalism and reliance on a saviour god in India which replaced for the majority of the population the belief that everyone is wholly responsible for their own salvation. It is not really credible that such a conception of a saviour god could have taken root as a result of a change in child-rearing practices.

Also, Spiro's characterisation of the personality and motives of monks is perhaps somewhat unfair. It is significant that their alleged narcissism is, nevertheless, as we have seen, not only tolerated but admired by laymen. Spiro believes this toleration of and reverence for the monk is the reflection of the laity's own inner desire to return to the infantile state. The character of the monk is that of the Burmese writ large. The reason most people do not become monks is because they would find the ascetic regime impossible to follow. Lay admiration of monks, however, might be alternatively interpreted. It may be that the pursuit of salvation is in the eyes of laymen indeed of over-riding importance for those who have the strength, conviction and tenacity to pursue it. After all, if existence is defined as unsatisfactory and meaningless one can hardly be too concerned with the plight of others. The fact that monks avoid attachments because they involve risk of hurt is interpreted by Spiro as emotional timidity. There are two possible motivations, Spiro argues, from which the relinquishing of attachments may stem – that which is sacrificial and heroic and in which attachments are given up for the greater goal of salvation, and that which is overcautious, timid and fears pain. But Spiro may be guilty here of posing the contrast too starkly. It does not follow that giving up attachments is due to fear of them nor that giving them up, even if it were out of fear of loss, is to make no sacrifice at all. Sacrifices are not, in any religious tradition, made simply for the sake of it but precisely to achieve a higher or greater goal.

Gombrich (1972) and Southwold (1983) also reject Spiro's contention that kammatic Buddhism is an adaptation of canonical nibbanic Buddhism and a deviation from orthodoxy. Popular Buddhism is as canonical as nibbanic Buddhism, according to Gombrich, and is not a heterodox adaptation of it. He argues that Spiro's view is founded upon a misunderstanding of the doctrine of karma. Spiro's claim that Buddhism teaches that even good and meritorious action always results in rebirth, since it has karmic consequences, is incorrect. If this was Buddhist teaching then salvation could only be achieved by the extinction of karma. Gombrich points out, however, that canonical Buddhism holds, in fact, that salvation is achieved by the extinction of desire. Only action performed from desire produces rebirth. The merit in an action depends upon the intention behind it. Good actions performed from the desire for reward have karmic consequences. Disinterested actions, as long as they are good, do not. Good action is a step on the way to salvation and is considered to be spiritual progress. The peasants who pursue merit are thus doctrinally quite correct in their understanding of Buddhism.

Gombrich acknowledges, however, that there is a difference between kammatic and nibbanic Buddhism. The difference is better characterised for Gombrich in terms of a discrepancy between what people say they believe and what their behaviour indicates to us they believe. It is this distinction which informs his own detailed ethnographic study of Sri Lankan Buddhism (Gombrich, 1971). It is misleading, he argues, to present as Spiro does the two forms of Buddhism as distinct cognitive structures. The cognitive structure which Spiro calls kammatic Buddhism, Gombrich claims, is really only in part nibbanic Buddhism and in part an extrapolation of people's actual behaviour. The actual behaviour of Burmese villagers would suggest that they do not really believe that all life entails suffering. Spiro consequently attributes to them a different form of Buddhism. The simple truth is, however, that they are not very good Buddhists, just as most professed Christians or Muslims are not very good Christians or Muslims. The values of Buddhism represent, as Spiro himself puts it, 'what the Burmese think they ought and would like to be – but aren't' (Spiro, 1971, p. 475).

Southwold goes further than Gombrich in making a similar point in his treatment of the alleged lack of interest of most laymen in attaining nirvana. In fact, while similar to Gombrich's argument, Southwold's point would apply equally to it. It is not legitimate to assume, according to Southwold, that the popular lack of interest in the goal of nirvana is a deviation from canonical Buddhist teaching. Nirvana is simply not available to most people, if anyone, for a very long time – not until the coming of the next Buddha, Maitreya – a very distant prospect. This view has abundant scriptural backing according to Southwold. Village Buddhists are uninterested in nirvana largely because it is something they have no hope of attaining in anything but the remote future. In this they demonstrate a perfectly rational and understandable prioritising of proximate and ultimate goals. It is not a deviation from orthodoxy to place a very low priority on something which has very low probability of attainment and to defer concern with something which can only be achieved in the very far and distant future. The emphasis on nirvana in any case, Southwold claims, belongs largely to a middle-class interpretation of Buddhism which not even many monks share, as Spiro's and Gombrich's studies confirm. This middle-class Buddhism, furthermore, has itself been largely shaped and influenced by prestigious *Western* interpretations of Buddhism which have emphasised certain features as the essential ones and which have fed back into the understanding of both monks and laymen in Buddhist countries. If anything, it is the layman's viewpoint that is more consistent with the scriptures than this middle-class Westernised Buddhism which has largely misread or misunderstood them.

Whether or not kammatic Buddhism is a deviation from or adaptation of nibbanic Buddhism, the distinction between them remains nevertheless valid as does that between what people profess to believe and what their actions indicate they believe. The two forms of Buddhism that Spiro identifies broadly address the transcendental and pragmatic needs that Mandelbaum distinguishes. Yet in Buddhist countries we find a complication to this model. The pragmatic needs are also catered for by non-Buddhist, pagan beliefs and practices in all Theravada countries – for example *nat* cults in Burma (Spiro, 1978) and spirit cults in Thailand (Tambiah, 1970). Sri Lankan cults, Obeyesekere (1966) has shown, centred on various deities and demons, are nevertheless integrated to some extent with Buddhist belief. The ultimate source of power and authority of these gods is said to be the Buddha who has delegated power to them. While the gods and lesser supernaturals are concerned with material and this-worldly matters, the Buddha is associated with otherworldly concerns. Ames (1964a; 1964b) argues similarly that Buddhism and magical practices are complementary even though pagan beliefs and practices are clearly distinct from popular forms of Buddhism (see also Evers, 1965). Ames (1964b) and Obeyesekere (1963) reject the idea that the relationship between canonical Buddhism and popular Buddhism is that between a great and a little tradition along the lines of Redfield's (1956) well-known distinction. In both its canonical and popular forms Buddhism, according to Ames, belongs to the realm of the sacred – *lokottara* in Pali. Magic and worship of gods belongs to the realm of *laukika* or the profane. Popular Buddhism, unlike magical practices, is concerned with merit making. Magical practices are concerned with practical, immediate, mundane ends.

Against the view that the concepts and values derived from the 'great' tradition of Theravada Buddhism are merely a veneer thinly formed over a mass of non-Buddhist popular concepts which constitute the true religion of the masses, as interpretations of the great–little tradition distinction often suppose, Obeyesekere argues that they are by no means so. The concepts of Theravada Buddhism, even in their popular interpretations, constitute the frame of reference by which ordinary people attempt to understand the deeper and fundamental facts of existence.

This suggests that a modification of Mandelbaum's distinction is necessary, at least as far as Buddhist countries are concerned. There appear to be three levels of concern – ultimate salvation expressed in terms of nirvana in Buddhism, long-term worldly goals expressed in terms of good rebirth through merit, and everyday immediate practical goals for which pagan practices are the appropriate means.

The complementarity of Buddhism and pagan systems can also be seen at higher levels than that of the village. Evers (1965) shows this in a study of the religion and social structure of central Sri Lanka centred on a large and important temple, the Great Royal Temple of Laukatilaka, the former state temple of the Gampola Empire. Clearly associated under the same roof of this temple are two distinct sets of religious paraphernalia – shrines, statues, and so on. One, associated with Buddhism and centred around the statue of the Buddha, is termed the *vihara* system by Evers from the Pali word for monastery. The other system relates to the worship of various gods and is termed the *devale* system.

These two religious systems are organised in quite distinct ways despite their close association. In the vihara system the religious specialists are monks as opposed to priests in the devale system. The ritual system is somewhat different and there is a quite distinct social, administrative and economic basis of organisation in each case.

Evers shows that these two religious systems, which exist throughout central Sri Lanka, complement one another. Basically they represent the two different value systems known as lokottara and laukika.

Some of the work reviewed in this section has raised broader and more historical issues than those so far discussed and has addressed the problems arising from Weber's reliance on scriptural sources in his work on the world religions. The conclusion has often been that this is an inadequate basis on which to generalise about the impact of Buddhism on behaviour and motivation and ultimately upon the development of these societies since the real Buddhism of the mass of the population differs so much from canonical forms.

Spiro (1971), for example, argues that while Weber was right that doctrinal Buddhism could not have given any impetus to economic development the point is hardly relevant since the mass of the population have not internalised nibbanic Buddhism. Kammatic Buddhism is, however, equally conservative in its impact. While he rejects the frequently made claim that the doctrine of karma has made the East fatalistic because it implies that whatever happens is predestined and promotes indifference to suffering and misfortune, he acknowledges that it does provide powerful support for the status quo. It proscribes structural change and explains present inequality as the result of karma and therefore inevitable. Fear of karmic retribution, however, is a strong agent for social control.

It does, however, allow the possibility of positional change for individuals since success and improvement within the course of this life can be attributed to good karma acquired in past lives. Success is a sign that one's karma is good. The doctrine of karma can always be used by the ambitious and has often provided a legitimation for the usurpation of power. (Generally speaking, however, Spiro reports, the poor attribute their position to bad karma while the better-off attribute their position to hard work). The doctrine, then, can provide strong incentives for economic action contrary to Weber's claims. Economic success is essential for acquiring merit by giving to monks and monasteries. Wealth is proof of good karma and of progress towards ultimate salvation as well as an important basis of prestige earned through giving in a religious context. The donation of wealth to monasteries, however, tends to dissipate it, inhibiting capital accumulation and thereby economic development. In any case, prevailing conditions in Burma did not favour investment. Arbitrary state predation tended to make it too risky and uncertain.

Other critics of Weber have taken issue with his claim that Buddhism was asocial and apolitical. Houtart (1977), for example, has argued that in order to build temples and monasteries the sangha needed considerable resources – more than could be acquired from alms giving. It had, therefore, to become a state religion. In its turn it diffused a functional ethic supporting tributary relations and contributed its part to the reproduction of the social relations of production. It legitimated the king's rule and sanctioned the process of deification of monarchs.

Tambiah (1976) has also emphasised the importance of the relationship between Buddhism and the political realm and the social and political doctrines of Buddhism from a somewhat different perspective. He points out that Buddhism developed a clear doctrine of the righteous ruler and examines in detail the significance of this concept in the history of the relationship between sangha and state in Thailand.

Ling (1976) also emphasises the social and political teachings of Buddhism – even more so than Tambiah. For Ling early Buddhism was not a religion but a social and political theory. The aim of Gottama was to institute a new form of social life.

In Northern India, in the Ganges plain, Ling argues, a process of political change was taking place at the time that Buddhism emerged in the sixth century BC. The small-scale society of the older tribal republics was giving way to the larger and more impersonal monarchical states. There was also a growth of urban communities. The whole process was accompanied by a degree of malaise and anomie which promoted dissatisfaction with current conditions of life and much speculation about the human condition.

Religious life in the area was dominated by the Brahmin elite who monopolised ritual practice and religious knowledge. Brahmin domination and practice were increasingly subject to question and criticism. Gottama severely criticised the practice of animal sacrifice and other Brahmin practices – more so than he did popular cult beliefs and practices of the time. In his approach to the latter, Ling claims, the Buddha was pragmatic and open-minded, taking the beliefs as a possible departure for a more abstract type of thought and analysis of reality and human nature.

The Buddha preached largely in the growing urban centres where a new individualism was emerging which, Ling argues, he sought to counteract. He did not teach salvation of the *individual soul*, Ling claims, but the obliteration of the self. The root of human ills, he thought, lay in private-property-owning individualism. Hence the regime of the monk.

Ling rejects the idea, however, that these teachings were otherworldly in character. He claims that there was a close connection between sangha and laity – that they were complementary. The Buddha was very much a social and political theorist in his view. The sangha was a key aspect in this, and its purpose was to set the example and show what was possible.

A second key element in the design of Gottama emphasised by Ling was that the monarch should be Buddhist and should promote

Buddhism, in short the concept of the righteous monarch. The Buddhists set out to convert those with political authority including kings and princes. Whenever Buddhism failed in this endeavour it tended to become a theistic religion of supernatural salvation, as in the case of Mahayana Buddhism in China. Ling goes so far as to see this as a degenerative process by which a social philosophy and programme – a form of civilisation – declines into the status of mere supernaturalism and religion.

Some support for Ling's position is provided by Chakravati (1987) who bases his interpretation on a more extensive analysis of the changes that were occurring in North Indian society at the time of the emergence of Buddhism. It was not simply the growth of individualism that undermined the tribal republics but a whole series of social and economic changes. There was, Chakravati claims, a tremendous growth of the economy. Following Kosambi (1965) he argues that agriculture intensified as a result of increased availability of iron implements. The communal control of land was giving way to private control in the hands of a landowning class which necessitated greater centralisation of power to uphold land claims and settle disputes. A more complex economic system was emerging with much greater specialisation, trade, use of money and urbanisation. This had profound implications for the structure of society and for social tensions. A much greater degree of stratification was developing, one aspect of which was the emergence of a class of wage labourers. The whole character of the tribal republics, then, was changing and we must see the emergence of Buddhism against this background.

Chakravati, consequently, gives considerable support to Ling's contention that Buddhism was concerned with establishing a better society free from the tensions and problems emerging as a result economic, social and political change. Weber was right that Buddhism thought in terms of a strict separation between the temporal and spiritual spheres as far as the earliest period was concerned. There is nothing in early Buddhist literature to support Ling's and Tambiah's claim of a close relationship between king and sangha, in so far as monks having any role to play in temporal affairs or kings any role to play in spiritual matters. The Buddha did, however, teach that the Buddhist monarch had a responsibility to institute an ideal society. The new political system would be based upon charismatic kingship responsible for stimulating social and political change and eliminating destitution and injustice. Over time, however, a closer relationship between king and sangha did develop in which the former took an active role in the affairs of the latter.

Other writers, while supporting the general point that extensive economic, social and political changes were associated with the emergence of Buddhism, have questioned Kosambi's claim that the fundamental technological stimulus was the increased use of iron implements (Sharma, 1983: Gombrich, 1989). Sharma has pointed out that there is no archaeological evidence for it. Nevertheless, the importance of increased urbanisation, commercial trade, the use of money and the transformation of tribal republics into states are all factors which Gombrich agrees were significant (1989). Also, it cannot be accidental, he points out, supporting Weber here, that both Buddhism and Jainism, which challenged everything that the Brahmins stood for, were founded by men of Kshatriya status, or that the fundamental principles of Buddhism were wholly incompatible with caste, or that organisation of the sangha shares certain features with that of the tribal republics. In the sangha there was no principle of rank but only seniority counted from the time of joining. Buddhism seems to have flourished in the new towns and among the reasonably well to do rather than among the downtrodden. He lays some stress on the process of urbanisation, which, he agrees, was associated with a degree of malaise, from the perspective and values of the old and now disintegrating tribal and rural communities. Also, urbanisation and increased density of population, because of problems of sanitation and hygiene, is usually associated with the more rapid spread of diseases and increased mortality, he points out, which may have tended to promote more spiritual rather than material aspirations, especially ones which take a rather gloomy view of material existence as Buddhism does.

Buddhism, according to Gombrich, may also have provided more practical benefits in the new commercial situation. In these more impersonal circumstances the knowledge that others with whom one has to do business subscribe to a universalistic ethic of right and wrong and that they hold the belief that the latter would receive its just punishment automatically as a consequence of the law of the universe, may have given confidence that one could put one's trust in business relationships in the absence of a community which would previously have censured dishonest behaviour. It would thus have been conducive to the promotion of trade and commerce. Buddhism, also, being attached to no particular community or locality, was easily transportable and suited to those who moved around, such as traders, and tended to spread along trade routes. The moral precepts of Buddhism also had some appeal for businessmen. Moral behaviour brings benefits such as wealth and a better rebirth. In short it taught that honesty was the best policy. Gombrich reminds us, however, against those who have claimed that Buddhism was similar in its appeal to businessmen as Protestantism was in Europe, that it was very different from Protestantism and that we should not forget that the most valued way of life for Buddhists is that of the contemplative monk.

It is the emergence of this ethical dimension as a integral aspect of the emergence of Buddhism, stressed by the writers discussed above and particularly by Gombrich, that produced the doctrine of karma, according to Obeyesekere (1980). In the process of reconstituting human relationships on the basis of an ethic more universalistic than that of previous tribal morality, karmic doctrine was not simply something that religious thinkers hit upon. Karmic teaching was the inevitably logical outcome of a process of ethicisation of a pre-existing rebirth doctrine. Obeyesekere argues that ideas of rebirth are or were by no means confined to India but have been widespread in primitive or preliterate societies. In tribal India, in all likelihood, rebirth was a central idea of belief systems but not originally linked, as it is not in many tribal societies elsewhere, to a karmic type of doctrine. The latter was the result of a process of ethicisation in which reward or retribution for actions in accordance with how they conform to moral values and norms became attached to the idea of rebirth.

On the basis of a cross-cultural comparison, with particular focus on Trobriand Island and Igbo belief, Obeyesekere notes that ideas of rebirth often exist without accompanying karmic notions or belief in an ultimate salvation such as nirvana. What is striking about these systems of belief is that there are no accompanying doctrines of reward or retribution in the next life, be it in a paradise or in a subsequent rebirth, for the moral character of conduct in this life. There is a separation between what is considered morally right or wrong action on the one hand and religious fate on the other. Often souls enter paradise whatever the conduct of their bodily hosts had been in life.

When a belief in rebirth is ethicised, that is to say when it becomes linked to notions of reward and retribution for moral and immoral conduct, the inevitable outcome will be a karmic type of doctrine. The process of ethicisation applied to a belief in rebirth must result in a belief that the nature of a person's rebirth carries a reward or punishment. If a person's circumstances in this life, then, are the consequence of actions in the previous life, so circumstances in this previous life must in turn be the consequence of those in a yet earlier life and so on in an unbroken chain. One ends up with the doctrines of samsara and karma. As for the doctrine of nirvana, this too is an inevitable and logical outcome of a process of thought. If an endless cycle of rebirths is thought to be unsatisfactory, perhaps because it promises no ultimate escape from worldly suffering, then salvation can only lie in escaping from this cycle of rebirths. This is precisely what nirvana is.

Comparative analysis shows that societies differ in the degree to which they ethicise their eschatological beliefs. At one extreme there are those, mostly tribal societies, which manifest no degree of ethicisation at all; at the other there are those, as is the case with Hinduism and Buddhism, in which ethicisation is total. This gives us some purchase on the question why ethicisation takes place and therefore why the doctrines of karma and nirvana became characteristic of Buddhism. It is clearly linked with the growth of social complexity, with, as Obeyesekere argues, the emergence of a specialised priesthood, a tradition of prophecy or similar social institutions which promote speculative thinking. One needs to go further than this, however, to ask why such institutions emerge in the first place. Here the relevance of the arguments of Ling, Chakravati and Gombrich are apparent. A set of social changes which transform tribal societies into more complex systems, no longer relatively isolated from one another but linked in complex sets of political, mercantile and military relationships, produces a more universalistic ethos and belief system as well as specialised groups devoted to the speculative thought which underlies these systems of ideas. It produces a tendency towards an ethicisation of eschatological beliefs in the process of creating more universalistic systems of moral belief. In India it produced Buddhism and, either independently or a result of the impact of Buddhism, it produced notions of karma and nirvana.

5 Chinese Religions: Confucianism and Taoism

WEBER ON THE RELIGIONS OF CHINA

In his study of the indigenous religions of China – Confucianism and Taoism – Weber is as much concerned with the overall structure and character of Chinese society as he is with the religious system. He is interested in those factors which would have tended to favour or inhibit the development of rational capitalism of which religion is one. In the first part of the study Weber outlines the particular features of Chinese society in order to show how they compare to those of the West. He considers the Chinese city, the system of government and administration, the official class who staffed these organisations and the way in which religion was organised on the institutional level. From the outset of his account it is clear that he does not find that everything in China bar religion is conducive to the development of rational capitalism. Rather he shows that despite being in some respects conducive to such a development, Chinese conditions and institutions were not on the whole favourable and often quite unlike those prevailing in the West.

Weber points out that the nature and position of the city in China differed from that in the West. It lacked political autonomy, had no citizenry and did not have at its disposal a military force for its protection. The Chinese city, in fact, was unable to act as a corporate body and had fewer guarantees of self-government than had the Chinese village. While the residents of the city in China did perhaps regard themselves as members of the community, they retained strong and overriding links with their own kinship groups. All important ties were with a person's kinship group or clan centred on its place of origin – a particular village. The survival of the clan as an important institution was connected with ancestor worship in which a person's relationship with the spiritual was through the medium of kinship, unlike those religions that have emphasised a personal relationship with God.

In China, then, there were forces which prevented the fusion of urban dwellers into an autonomous status group as occurred in the West. A second aspect associated with the city in China relates to its origin. In China few cities grew up, as they often did in the West, as a result of foreign trade. Also, in the West cities were often established by princes as a means of raising revenue but could not be governed and ruled by princes because they lacked the means of administration and because cities could resist the interference of princes by using their militias to close the gates and defend the city against them. In China the city was highly dependent on the central bureaucracy. This was the consequence, according to Weber, of the fact that the city was dependent for its prosperity upon the imperial administration of water resources – of rivers and irrigation systems. The Chinese city, Weber claims, was the product of rational administration and there was 'an absence of fixed, publicly recognised, formal and reliable legal foundations for a free and cooperatively regulated organisation of industry and commerce, such as is known in the Occident' (1951, p. 20).

This is one important difference, then, between China and Europe. In Europe the character of the city was an important factor in the development of capitalism. The autonomy of the city and its involvement in trade and commerce allowed an accumulation of capital relatively free from the predations of the nobility and the state. Once other conditions were favourable for the development of industrial capitalism the wealth of the powerful merchant class could be invested in manufacturing enterprises. True, the guild regulations of the cities often prevented investment of this wealth within the city itself but outside its limits the guild regulations did not apply and new centres of manufacturing grew up.

None of this was possible in China. The city was not as important as a trade centre. Whatever money was earned in urban centres was subject to the arbitrary appropriations of the state. Kinship obligations tended to dissipate wealth away from the cities to the rural areas.

Another crucial difference between China and the West identified by Weber was the nature of the state and of government. In China patrimonial government prevailed and with it the associated traditions of prerogative and favouritism. Rational capitalism, Weber said, is particularly sensitive to political factors of this kind and is greatly impeded by them. The patrimonial state embodies a system of law inimical to the development of rational capitalist enterprise.

Patrimonial bureaucracy was associated in China, according to Weber, with the need to control the rivers and with large-scale irrigation. When translated into religious conceptions we get the idea of a god who is like a king. In both Egypt and China and in irrigation civilisations generally, the peasantry see the king as having 'created' the harvest. The king is thought to be responsible for general welfare.

This becomes the model for conceptions of gods and deities. They are seen to have created the world and man and this idea is promoted by the centralised bureaucratic administration.

Associated with this patrimonial bureaucracy during the period of the unified Empire was a system of administration characterised by a lack of regional autonomy in contrast to the West. In China the provinces and local groupings were more dependent on the central government, although this should not be exaggerated, Weber comments, since China covered a large area within which communications were no better than in the West. The crucial difference was that in China local groupings were never able to unite against the centre to win a measure of autonomy.

Just as important was the system of local administration whereby officials were appointed and could be removed by the central authority. They had no permanent rights to their offices nor to the prebendal land attached to the office.

Clearly such crucial differences between China and the West prevent Weber from using the case of China to test his Protestant ethic thesis. Not only was the religious system different but so were many key institutions of the society. On the other hand, Weber did believe that religion was also an important factor. For example, he says that 'rational entrepreneurial capitalism... above all has been handicapped by the attitude rooted in the Chinese "ethos"...' (1961, p. 104), and speaking of this mentality, in so far as it was a set of practical attitudes towards the world, '... in view of their autonomous laws, one can hardly fail to ascribe to these attitudes effects strongly counteractive to capitalist development' (ibid., p. 249).

We must conclude, then, that Weber's study of China, as with his other studies in the world religions, does not conform to any simple strategy or fit any clear methodological programme. It simply sets out to analyse in an exploratory way the complex interlocking sets of variables operating through a vast period of history, focusing on prominent or dominant features and relationships. In the Chinese case, while the religious mentality of inner-worldly asceticism which Weber believed played a significant role in the development of Europe was lacking, many crucial aspects of the society were, in any case, wholly inhibitive of the development of rational capitalism. The religious mentality of China, furthermore, was itself shaped to a considerable degree by the prevailing political, economic and social conditions. In fact, to a large extent what Weber tends to demonstrate in *The Religion of China* is the way the Chinese religious mentality is closely related to and reflects the outlook of the dominant status group, its position in the society and its interests. He shows how the mentality of the dominant social group disposed them to a particular world view which gave Chinese civilisation its characteristic ethos.

The organisation of religion in China, Weber points out, was characterised by an absence of prophecy and of a powerful priesthood. The emperor was also the high priest and, in general, there was a fusion of official religious and political functions.

The state cult, however, may be contrasted with the popular cults of the masses. Ancestor worship was central here, of course, but in addition there were numerous popular cults centred on a variety of deities. Such popular cults were tolerated by the political authorities because they were considered a useful aid in keeping the masses quiescent. The situation in China was thus very different from that in the West where Christianity was upheld as the religion of both the dominant groups in society and also of the common people and where there was no fusion of political and religious authority.

In the early periods in China, before the unification, the gods were related to fertility and the harvest or were ancestral spirits. Later, with an increase in the power of princes and nobles, a personal God of Heaven emerged. With the growth of imperial power the sacrificial rites to Heaven became a monopoly of the emperor while princes sacrificed to the spirits of the land and to the ancestral spirits.

Increasingly, the spirits assumed a more impersonal character, especially the main ones. As a result of a long period of unbroken peace and stability a conception of an ordered universe grew up. As part of this universe the world of man was seen as governed by an impersonal spirit or principle of order and harmony. The main object of the state cult and of all official religious activity was the promotion and maintenance of this order and to ensure that the world of man was in harmonious relationship with the heavenly order. The official religious outlook was, understandably, antagonistic to ecstatic and emotional religiosity and to religious movements with such characteristics and tended to suppress them.

Weber contrasted this situation with that of the Middle East and particularly with Palestine and the Israelites. The Chinese emphasis on an impersonal, eternal, timeless principle of order and antipathy to ecstatic and emotional religiosity or belief in personalised wrathful gods was not an outlook capable of providing an ethic likely to stimulate innovation and change, as was the case with the ethic which developed in the Middle East with its emphasis upon the possibility and likelihood of change and the transformability of the world.

The specific social and political factors which supported the official religious outlook in China may be summarised as follows.

1. The dependence of the government upon appointed officials.
2. Appointment to office on the basis of success in official examinations and not on the basis of birth or status.
3. The derivation of income by officials from their powers and rights to keep back any taxes they were able to levy and collect in their area of jurisdiction over and above the stipulated amount payable to the central government.
4. The role of kinship groups, the sibs as Weber terms them, in supporting and financing candidates for the examinations through which they hoped to achieve lucrative office. In fact the persisting importance of kinship supported by the ancestor cult was a very significant factor in China.
5. The lack of emphasis on specialised skills and knowledge and in fact the general deprecation of specialisation among the dominant class of officials as unbecoming to a gentleman.
6. The strong emphasis on a purely literary education in the classical texts as the only one appropriate for a gentleman.
7. The consequent weakness of central administration at the local level, which, given the large area and poor means of communication, meant that no adequate legal foundations existed for the development of commerce and ultimately capitalistic enterprise such as developed in the West.

The combination of all these factors made China a very stable and conservative culture lacking dynamic characteristics. This was reflected in and supported by the religious system.

The way in which the social and political structure of China partly determined the outlook of the dominant group and the way in which this outlook in turn influenced the character of Chinese civilisation can best be seen in an examination of the social position of the official class, the literati, its concerns and its adoption of Confucianism. This Weber sets out to do in the second part of *The Religion of China*.

The dominant group in China, as we have seen, was the officials or literati. They were also the educated class and were appointed to office on the basis of educational qualifications. They were, consequently, China's intellectual class.

The Chinese intelligentsia, unlike that of India and the West, were not churchmen. Very often in history, literacy, knowledge, education, philosophy, and so on, have been the monopoly of priests. The Chinese literati were, however, not priests but educated laymen. In theory, rank in China depended upon educational qualifications rather than on wealth or birth. In reality, however, wealth was important since acquisition of education and qualifications depended to a large extent upon the availability of sufficient finance to undertake the long education required for success in the examinations.

The literati were also administrators and bureaucrats. The ideal for an educated person was to obtain an official position in the imperial administration. These positions could be very lucrative and carried high social status. The literati were, consequently, strongly opposed to feudal tendencies and their rise to dominance was closely associated with the decline of feudalism in China and the emergence of the centralised state.

It is significant that Confucius and Lao Tzu, the putative founder of Taoism, lived at the time of the Warring States, that is around 500–250 BC, a time when a feudal-like situation was giving way to centralisation through the formation of larger and larger and increasingly bureaucratically organised states.

The position of the literati in these states, and ultimately in the single dominant state that resulted, was that of 'certified claimants to office prebends' (Weber, 1951, p. 115), that is they held official positions in the bureaucracy which they acquired by merit measured in terms of the number of examinations they had passed. They derived their income largely from the office they held in the form of tax revenue or revenues derived from lands set aside specifically to provide an income for the incumbent of the office. Weber argues 'that this relation to state office was of fundamental importance for the nature of the mentality of this stratum' (ibid., p. 112).

The competition for office resulted in the development of a unified orthodox outlook which was compatible with and adjusted to the circumstances. This orthodoxy found its expression in Confucianism. The fact that competition for office was channelled through the examination system meant that aspirants to office had to acquire an extensive and elaborate education in the classics and had to pass numerous examinations. The intense competition ensured that the literati became thoroughly inculcated with and immersed in a particular set of attitudes and orientations towards the world, life and society.

Chinese examinations were not designed to test specific skills. 'The examinations of China tested whether or not the candidate's mind was thoroughly steeped in literature and whether or not he possessed the ways of thought suitable to cultured men and resulting from cultivation in literature' (ibid., p. 121).

The type of education required for success in these examinations was secular, non-military, literary and bookish in character. It emphasised writing and the study of written texts to an extreme degree. This, Weber thought, was related to the nature of the Chinese system of writing.

The major task of education was the unfolding of the *yang* substance in the soul of the student. A fundamental feature of Chinese thought is that of an opposition between two forces or principles which though opposite to one another are also complementary. These forces are known as *yin* and yang. The opposition and union of yin and yang was conceived as providing the basis of all existence and being. Yin is associated with earthly substance and yang with heavenly substance. Yin was associated with the evil spirits or *kuei* and yang with the good spirits or *shen*. Good spirits were responsible for the preservation of order and harmony in the world. The aim of education, then, was the promotion of the yang aspect of human nature and the yang character of human beings above the yin aspects. In popular belief this resulted in the individual having power over the shen spirits and, consequently, magical power.

In this way a sound education enabled the official to ensure a harmonious administration in his area. A predominance of the *yin* principle, associated with restless evil spirits, would result in disorder and disaster. Both natural and social disturbances and misfortunes would be attributed to the faulty education of the official in whose area these things occurred. The official's own faults would be attributed to a faulty *education*.

This was because in Confucian thought no man was believed to be either inherently bad or good – it was simply a question of whether he had received an adequate education the effect of which was to bring out all the desirable characteristics in human beings. A man who had attained high educational qualifications enjoyed enormous prestige and even a reputation for magical power in the eyes of ordinary people. A prominent and greatly respected mandarin might become the object of a cult after his death and sometimes even during his own lifetime.

The emphasis on harmony and order which was so characteristic of Chinese thought can be readily seen to fit, Weber argued, the social, economic and political position of the literati. It is an outlook that one would expect to find among the officials of a large bureaucratic apparatus. Men in this position nearly always desire, above all, that things go smoothly, that there should be no disorder, that affairs be conducted without friction or disruption. Their livelihood, careers, status and sense of their own worth are bound up with such aims. As Weber put it, the outlook of this group was oriented towards 'the practical problems and status interests of the patrimonial bureaucracy' (ibid., p. 127).

Since this status group was the dominant group in China it influenced the whole character of Chinese civilisation. As there was no organised and powerful priesthood the literati had no real intellectual competitors. Their particular outlook was thus able to influence to a considerable extent the tenor of Chinese thought and culture.

The vast mass of the population, on the other hand, remained attached to magical and ritualistic cults of various kinds. These were tolerated by the state and the bureaucracy which, while it looked down on them, tended to see them as useful instruments for the management of the people and for keeping them quiescent.

On the whole, the literati rather despised religion. Confucianism is in many respects a secular doctrine rather than a religion. The Chinese language has, significantly, no word for religion. In Chinese, Confucianism is known as 'the doctrine of the literati'. Confucius, or Kung fu-tzu, lived between 551–479 BC. This was still a feudal age but increasingly, as we have seen, the feudal social system was giving way to more and more centralisation in larger states which would culminate eventually in the unified Empire. The writings attributed to Confucius reflect a change in outlook mirroring this movement from feudalism to centralised administration. They were largely concerned with political life and social behaviour. They give accounts of and comment on political events, wars, victories and so on, but in these writings victory is no longer attributed to sheer heroism and military superiority but is interpreted in terms of moral right and divine providence. The glorification of the old heroic virtues of the feudal age is absent. Rulers and princes are advised to follow ethical precepts and to seek to promote earthly harmony in accordance with heavenly order. Weber believed that Confucius may have been important largely because he revised classic texts in such a way as to play down the glorification of war and victory for its own sake linking instead such events to moral right and spiritual values.

The Confucian doctrine was essentially inner-worldly, materialist and atheistic, or at least agnostic, according to Weber. Ideas of a personal God, immortality, a supernatural plane of existence and so on tended to decline under its influence. It was not a salvation religion expressing a negative attitude to hopes for a future life. It was concerned with the here and now and the influences which were significant for conditions prevailing here and now, whether or not these influences were seen as supernatural. Confucianism emphasised acceptance of and adjustment to the world, to its conventions and prevailing conditions. There was no idea of withdrawal from the world.

Confucianism tended to be somewhat ascetic in that passions and enthusiasms, ostentation and display ought to be minimised in the interests of harmony and order but the possession of wealth was not considered undesirable in itself. What was to be avoided was any striving for wealth, especially through business activity, since this was likely to stir the passions and to lead to a loss of poise, dignity and harmony. The ideal was to have a good income from an office; an income which was customary, regular and not the product of a constant striving to *make* money.

Confucianism was strongly oriented towards acceptance of the world as it is and to accommodation to the status quo. The ideal state was a 'welfare state' in which everyone received their adequate due and in which regularity, order and harmony reigned.

One of the key ideas of Confucian thought was that of propriety (*li*). The ideal standard for behaviour was characterised as comprised of poise, dignity, elegance, mastery of the complexities of Chinese etiquette, and above all calmness. It is significant that the word li originally applied to religious rites but was broadened to cover all customary practices governing social interaction (Smith, 1974, pp. 75–6). Most important was the suppression of passion in any form. Self-control and reserve was essential in all circumstances. All passions were thought to disturb inner harmony which is the source of all that is good.

A second key idea was that of filial piety (*hsiao*). This was the model for all relationships of authority and was considered to be the highest of all virtues. Weber said 'filial piety was held to provide the test and guarantee of adherence to unconditional discipline, the most important status obligation of bureaucracy' (1951, p. 158).

It can readily be appreciated that this Confucian ethos was not one which could have had any revolutionary or transformatory consequences for society or which was likely to stimulate change or promote economic development, even if other conditions had been favourable for it.

But were there any other religious traditions in China which might have had a different impact? Confucianism had little relevance for the religious needs of the masses. As Weber put it 'the proud renunciation of the beyond and of religious guarantees of salvation for the individual in the here and now could be sustained only among cultured intellectuals' (1951, p. 173). The ordinary people were more involved in magical practices, cults and ancestor worship. There was, however, another great indigenous tradition in China which in certain forms did have a very great influence upon the mass of the population. This was Taoism. Weber, consequently, subjects this to analysis to ascertain if it could have provided an alternative ethos to that of orthodox Confucianism or could have had a different sort of impact.

Taoism was a development which derived from a tradition of long standing in China, according to Weber. The Confucian who failed to obtain an official appointment would often withdraw into a different style of life. He would become an anchorite. There had been anchorites in China from the earliest times. Anchoretism was traditionally associated with the quest for salvation through magical and macrobiotic means. From this tradition it was possible to develop a mystical attitude towards the world and it was this that Lao Tzu, the putative founder of Taoism, did. Unlike Confucius, Lao Tzu did not seek office but taught that withdrawal from worldly activity was the way to wisdom.

Taoism and Confucianism shared many things in common – they were both based upon the classical literary texts. They shared the idea of the Tao or heavenly order. The same person might be a Confucian while holding office but on retirement take up a more Taoist attitude and way of life.

The followers of Lao Tzu, however, in developing the doctrines of Taoism, which in its original form was philosophical and relatively unconcerned with salvation, gradually increased the differences between itself and Confucianism. Taoism lent itself to adaptation and accommodation to the needs of the masses. Its magical and soteriological aspects were emphasised and it became a popular cult. We can thus distinguish philosophical Taoism and the Taoism of popular cult.

Although Lao Tzu taught withdrawal from worldly involvement, Taoism was not essentially otherworldly. Withdrawal from worldly involvement was not achieved by resolute rejection of it but by acceptance of the world and accommodation to it. This accommodation could be achieved by the minimisation of strenuous activity. The

Taoists sought to achieve a kind of 'apathetic ecstasy' (ibid., p. 181). The aim was to remain in the world but devoid of worldly interests and desires – to live in the world while at the same time seeking release from all striving. This, then, made Taoism essentially inner-worldly and mystical.

Weber perceived a certain contradiction in Taoism. The fully consistent development of its ideas and, in fact, the ideas of any form of mysticism leads in the direction of an otherworldly outlook and the rejection of inner-worldly activity. Taoism did not draw this conclusion, however. Derived as it was from the same social stratum as the literati it could not help but retain an inner-worldly concern with life as it is lived in this world, with harmony and order, and with good government.

The macrobiotic ideal of Taoism reinforced this tendency. Lao Tzu emphasised the enjoyment of life *per se*, that is the prolongation of life by inactivity. It is clear that ideas such as these cannot have any practical results for the world and for change. Taoism was, in fact, opposed to all innovation as something which would upset the balance of the world and thereby release restless spirits destroying harmony.

The macrobiotic and magical side of Taoism appealed to the mass of the ordinary population and those followers of Taoism who emphasised these aspects brought about a fusion of the escapist doctrines of the intellectual side of the teachings on the one hand and the mundane practices of the Chinese magicians on the other.

Taoist magicians became particularly prominent in China and since they made their living from their practices they had an obvious interest in promoting magical beliefs among them. The Confucians had never entirely rejected such ideas themselves because of their usefulness in keeping the masses quiescent. Belief in magic thus served many interests.

A whole variety of techniques grew up which Weber considered to have had an important influence on Chinese life. He mentions, among other things, chronomatics, astrology, macrobiotics and geomancy. All this was bound to have consequences for economic development, and largely detrimental ones according to Weber. He mentions, for example, how mining was inhibited due to the belief that it would disturb the spirits of the earth. Geomancy hindered the development of industry and communications since workshops and factories could not be sited at the most convenient places nor roads follow the shortest routes, and so on.

Taoism was not always tolerated by Confucian orthodoxy. Its priests often competed with the literati for power and influence and both Taoism and Buddhism were suppressed by the authorities whenever they threatened the material position of the literati. They were seen to be a threat usually when they attempted to set up organised religious communities and attempted mass instruction in mystical and magical beliefs and rituals.

Whether tolerated or persecuted, however, Taoism could not have provided any greater stimulus for change or development than Confucianism. Much the same can be said for Buddhism, the other major religious tradition, but an imported one, that gained widespread support in China. Weber analysed the impact of Buddhism in his study of the religious traditions of India where it originated. There was, then, no religious tradition in China which could have provided any strong motive for salvation or an ethic which taught that the world as it exists is inadequate and must be changed. Neither Confucianism nor Taoism provided a prophetic saviour figure whose teachings might have had an impact on the way in which the society developed.

In the final part of *The Religion of China* Weber contrasts Confucianism with Puritanism, comparing the rationality of these outlooks and the implications that this might have had for the development of Chinese civilisation in relation to that of the West. He uses two criteria for determining the level of rationality of a religious orientation in this discussion – (i) the degree to which it has divested itself of magic and (ii) the degree to which it has systematically unified its conception of the relationship between God and the world and therewith its own ethical relationship to the world.

By the first measure Puritanism is more rational than Confucianism because while the latter did not exactly foster magic it tended to tolerate it and to retain a certain magical residue in itself. In no other religion, in contrast, has magic been so thoroughly deprecated and eradicated than in Puritanism.

Both Confucianism and Puritanism are relatively rational orientations to the world according to Weber but in very different ways. 'Confucian rationalism meant rational adjustment to the world; Puritan rationalism meant rational mastery of the world' (ibid., p. 248). Weber believed that Puritanism had the edge over Confucianism. For example, he said of the latter 'this ethic of unconditional affirmation of and adjustment to the world presupposed the unbroken and continued existence of purely magical religion' (ibid., p. 229).

The implications of this attitude of adjustment were that tension with the world was reduced to a minimum. There was no ethical prophecy, no supramundane God making ethical demands upon man. Hence there was no leverage for influencing conduct through forces freed from tradition and convention. Kinship organisation, for example, remained intact in China whereas Puritanism shattered it. Puritanism transformed all activity into rational enterprise. Confucianism preserved everything that was traditional.

THE STUDY OF CHINESE RELIGION SINCE WEBER

Criticism of Weber's analysis of Chinese religion has centred largely on his assessment of its social and economic impact and in particular on his characterisation of Confucianism. Metzger (1977) considers that Weber was quite wrong in his estimation that Confucianism was devoid of any sense of tension with the world and thus lacking in potential for change. Fundamental to Confucianism, and especially in its neo-Confucian form, according to Metzger, was a tension between the ideal of achieving a state of oneness with the divine, the *Tao*, but the inherent elusiveness of the divine. While imminent within reality rather than separate from it, the divine was considered almost imperceptible in its subtlety. The only way to deal with this problem for the Confucian sage was through the pursuit of moral cultivation thus focusing attention on the inner realm of the self. This pursuit was presented in terms of a philosophy which in effect constituted a process of salvation. The emphasis of the Confucians upon the elusiveness of the divine which separated them from it played the same role as the tradition of prophecy among the Jews. In Judaism, prophecy bridged the gap with the divine which had come about through original sin. In Confucianism, the separation from the divine, in the sense of a human incapacity to fully perceive and understand it, was expressed in this idea of subtlety and elusiveness. There was, then, a tension between the ideal and reality within Confucianism. It was also, according to Metzger, one which had transformative capacities but not without, he acknowledges, a tendency at times to lapse into acceptance of the status quo. If Confucianism did manifest a tension with the world it was not of a kind which produced the transformative capacities of certain currents in Western Europe.

Metzger's work received considerable discussion, in particular in a Symposium published in the *Journal of Asian Studies* in 1980. Here Harootunian argues that Metzger illegitimately reads features into neo-Confucianism as a result of his concern with the Weberian thesis. It is the agenda of Weber's Protestant Ethic thesis that leads to him to find in neo-Confucianism the alleged tension with the world as well as forces creating anxieties in the individual of a kind similar to those felt by Calvinistic Protestants. Chi'en charges Metzger with ignoring many other systems of thought relevant to the issue in concentrating too exclusively on neo-Confucianism. Chang argues that Metzger fails to distinguish clearly enough between tension with the world on the one hand and the transformative capacities of such tension on the other, a distinction which is quite clearly made by Weber himself.

Eisenstadt (1985) makes a similar point. While there was a tension between the transcendental and mundane order in Confucian China, according to Eisenstadt, this tension was conceived in secular rather than religious terms. Resolution of the tension was seen by the Confucians to lie in the performance of worldly duties and obligations within the existing social framework. This was not necessarily conservative or non-transformatory in its impact. Confucian notions of the imperfectability of the mundane order, its consequent partial legitimacy, a consequent critical attitude towards it and a need for stringent self-discipline in pursuit of a moral ideal, all carried transformative implications yet they were very limited in their effects because they remained within a secular context. As a result, the transformative potential of the Confucian ethos was not realised until China was exposed to modernity through the impact of Western culture and influence. The result was a revolutionary transformation.

Berger (1987), in seeking to explain the economic success of East Asian countries and the vigour of capitalism in the region considers one important factor to be the values of pragmatism, materialism and capacity for delayed gratification which can be linked to certain values embodied in popular or bourgeois forms of Confucianism which aided the process of modernisation. An emphasis upon the work ethic, self-discipline, activism and espousal of rational innovation provided an equivalent to the Protestant ethic that was conducive to economic success and development but without the individualism characteristic of the West.

Garrett (1992) argues that Confucianism was not able to generate a capitalist ethos *de novo* but in the context of an existing capitalist framework, once imported from the West, it is capable of providing the kind of personal motivation for economic achievement that Weber thought crucial to the development of the West. This view is not actually entirely dissimilar to Weber's own position, at least in certain interpretations of it. It can be argued that Weber considered ascetic Protestantism to have invigorated and imparted a dynamism to an already existing nascent capitalism (Fischoff, 1944; and see below, Chapter 7).

Among more general treatments of Chinese religion one of the most comprehensive studies which takes a sociological approach is that of Yang (1961). It is, unfortunately, largely and uncritically functionalist bringing in Malinowskian uncertainty where functionalism seems to need supplementing. Most aspects of Chinese religion are interpreted by Yang as integrative of various levels of Chinese social structure. The ancestor cult promoted integration of the kinship group, the worship of various local gods and deities promoted integration of the community, the state cult integrated the nation and was intended to legitimate the regime and the rule of the Emperor. Deities related to agriculture, on the other hand, derive, Yang argues, from the inherent uncertainties of peasant life at the mercy as it was of the forces of nature. The cults associated with various crafts and trades are similarly attributed to the uncertainties attached to them. In general, he claims, the more uncertain or dangerous the occupation the more superstitious its members. Peasants were the most devoted to their cults. The business class were used to taking calculated risk and consequently less superstitious, worshipping only gods of wealth. The Confucian literati were the least inclined to supernatural beliefs, resorting to them only in the context of the examinations, an inherently uncertain and anxiety laden aspect of their lives.

Yet Confucianism itself, Yang points out, supported many of these practices and cults as of social value in promoting order and stability while rejecting their supernatural aspects. Yang implies that the Confucians recognised the social functions of these cults. He does not see the possibility, however, that this tolerance of them by an otherwise anti-magically oriented class might have been a rationalisation consistent with the strongly conservative bent of Confucianism which was inclined to find everything traditional somehow of value. In doing so it naturally would have attempted to use the magical and supernatural beliefs and practices of the populace in a way conducive to good order, as Yang himself acknowledges.

The ambivalent nature of Confucianism and the limitations it imposed regarding religion and supernatural belief can be seen particularly clearly in its attempt to legitimate the regime by the doctrine of the Mandate of Heaven. Confucianism found it necessary to legitimate the power of the state by investing it with sanctity and divine character. Yet Confucianism was in other respects anti-supernaturalistic and upheld the value of government and selection for office by merit, demonstrated in the examination system. Such ideas could not be applied to the position of the monarch, however. Confucianism was unable, as a consequence, to develop a satisfactory theory of the origins of imperial power, concentrating instead on formulating a body of ethico-political principles that would define the duties and guide the actions of whatever ruler was in power. Some supernatural legitimation was needed, however, to justify the regime in the eyes of the masses and this Confucianism found in the doctrine of the Mandate of Heaven by which whoever won power was said to have the mandate, and whoever lost power was said to have lost it for his faults. This was supplemented with the theory of yin–yang and of the Five Elements. The succession of dynastic power was believed to be governed by the rotation of the influence of the five elements, of earth, air, fire, water and wood. These were connected with the movements of the stars which, in turn, governed the mystical operation of time and, thereby, the course of human events. It is hardly surprising that such a doctrine became at times severely strained in its credibility and failed to fulfil its integrative and legitimating role. It worked only so long as there was a reasonable degree of stability and not too frequent disruption but could not cope with constant and rapid change.

Such was the case, Yang argues, during the second century AD when the Han Empire suffered severe disruption and violent power struggles. Widespread corruption, concentration of land ownership, increasing landlessness and ruinous taxation led to a breakdown in the legitimacy of the state and in confidence in Confucian ideology. Much of the population turned to Taoism.

Yang attributes the successful introduction and spread of Buddhism in China to this social malaise and disruption. Buddhism found fertile soil towards, and for some time after, the end of the Han period when added to internal difficulties there was a constant threat from marauding nomadic groups such as the Huns, Mongols and Turks. Buddhism offered a salvation doctrine which was eagerly received at such a time of insecurity and confusion.

The response of Confucianism was to incorporate much of the Buddhist outlook, especially in its Mahayana aspects, into itself, creating what is known as neo-Confucianism. For example, the neo-Confucians adopted the Ch'an Buddhist formula of meditative mental concentration in order to achieve sudden enlightenment. Confucianism was thus able to regain its pre-eminent place once again with the eventual restoration of peace and order in the Empire.

Confucianism, however, remained, as it had always been, essentially a socio-political doctrine only partially religious in nature. The consequent absence of any separate religious sphere in Chinese society having official or socially recognised status meant that religion remained for the most part diffused throughout Chinese society. This gave to the social environment as a whole a sacred atmosphere strongly supportive of the values and traditions of long established institutions. This may account in part for the well-known conservatism and stability of Chinese society, Yang argues. It is often argued that there was a clear distinction between elite and popular religion in China (Wolf, 1974b), Confucianism being the religion of the dominant class of literati while magical Taoism and the many supernaturalistic cults represented the popular religion of the masses. Yang, despite seeing Confucianism as not primarily a religion in the theistic sense, rejects this view. The Confucians, he points out, shared with the rest of the population a basic system of belief in Heaven, fate and various supernatural conceptions that were part of the general pattern of Chinese religious life. There was a close interlocking of official Confucian and popular cults which Weber failed to appreciate in characterising the official cults as mere formality and convention. Smith (1970) has also argued that the literati had a distinct sense of the sacred and the transcendental in their conception of Heaven even if they lacked formal beliefs and doctrines concerning it. What gave meaning to life for them was a sense of relatedness to Heaven and to the natural order.

Yang (1957) sums up the relationship between Confucianism and popular religion as one of domination of the latter by the former. This resulted from the separation between ethics and religion, the organisational weakness and the diffused nature of religion in China.

In China, Yang points out, unlike most other cultures and civilisations, ethical values were not primarily the province of religion but of Confucianism. Religion tended to lend supernatural sanction to Confucian values and Confucianism was happy to make use of religion in support of these values. They were mutually supporting systems. This is particularly true of popular religion, diffused as it was through the institutions of Chinese society and without its own autonomous organisation or institutional basis. Even in the case of the organised religions of Buddhism and Taoism, however, the ethical values of these systems did not have the influence over the mass of the population that Confucianism or popular religion did, but only over a minority of particular devotees, monks, priests and virtuoso followers. Buddhist and Taoist values were also less applicable in the practical sense to

Chinese social structure than were those of Confucianism. The organised religions were, in any case, only loosely organised. There were no central overarching authority structures, organised priesthoods, or even local structures in either Buddhism or Taoism. Monasteries and temples were largely autonomous units, there was no central system for recruitment or training of priests and the relationship between laity and priest or monk was ad hoc, limited to specific purposes and largely contractual – in other words there was no organised parish or local religious community. This organisational weakness applies even more, of course, to diffused popular religion, including ancestor worship.

The organisational weakness of religion in China deprived it of any independent structural position in social organisation leaving Confucianism to play the central role in the traditional order. The state, also, almost always followed a policy, in Chinese history, of acting to suppress any attempt to establish centrally organised religious institutions. This was a major reason for the continued organisational weakness of even the relatively organised religions of Buddhism and Taoism. The state saw independent religious organisations as a potential threat to stability.

A second factor which tended to promote weak organisation in Chinese religion was the very fact of religious pluralism and eclecticism. The existence of popular cults, Confucian cults, Buddhism and Taoism meant that the Chinese tended to use each for different purposes and in different contexts thereby undermining the authority of all of them as far as commanding the loyalty of a lay following in any organised manner was concerned.

Yang's view of the unity of Chinese religion is strenuously supported by Freedman (1974) who points out that recent studies of Chinese religion have tended to be anthropological and ethnographic in orientation concentrating on peasant religion in small communities to the neglect of the tradition of Confucianism and therefore failing to see the connections between popular and elite levels. The view that the elite was characterised by rational agnosticism and the masses by indiscriminate superstition is one which actually expresses the elite's own view of the differences between the main strata of the society rather than that which the impartial outside observer is constrained to take by the nature of the facts. Chinese religion was based upon a conception of authority that in the last analysis would not allow the religious to separate off from the secular. The Chinese state, he points out, has been and remains today remarkably successful in muting religious authority.

Other writers have stressed the complementarity of Confucianism and Taoism. Garrett (1992) points out that the Confucian requirement of self-discipline and submergence of personal identity and destiny in accordance with a conception of an unchanging and unchangeable principle of order, the Tao, created unbearable psychological tensions in the individual. The individual's perception of his or her relationship to the fundamental order of the world was expressed in the Chinese preoccupation with fate. Taoism, especially through its legitimation of magical and divinatory procedures, provided a means of discerning what fate might hold or for overcoming problems so giving a sense of release from the tight constraints of a Confucian world quite beyond human control. This was particularly important for the less advantaged. Taoism thus functioned at an individual and personal level whereas Confucianism was dominant in the sphere of public social relations, but each reinforced the other.

Sangren (1987), in a study of religion in Taiwan, however, notes that Taoism in its emphasis on a primal chaos (*hun-tun*) rather than order was, at least at certain periods in its history, profoundly opposed to Confucianism. The Taoist conception precludes the possibility of legitimating social institutions and structures. While Confucianism sets order, yang, against disorder, yin, there is, nevertheless, an order within the relationship between the two. Order is unthinkable without counterposing it to disorder; the notion of order implies the notion of disorder. In Confucian thought order thus has a kind of priority in the last analysis. Taoism, on the other hand, counterposes a primal chaos against the ordered relationship of yin and yang and in doing so denies the primacy of order. The order in human society is necessarily seen, therefore, as a conventional and humanly contrived rather than inherent one. As such it cannot be legitimated in terms of a conception of a fundamental order in nature outside and beyond human choice and decision. Taoism, also, may have shared with Buddhism, which emphasised salvation outside the established relationships of family, community and state, the role of providing a renunciatory counterpoint to the Confucian hegemony of order.

A quite different approach to the question of the unity of Chinese religion is that taken by Baity (1975) in his study of temples in a Northern Taiwanese town. Baity considers that the distinction between great versus little tradition is not able to express the underlying unity in Chinese religion. Neither can this be expressed in terms of the conventional categories of Confucianism, Taoism, Buddhism and folk belief and practice. Rather one has to attend to the distinction between public and private, pure and impure, yin and yang to make sense of the diversity of Chinese religion. In examining the role of various temples in the town it is apparent that no single temple can offer the full range of services required by residents; collectively, however, they do so. While the residents will tend to give quite contradictory accounts of the role of the various temples it can be seen that there is an underlying order in their collective operation which is not an arbitrary amalgam of Taoism, Buddhism and Confucianism. For example, the distinction between ancestral halls and community temples is best conceived in terms of a private and public division. Since both would be polluted by contact with death neither can be used to store the bones of the dead. This is where Buddhist monasteries take over. They are somewhere between the public and the private and are immune to pollution by death. Overall, then, the system has a logic and a coherence.

This can be seen through consideration of other contrasts. Since ancestor spirits are yin in relation to gods they cannot be propitiated or venerated in temples devoted to gods. As a result there is a specialisation of temples in different types of ritual and service relating to the dead; ancestors are venerated in ancestor temples but other spirits of the dead, such as ghosts, cannot be propitiated in these temples so this must be done in community temples. Also, private ghosts, namely ancestors, belong to the private realm whereas other spirits of the dead, the hungry ghosts, belong to the public realm; they are the ghosts of the community.

Baity examines practices relating to mourning, the treatment of corpses, funerals, burials and a variety of rituals and services, showing that the same underlying logic is at work. A fundamental distinction in such rituals is that between services relating to the living and those relating to the dead. In popular conception these two spheres are associated with Taoism and Buddhism respectively. In reality both types of service are performed in both Taoist and Buddhist temples and in each case priests or monks from the other religion are present. There is a division of labour within both the Taoist priesthood and Buddhist sangha in terms of types of service and those who officiate rather than a division of labour between them. But because Buddhist institutions monopolise a certain type of service for the dead which cannot be held in non-Buddhist temples there exists in popular perception a close association between Buddhism and services for the dead. Despite the division between Taoism and Buddhism and the popular understanding of this there is an overall unity in the system as a totality which is revealed by focusing upon the distinctions mentioned, purity versus pollution, private versus public, and so on.

Whether this is true generally for Chinese religion, or for Taiwan as a whole, it is difficult to say. A point that Watson (1976) makes gives cause for caution in too readily seeking to overgeneralise from a particular case. We should not forget, he argues, that ethnic differences in regions like Taiwan and elsewhere tend to generate religious diversity. Different ethnic groups often actively seek to express their identities and to reinforce boundaries through creating religious distinctions.[1] On the other hand, as Sangren (1984) points out, the use of sacred symbols to differentiate one group from another presupposes a common intelligibility of the sacred symbol system. The marking of boundaries by the use of religious concepts and symbols cannot be taken to indicate that there is no shared system of ideas and categories.

In some ways, this debate about the unity of Chinese religion seems to be a false one. Where there are similarities and differences one sees the similarity and another sees the difference. As Weller (1987) points out, those who focus upon the society as a whole tend to find an underlying unity whereas those who focus on particular groups find diversity. In his study of Taiwanese religion Weller seeks to show how a common experience produces an overall common religious perspective but also how within this commonality diversity of experience nevertheless produces diverse interpretations and understandings of the religion and its elements.

In one particular respect, there is a high degree of uniformity in Chinese religion. At all levels its beliefs closely reflect the bureaucratic character of the traditional Chinese system of government staffed by the Confucian literati. Even popular cults took a form which mirrored the hierarchical nature of the bureaucratic structures. Many writers have noted how the organisation of the supernatural realm was seen to be on the pattern of the temporal government and functioned in much the same way in maintaining order and discipline (Yang, 1961; Jordan, 1972; Wolf, 1974b; Feuchtwang, 1974; Weller, 1987). Opinion differs, however, on the extent to which Chinese religion can be assimilated to this pattern. In many respects, the gods had the character of government officials. Wolf (1974b) points out that many deities were responsible for a discrete administrative district in just the same way as local officials were. In some parts of China the image of the city god is dressed in official robes and is flanked on either side by secretaries. His temple is laid out along the same lines as a government *yamen*.

Feuchtwang (1974) notes that diviners and priests present petitions to the gods as if they were administrative officials and offer guidance to their clients in sacred protocol. Ahern (1981) shows how the use of written documents was an essential technique in influencing the gods to grant desired benefits. In general, she argues, the way to deal with gods in China was to utilise the same techniques and procedures of appealing to or drawing upon bureaucratic authority that one would use in political and administrative life.

We may agree with Yang, then, that Chinese religion, at least at the official level, was an attempt to give moral significance and meaning to the vagaries of life and to the social and political order. It attempted to do this by 'moralising' popular supernaturalism. But it did so by use of the analogy of the imperial administration. We may go further than Yang in noting that not only did the ethos of Confucianism give meaning to life in China but the Confucian order also provided a model for the meaningful ordering of the whole cosmos.

Yet the 'imperial metaphor' as it has been termed takes us only so far in understanding Chinese religion. Feuchtwang (1992) points out that while there were many close parallels between imperial organisa-tion and religious order there were also differences and it was in the differences that one finds what made Chinese religion timeless. Sang-ren (1987) notes that it is a past imperial system that provides the present day model of celestial bureaucracy. Taiwan, also, has under-gone much political change in the last hundred years under Repub-lican, Japanese and independent administrations but this has not been reflected in changes in the character of the imperial metaphor which suggests that the celestial order is not just a simple projection of the social order.

It is important to remember, also, that conceptions of gods and their relationships reflect not simply the hierarchical and bureaucratic polit-ical and administrative order but also the conflicts and competition characteristic of political life. Popular interpretations of gods in Tai-wan, reflect, according to Weller (1987) ethic differences, local opposi-tion to national control and local political manoeuvring.

Dean (1993), in his study of Taoism in South East China, stresses that Taoist ritual embodies modes of communication with the divine quite unlike the modes of communication that existed between citizen and official. Taoist priests took on god-like attributes in ritual and became identified with gods acquiring in the process power over beings within the pantheon. The relationship that common people often had with gods was characterised by a devoutness and deep sense of divine benevolence and protection which far surpassed in intensity anything that could be said of the relationship with bureaucratic officials.

The relationship between social and celestial order is much more complex according to Sangren (1987) than it has often been presented. In his study of a Taiwanese community he seeks to show that while indeed a metaphor for social order the imperial metaphor was much more than this. In his view it played an active role in the patterning of social order and social relations in the process of their production and reproduction. The heavenly order resembled the social order not because it was a mere expression of the latter but because both were constituted in the same set of processes. In this sense the relationship between mundane and celestial orders is even more intimate than the imperial metaphor notion recognises.

Complexities in the relationship between the mundane and celestial order can be seen clearly in examining the role of female deities in Chinese religion (Sangren, 1983, 1987). Sangren notes that in Taiwan conception of deities as imperial officials is confined primarily to territorial cults. Buddhist temples, pilgrimage centres and sectarian cults are not usually associated with clearly defined territories. Female deities are prominent in all these non-territorial cults including Kuan Yin, Ma Tsu and the Eternal Mother. These deities embody only the positive aspects of womanhood as conceived in Chinese culture unlike male deities which resemble more closely their earthly counterparts in terms of both their authority and their weaknesses. Male deities are susceptible to bribery, threat and so on. Female deities, on the other hand, are perfectly just and upright. This difference can be understood, according to Sangren, in terms of an inherent contradiction in the female role in the Chinese family structure.

In patrilocal Chinese families a wife is under the authority of the mother-in-law and receives little support from her husband. She will usually turn to her children for emotional support. Mothers are allies in the eyes of sons against paternal authority. The bond between mother and sons can act to postpone fission of patrilineal households. From loyalty to their mother otherwise intensively competitive sons may remain together. Their young wives have an interest in early division and independence for their husbands in order to escape the authority of their mothers-in-law. The mother-in-law will wish to postpone division for as long as possible. So women in the Chinese domestic setting play a divisive and unifying role depending upon their situation as mothers or as wives.

It is the unifying role of mother that is expressed by the perfection of female deities. Kuan Yin, Ma Tsu and the Eternal Mother are all unifying symbols in Taiwanese religion. Ma Tsu as the focal deity of nationwide pilgrimage cults transcends local allegiances; Buddhist female deities integrate the socially marginal and anomalous. Just as earthly mothers mediate between children and fathers so female deities mediate between worshippers and the other gods who are less easily approachable. The Eternal Mother, the female deity of sectarian cults, represents, according to Sangren, the alliance between mothers and sons against fathers. Just as mothers ally with sons to circumvent paternal authority so in the sectarian cults one finds a millenarian ideology which seeks to subvert the hierarchical authority of the celestial bureaucracy through appeal to the Eternal Mother.

In these roles it can be seen that while female deities in many respects parallel features of the mundane social world they differ considerably from mothers. They exhibit only one side of the motherly role and are much more powerful than women in the mundane world. The Eternal Mother is to her worshippers the creator of the world and controls all heaven and earth and is thus vastly superior to any god of the orthodox, male-oriented cosmology (Weller, 1987). Weller agrees with Sangren that while the cults of female deities express the nurturing role of women in contrast to the masculine role, they possess also the power of opposition to the male-dominated bureaucracy thereby expressing the experience of women and also the feelings and aspirations of potentially rebellious sections of society.

The legitimating and unifying in contrast to the oppositional role of gods and goddesses depends a great deal upon context. In Sangren's terms they can express either order or disorder, yang or yin, according to context and interpretation. Goddesses such as Ma Tsu in their oppositional potential are clearly a threat to the social order. The reaction of established authority to such goddesses has often been to attempt to co-opt them into the official pantheon. This requires emphasising their yang aspect by appointing them to a celestial office. Ma Tsu was thus endowed with official titles and honours and included in official rites. Yet she remains essentially yin in nature and potentially expressive of opposition to male, bureaucratic, hierarchical order.

The state in China always demonstrated a readiness and ability to incorporate popular deities and cults. In doing so, of course, the state legitimated them and as a consequence the pattern of local social and political relationships and the powers that local and popular cult deities were believed to have. Local communities, in their turn, acknowledged their place in the wider hierarchical order of society in so far as they accepted this state legitimation. This reciprocal legitimation demonstrates an underlying similarity of structure in orthodox and unorthodox systems of ideas. The simultaneous unity and diversity of Chinese religion is likened by Sangren to the drawing by Escher in which a flock of white birds flying to the left can be seen from a different perspective as a flock of black birds flying to the right. The same hierarchical order, which from the perspective of orthodoxy and established authority encompasses all under heaven within one household, from the popular perspective divides society in a hierarchy of competing communities.

6 Judaism

WEBER ON ANCIENT JUDAISM

Weber's study of the social and religious developments of ancient Palestine was of crucial significance within his overall programme. The religious outlook and ethos of Judaism stands in clear contrast with that of the East, that is with China and India.

This very different outlook that developed in the Middle East was of great importance for the whole character and development of Western, that is European, civilisation. This religious outlook and ethos was incorporated into Christianity and through Christianity and the culmination of certain elements of it in Protestantism it had great importance for the development of European civilisation. We have seen that Weber considered the characteristic feature of Western civilisation to be rationalisation of all spheres of activity, one of which is, of course, the rationalisation of productive activity in the form of capitalism.

Weber, in Ancient Judaism, is looking not so much for the origins of that mentality which was to create rational capitalism but for the origins of the overall Western mentality and ethos which promoted the general rationalisation which in his view characterised western society. And he is seeking to contrast this tradition with that of the East, with China and India. He attempts to uncover the specific circumstances and conditions, social, political and economic, which promoted the development of this very different ethos in ancient Palestine.

In the East, according to Weber, as we have seen, religion was characteristically other-worldly, mystical and elitist. The higher religions were suited only to monks, leisured intellectuals and religious virtuosi. Prophecy was largely exemplary. In Palestine and in Christianity we see the very opposite of this. These religions tend towards asceticism and often of an inner-worldly type. Prophecy is ethical and there is no division between an elite and the masses in so far as the possibility of salvation is concerned.

All this was of great significance, in Weber's view, in the development of the West. In the East the predominant religious outlook favoured conservatism and traditionalism. The world was seen as unchanging and eternal – unchangeable, in fact. Or it was seen as illusory and transitory. This meant that the religious impulses were inclined to an otherworldliness. There was no point in activity or striving in this world or in attempting to change aspects of it.

Among the Jews quite a different view came to prevail. The world was seen to be totally unacceptable and change was certain. In fact, the world in Jewish eyes was subject to immanent transformation. The Jews developed a conviction of the inevitable and complete overturning of the existing world order. 'The whole attitude to life of ancient Jewry was determined by this conception of a future God-guided political and social revolution' (Weber, 1952, p. 4).

This attitude was carried over into Christianity where it had profound consequences given the particular environment and circumstances that prevailed in Christian Europe. As Weber states, '... in considering the conditions of Jewry's evolution, we stand at a turning point of the whole cultural development of the West and the Middle East' (ibid., p. 5).

This importance of Judaism and its specific character is related to the position of the Jews as a pariah people, that is as a guest people ritually separated from their social surroundings. Weber claims that we can derive much of the fundamental outlook of the Jews from this fact. He compares the Jews with the pariah tribes of India. In India, of course, the caste system existed and because of it these pariah groups were led to adopt a very different outlook to that of the Jews. The caste system gave them hope of improvement in their condition in later reincarnations and kept them in conformity with caste dharma. Their response to pariah status was thus conservative and tended to maintain the status quo.

Quite the contrary prevailed in the case of the Jews, who hoped instead for a radical transformation of their condition in the present world. Unlike the Indian low caste pariah groups they did not look upon the world as eternal and unchanging. For them it was a creation of a powerful god and the circumstances that prevailed in the world were seen as a direct product of their own conduct, as a people, and their relationship with this god. It was thus susceptible to change and the Jews could believe in an eventual transformation of their status and position in the world. They developed a sense of a unique destiny in history and interpreted historical events in the light of this conception and their moral and ethical condition as a people. This was, then, an innerworldly orientation and a salvation doctrine of a rational and ethical type.

How was it that the Jews became a pariah people and how did they acquire their distinctive traits as a people? Weber sets out to answer these questions beginning with an examination, as in his studies of China and India, of the economic, social and political conditions and institutions prevailing in Palestine from early times and a broad survey of historical developments.

The inhabitants of Palestine in the early period were largely tribal peoples living between two great centres of civilisation dominated by centralised, bureaucratically governed states – Egypt and Babylon. Both periodically threatened Palestine and its peoples and sometimes brought it under their domination, although usually only temporarily. For the tribal peoples of Palestine and in particular for the Israelite tribes, many of which were nomadic or partly nomadic, Egypt was alien and despised. This hierarchical, centralised bureaucratic state imposed compulsory labour services upon its population and upon subject populations in the construction of irrigation and flood control systems, temples, royal palaces and so on. It was ruled by a priestly hierocracy preoccupied with the cult of the dead and the afterlife. It was, for the free pastoralists and semi-nomads, a wholly alien style of life and culture. For the Israelites it was the 'house of bondage' from which they had been led to freedom by Moses.

The Israelites had probably entered Egypt somewhere around 1700 BC, a time of extensive migrations, as a largely nomadic people who grazed their flocks in the Nile Delta region. Subsequently, the position of the Israelites seems to have become oppressive. The outcome was the Exodus which perhaps occurred around 1400 or 1300 BC and the eventual settlement in Canaan some time after 1300 BC – a settlement made possible in the traditional story as result of a conquest assisted by the Israelite god Yahweh.

The Israelites, however, continued, to be threatened by Egypt and by Babylon as well as by many invading and neighbouring tribes and peoples – Philistines, Bedouin, Midianites, Moabites, Ammonites, Arameans and so on. There was also a great deal of internecine warfare among the Israelite tribes themselves. This unstable political situation is attributed by Weber to the climatic and geographical features of the area and the variety of modes of economic production and ways of life.

The basic division was that between the grain growing and cattle breeding farmers of the central and northern areas and the nomadic and semi-nomadic pastoralists on the margins of the desert lands. There was often a conflict of interests between the settled population and the herdsmen. The latter would sometimes unite under the temporary direction of a war leader in order to expand their grazing lands at the expense of the settled farmers.

As the settled area grew in power and importance, and as trade developed which increased the importance of the towns and cities, new divisions and conflicts emerged. In the cities a noble stratum of warriors and landowners developed. The cities often developed from the castles and fortresses of warrior chiefs who with their personal followers dominated the surrounding area. The urban dwellers, Weber claims, were an 'armed patriciate' whose wealth enabled them to equip themselves for warfare: '... the early Israelite city at its height was an association of hereditary, charismatic sibs economically qualified to bear arms' (ibid., p. 20).

These sibs were also engaged in trade. Palestine was at the crossroads of numerous trade routes and the city population acted to a large extent as middlemen. Capital from these sources was used to acquire land and to reduce, ultimately, the peasantry to debt slavery.

The peasant stratum was comprised of the rural population of lands surrounding the cities. At first they were free landowners or tenants but with the growth of urban power they were reduced to dependence upon and domination by this group. At one time the backbone of the Israelite army, their importance was progressively eroded with the development of methods of warfare requiring costly armour, chariots and horses.

Finally, the semi-nomadic sheep and goat herders occupied a situation midway between the settled population and the fully nomadic Bedouin of the desert regions. They were only ever temporarily united under the leadership of warrior figures specifically for purposes of warfare. For Weber they were a very important group, however, whose outlook was to have a profound influence within Judaism.

At times the urban patriciate, the peasantry and the herdsmen would unite in alliance against the Bedouin and other mutual enemies. At other times there would be internal conflict between them. The early tensions between herdsmen and peasant became overlaid increasingly with that between landlord and peasant. This was intensified with the development of more centralised administrations and the formation of the Jewish state under Saul, David and Solomon.

Originally the Israelite tribes had formed a loose confederation or alliance for purposes of warfare. Weber tells us that 'Israel as a political community was conceived as an oath-bound confederation' (ibid., p. 75). There were no permanent central political institutions involved in this confederacy. The oath that Weber refers to consisted of the covenant with God, the *berith*, symbolised by the famous ark of the covenant. The confederacy, then, was held together by limited common interests expressed in terms of a common religious basis. A confederation of this kind was advantageous, Weber argues, for survival in the prevailing conditions of conflict and tribal fragmentation. It was thus the result of particular historical and religious circumstances but once in existence it spread to incorporate a wide variety of groups because of its ability to provide some measure of security in an uncertain and dangerous world. 'Israel', then, was not the name of a tribe or people but of an association or as Weber put it of a 'cult league' (ibid., p. 81).

With the growth of the power of cities and the warrior elite, made increasingly important by the emergence of new methods of warfare, the role of the confederacy changed. Under Saul and David there was greater reliance on the dominant warrior kinship groups and upon mercenary and slave armies. Even so, the Israelite kings could never be entirely independent of the rural tribespeople in military matters. The subject population usually attempted to resist the power of centralised rule and domination.

Under Solomon a centralised urban despotism on the Egyptian pattern was established. This led to constant opposition and criticism from the rural population which continued after the division of the state into a northern kingdom, Israel and a southern kingdom, Judah. In the north the tradition of opposition to kingship remained because of its association with non-Yahwistic religious practices. In Judah the retention of a more pure form of Yahweh worship, at least for much of the time, reduced to some extent opposition to kingship.

This, then, is the historical, political, and religious background against which we must see the development of Judaism and the Jewish outlook and the development of the great prophetic tradition. The social divisions and conflicts were, according to Weber, largely bound up with religious matters in the history of the Jews and with the characteristic religious ethos which developed in this situation of conflict between the dominant, ruling, land-owning aristocracy and the rural population.

The religion of the Jewish people developed over a long period of time and, Weber argues, its features can be traced to and understood in terms of the particular circumstances which prevailed in Palestine during this era. Yahweh was originally a god of war and of a confederacy which was formed for purposes of warfare. He was also a god of catastrophe and destruction. The Jews had entered into the covenant with this god because, they believed, he had chosen them above all other peoples and had committed himself to the promotion of their interests on certain and absolutely binding conditions. They were charged with the duty of carrying out his commandments and above all they were obliged to worship him and only him as the one true god. These were the terms of the covenant that Moses was said to have entered into with God on behalf of the Israelites at the time of the Exodus when he had led them out of Egypt to the promised land of Canaan.

The commandments that had to be obeyed by the Israelites comprise the Jewish law handed down from the time of Moses and codified in the Torah. In this way Jewish belief was given a characteristically ethical aspect. The fortunes of the Israelites, they believed, depended upon their strict obedience to the teaching of the Torah. This contained not only beliefs and teachings of a religious nature but included also the social law and norms governing all aspects of social organisation and life. Yahweh was thus the god of the social order as well as the war god and guardian of the fate of Israel.

The Jewish law, then, was, in the perception of the Jews, not something necessarily eternal and founded in the nature of things. It was the product of an agreement, a contract and as such could be changed just as the terms of any contract could be changed. The social order, likewise, was seen as something not necessarily fixed and immutable. It was a question of Yahweh's will.

A unique feature of Judaism was that it was from a relatively early stage largely monotheistic. At least it is commonly said that the most important feature of Judaism was its monotheism which, of course, was carried over into Christianity as one of the most important contributions of Judaism to Western religious thought. Some, however, have disputed the monotheistic nature of early Judaism. It is not entirely clear whether it was a belief in a sole, all-powerful deity – a belief which recognised the existence of no other deity at all and unlikely in the early period. Was it, alternatively, the exclusive worship of one deity among several that were believed to exist – one with whom Israel had a sacred and exclusive contract? In short monolatry rather than monotheism. Or was it a belief in and worship of a single god who was one among many but superior to all others – henotheism?

Weber points out that probably all these conceptions coexisted with one another in the early period and that different conceptions tended to be favoured by different social groups. The warriors probably tended to believe that Yahweh was the god of his own people while other peoples had their own gods. The royal families and urban strata considered their god to be localised in the temple of the city. Elsewhere other local gods prevailed and when in any particular city it was wise to worship its god. The semi-nomadic stockbreeders had a rather different attitude to the urban and settled populations. They tended to believe that Yahweh was with the Israelites wherever they happened to be. For them God was not localised and his power operated in all places. This was probably the belief of the confederacy and gave rise later to the idea that when the Israelite army took the ark of the covenant into battle Yahweh was with them. It was a conception which implied that Yahweh was superior to any other god since he brought victory to the Israelites provided they had kept to the terms of the covenant and had obeyed the law. Other gods, then, were of little significance. This was a more universalistic conception and it was a short step from this to full monotheism – a short but not an easy one, as we shall see.

The semi-nomadic stockbreeders also tended to favour the worship of Yahweh by sacrifice rather less than the settled and urban populations, emphasising the keeping of his commandments rather more strictly. In early times there had been no special priestly hierarchy responsible for offering sacrifices to Yahweh.

From such attitudes there emerged a tradition of pure Yahweh worshippers, strongest among the semi-nomadic groups and which was more monotheistic, less interested in sacrifice and ritual, and more concerned with keeping the commandments of God; a religious orientation that was more ethical, which saw God as more universalistically powerful and which saw him as a jealous god who would not tolerate the worship of rivals. This tradition of pure Yahweh worship was of great importance in the development of Judaism, Weber believed.

The pure Yahweh tradition was, Weber argued, strongest in the South. In the North there was a much greater tendency to acknowledge the existence of other gods and even to worship them. In Canaan there were many local gods or *baals* with associated cults. The settled Israelites tended to indulge in these cults alongside the cult of Yahweh. Pure Yahweh worshippers were strongly opposed to this as being against the commandments of God. They were opposed to the representation of gods in the form of idols – the graven images which the commandments forbade them to make.

Apart from contravening the law the baal cults were seen by pure Yahweh worshippers as rivals to the cult of Yahweh, reminiscent of Egyptian cults and, consequently, anathema to them. These cults were often associated with ancestor worship which tended to strengthen the power of kinship groups and particularly dominant or ruling families, again something which was anathema to the pure Yahweh worshippers.

The struggle between these two traditions continued over a long period and gave rise to the prophetic tradition in Judaism which Weber considered to be of great significance. The Biblical prophets were active also at a time of political unrest and flourished during a period of political decline. This period begins in the ninth century.

Also important for the development of Judaism were the priests. If the prophets were experts in ecstatics, revelation and insight it was the priests or Levites who were the experts on ritual and law. There is some uncertainty, Weber recognises, as to the relationship between the Levites as priests, on the one hand, and members of the tribe of Levi, a military tribe, on the other.

In the early days of the confederacy there seems to have been no collective organisation of priests. Political leaders employed priests to carry out sacrifices at various shrines which they owned as private property. Sacrifices to Yahweh were performed on behalf of the confederacy as a whole by the political leaders themselves and not by priests.

The priests, then, were ritual specialists employed from time to time by secular authorities. Their services seem to have been valued by the political leaders as their knowledge of law and ritual enabled them to advise clients on how to win the favour of Yahweh. Many Levites also became involved in the baal cults and in non-Yahweh worship.

Weber likens the Levites to the Brahmins in India. Like them the Levites tended to segregate themselves ritually by the adoption of prescriptions relating to purity and pollution. This made those of them who did not compromise with the baal cults particularly strong opponents of them since they had taken over elements of Egyptian religion and the cult of the dead. Death and tombs were polluting to true Yahweh worshipping Levites.

As a result of this opposition the pure Yahweh worshipping Levites came into opposition with the priests employed by the kings. With the rise of kingship the royal priests and political authorities attempted to establish a monopoly of ritual relating to Yahweh. In the long run the advocates of pure Yahweh worship won out but not without a struggle. It is a fact which requires explanation. Weber relates it to the prevailing political conditions.

Pagan cults flourished in the northern kingdom after it separated from the southern kingdom in 931 BC. The southern kingdom was not entirely free of it either but on the whole, Weber argues, the tradition of pure Yahweh worship was much stronger there. In 722 BC the Northern kingdom was destroyed by the Assyrians and much of the population were exiled to Babylonia. The southern kingdom survived for some time but was under constant threat and often had to pay tribute to the Assyrians. It was these disastrous experiences which ultimately led to the triumph of Yahweh worship. These political events were interpreted as punishment by Yahweh for the failure of the Israelites to keep the commandments of the covenant and to maintain pure Yahweh worship. Judah itself became a vassal state of Assyria and its independence was entirely lost in 587 BC when, after it rose up against Assyria and was defeated, the temple in Jerusalem was destroyed and again a large section of the population, and particularly the priests, were exiled.

The covenant was between God and the Israelites collectively as a people. They considered themselves, therefore, collectively responsible for any backsliding on the part of a section of the nation and liable to collective punishment for it. Military defeat could thus be interpreted as such a collective punishment. God's retribution for sin thus tended to take a political form and to work through political events. It was in this way that the political fate of the Israelites was seen as being bound up with their worship of Yahweh. It was in this way that they acquired a sense of a specific and special historical destiny as a people. It was in this way that their religion acquired a uniquely ethical character rather than a ritualistic one.

The prophets played a crucial role in this process. Weber traces various types of prophecy in the history of Israelite society. In the early days of the confederacy military decisions were often made on the basis of prophetic insight gained during an ecstatic experience by the leader. There were also specialists in this kind of thing – professional ecstatics known as *nebiim* (singular *nabi*). They were magicians and sorcerers, Weber tells us. They also acted as war prophets, inciting warriors into battle and working magic to ensure victory. They considered themselves, while in an ecstatic state, to be seized by the spirit of Yahweh. Very often military leaders were indistinguishable from such prophets.

Weber mentions several other types of prophet. The seers or oracle givers (*roeh*) who were not ecstatics. They would typically interpret dreams.

Towards the end of the early period, that is the period of the confederacy, a new type of prophet appeared among the stockbreeding tribes in the South. They were not ecstatics but claimed to have contact with or be able to hear the voice of Yahweh and transmit his will to the political authorities. At first they would transmit the will of Yahweh when asked to do so. Later they began to pronounce on political and other matters to the authorities without being asked. The predictions they made were often pessimistic and they were often unpopular with the authorities as a result. Eventually their pronouncements became overtly critical and addressed to the people rather than to the authorities, and they formed or represented a group opposed to those who held power in the state.

The prophet Elijah, Weber argues, represents the climax of the older, and the beginning of the new tradition of Biblical prophets. Elijah spoke to the masses, to the people, as much as to the political authorities. Later prophets were to become the intellectual leaders of the opposition against kingship, centralisation, social injustice and crippling taxation. They were the leading figures of pure Yahweh worship and old traditional freedoms.

The classical prophets were, then, not responsible for the specific content of the ethic of Judaism – the teachings of the Torah. This was the contribution of the priests. What the prophets did was to promote '... the systematic unification by relating the people's life as a whole and the life of each individual to the fulfilment of Yahweh's positive commandments' (ibid., p. 255).

The pre-eminent concern of the prophets was the destiny of the state and of the people. This meant that they were inevitably mixed up in politics but they were, Weber points out, always independent of and usually opposed to the existing political authorities. Despite this concern with political questions they did not pursue definite political interests, Weber claims. They were not really interested in political matters in their own right or in social reform of any kind. Their concerns, Weber tells us, were absolutely religious and wholly oriented to the fulfilment of Yahweh's commandments. It was this overriding concern which brought them into opposition with the authorities. The prophets stood for the old confederacy and all those values associated with it, and in particular the ancient law. This concern, Weber says, always assumed the form of emotional invective against the overlords. They condemned the innovations of kingship, luxury, courtly life, worship of idols and strange gods, and oppression of the people.

The classical Biblical prophets were not, then, advisers and rarely gave their prophecies on request but always spontaneously. They never gave prophecies for payment or other reward. They were very different from those who made a living from prophecy and prediction. They were an independent force receiving little support from any quarter. The peasants were not particularly well disposed towards them because they frequently criticised their involvement in fertility cults and veneration of baal spirits. They certainly received no support from the kings who at best tolerated them and often persecuted them. They were frequently critical of the priests and their inclinations towards ritualism. They tended to see such things as if not wrong then as at least worthless.

The prophets considered themselves to be the voice of Yahweh and felt themselves compelled to make known his intentions to the people. They were not mystics, nor did they believe that they possessed superior wisdom or ability to communicate with Yahweh. They considered themselves to be simply the tools or instruments of Yahweh. They were, consequently, not exemplary prophets of the kind common in the Far East. They were ethical prophets who interpreted events in terms of the people's and their rulers' conduct.

Because of the periodic political and military disasters that befell the Israelites and because of the backsliding conduct of the rulers, the message of the prophets was more often than not one of doom and destruction. Their prophecies often seemed to contradict the trend of events. They would often predict disaster when things seemed to be going well which tended again to make them unpopular much of the time. Popularity, however, Weber points out, was not one of their motives. Their independence and their burning conviction that they were tools of Yahweh made them indifferent to public opinion and able to fly in the face of expectations and popular feeling. Jeremiah preached submission to the Babylonian king Nebuchadnezzar. Amos prophesied disaster at a time when the northern kingdom was apparently strong.

Sometimes, however, the prophecies were more optimistic. Isaiah predicted that Jerusalem, even though it stood helpless, would be saved when the armies of Sennacherib approached after devastating the whole of Judah.

For the most part the predictions of the prophets came to nothing. But sometimes they were right and this gave them great prestige and influence. Incorrect predictions were soon forgotten. But occasionally a prediction was dramatically fulfilled and this was never forgotten. Isaiah's prediction, for example, did come to pass; Sennacherib's army withdrew without attacking Jerusalem due to a severe outbreak of disease in its ranks.

This type of prophecy had a profound effect upon the direction religiosity took in Palestine, according to Weber. The orientation of the prophets was this-worldly and was not concerned with some other realm of reality. Yahweh's commandments and his promises were concrete, positive and this-worldly. This inhibited contemplation of the meaning of the cosmos. Man's duty was to ensure that his conduct was in accordance with the law of God rather than the acquisition of knowledge of the meaning of the world. Also God was not a god of order but of action.

It was not so much the actual content of the religious ethic that was affected by this style of prophecy, Weber argues. The commandments of the religious ethic, although they had their distinctive features, were not so very different from those of other nations. What was crucial was the way the underlying central religious mentality was shaped by it.

One important factor was the way prophecy promoted the notion of faith. Despite all the misfortunes which beset the nation the people had to retain faith in their covenant with Yahweh, and in the ultimate deliverance from misfortune that he had promised them. This had the further consequence that the greater the disaster that befell the Jews the more ardently they worshipped Yahweh. Despite all indications to the contrary they retained a conviction in the sincerity of their god and the fact of their ultimate deliverance.

Related to the idea of faith was that of humility. Deliverance would come only if the people acknowledged their complete dependence upon Yahweh. Their fate was seen to be entirely in his hands and no action of their own other than obedience to God's commandments could ensure their deliverance. Every disaster of the state was interpreted as punishment by Yahweh for the pride of kings and rulers who took the honours of victory for their own and had the audacity to think that they could affect the outcome of things entirely by their own actions. For the prophets every event was due to Yahweh's will and nothing else. The enemies and destroyers of Israel were simply the instruments of Yahweh's wrath.

After the ultimate disaster of the destruction of Judah and of the temple all the elements of the religion outlined above received even greater emphasis: the desire for deliverance and the overturning of the present world order; the necessity for complete faith in Yahweh in the face of such a complete disaster; the necessity for humility in the face of total impotence to bring about change by one's own efforts.

The characteristics of Judaism can be understood, then, as the consequence of the position of the Jews threatened by bureaucratic

Empires which sought to enslave them. It was their position on the margins of the main centres of civilisation that was significant for the development of their distinctive religious outlook and the triumph of pure Yahweh worship. In fact, Weber argues, new religious conceptions have generally emerged in areas on the periphery of great civilisations and rarely in the centres of them. Areas which lie outside but which are subject to the influence and pressure of the main centres of civilisation have been more fruitful in the development of new religious ideas. This is because people living in such regions are constantly led to question the meaning of events. Those living in the main centres of civilisation have little cause to question things or to find answers which are new and original. They are enmeshed in the culture and accept it as given. They take the way the world is for granted. Those outside find it deeply puzzling. As Weber puts it 'the possibility of questioning the meaning of the world presupposes the capacity to be astonished about the course of events' (ibid., p. 207).

The pure Yahweh worshippers saw the meaning of events affecting the Israelite people in terms of the covenant. The triumph of pure Yahweh worship also owed a great deal to the intellectual stratum, the Levites. It was also the achievement of this intellectual stratum, Weber claims. They were the guardians of the law – the Torah. The fortunes of Israel depended upon strict obedience to the teachings of the Torah. The achievement of the Yahweh priests and the prophets in making these teachings the religion of the Jews was all the more remarkable because this was not a set of ideas which had any great immediate appeal for the mass of ordinary people inclined as they usually are, Weber reminds us, towards magic and ecstatic, orgiastic religious cults. Yahweh was a god whom a stratum of prophets and Torah teachers sought to impose upon the people and not always without resistance. Yet the intellectual stratum was successful in making Yahweh worship the religion of the plebeian strata. 'The literati believed in their ability to develop, and actually did develop, puritanically sincere, anti-orgiastic, anti-idolatrous and anti-magical devoutness among circles which were largely plebeian in character' (ibid., p. 224).

In this religious ethic pre-eminence was placed on obedience and ethical conduct rather than cultic and ritualistic activities. The contrast with oriental religions could not have been greater. In China the higher religious and ethical ideas were those of an educated stratum of cultured gentlemen whereas in Israel they were shared by ordinary people. Here and only here, Weber says, plebeian strata became exponents of a rational religious ethic.

Since Yahweh was a god of political destiny he was not a god with whom one could seek mystical union by contemplation. He was a god who one had to obey, a personal master. This precluded the development of any kind of speculation about the 'meaning' of the world of the kind that was common in Indian religious thought.

The plebeian strata had become by now demilitarised. Accordingly, the demilitarised plebeian strata changed their conception of the future paradise which was to come about as a result of their contract with Yahweh. The idea became dominant that man's original state was one of peace and contentment. Even the animals were his friends. In other words the idea of Eden came to prevail. The future paradise was seen as a return to Eden, a place of peace and abundance. Weber says that these are the hopes of quite pacifistic unmilitary peasants.

Also the idea of a super-human hero who would overthrow Israel's enemies and destroy the strange gods grew up – the idea, in other words, of a Messiah who would overturn the present world order. Only those true to the pure Yahweh cult and those who had kept Yahweh's commandments would survive the holocaust. Again the religion was given a characteristically ethical turn in this development of its eschatological doctrine.

The Judaic ethical system at this time was not yet wholly inner-worldly and ascetic, Weber acknowledges, but it was rationally systematised to a large extent.

After the exile and as a result of it a number of new features were added to the religious outlook. This was largely due to the priests who had been deported en masse. The most important new feature was the ritual segregation of the Jews from surrounding peoples, their transformation into a pariah people. Weber interprets this development as a result of the fact that this second wave of exiles did not wish to suffer the fate of the earlier wave. Those who had been deported after the destruction of the northern kingdom were largely absorbed and had lost their identity. One way to avoid this happening again was to stress everything that was distinctive about the Jewish way of life – religious regulations, customs, codes of conduct, and so on. All the old prescriptions of the Torah were reinterpreted more rigorously and in a more exaggerated way.

A second reason for the adoption of this policy was to promote cohesion among the exiled community. The Jews had now ceased to be a political unit and were instead a confessional community. It was no longer a tribal, familial or national affiliation that united them but a religious one with its distinctive set of laws and customs.

The importance of the law for ritual segregation strengthened the influence of the priests who were the interpreters of the Torah and learned experts in the law. The priests became paramount and the age of the prophets came to an end.

After the conquest of Babylon by the Persians, the position of the priests was strengthened even further. The Persians used the priesthood to rule the Jews and to rule Palestine. They allowed the exiled Jews to return to their home. The temple was re-established as the sole centre of the cult of Yahweh around 517 BC.

With this development, a number of further changes in the religious ethic came about. The most important was a shift in emphasis away from the idea of misfortune as a punishment for sins and towards the idea that suffering has positive value for salvation. The priests increasingly emphasised the role of Yahweh in assisting the unfortunate to attain justice and of compensation rather than simply interpreting misfortune as divine punishment. One reason for this was that it was precisely the most pious who were the most persecuted because it was these who most strictly segregated themselves.

The idea arose that Yahweh had allowed Israel to suffer an unpleasant fate because by such means it would be purified and made fit to be the chosen people destined for world influence and the historic role of bringing salvation to all.

Of these various changes in belief Weber remarks 'the meaning of it all is plainly the glorification of the situation of the pariah people and its tarrying endurance' (ibid., p. 375).

Not only humility and endurance, but meekness and non-resistance were extolled. In all this it can readily be seen, Weber argues, how the prophets and priests had lain the foundations for Christian belief in Palestine. A religion of faith, which was anti-magical and which emphasised regulation of life in accordance with moral law as the way to salvation, was established. It was readily comprehensible and appealed to ordinary people. This unique product was to have profound consequences for the development of the whole of Western civilisation, according to Weber.

THE SOCIOLOGY OF ANCIENT JUDAISM SINCE WEBER

For the most part, as Petersen (1979) notes, Weber's work on ancient Judaism has been ignored by specialists in the field. Nor have such specialists often adopted a sociological approach. Also, few sociologists have undertaken studies in this area. An early, but much neglected, exception was Antonin Causse, whose conclusions were in many respects very similar to those of Weber. Kimbrough (1969, 1972, 1978) has argued, contra Hahn (1970) who claims that Causse's insights were derived directly from the work of Weber, that Causse's work (especially 1937) was quite independent. Causse, like Weber, saw the Israelite prophets as playing a central role in combating through religious means the laxity, centralism and oppressiveness of the more hierarchical society instituted in Canaan under the monarchy. Hahn (1970) characterises this view, as Turner more recently (1974) has characterised Weber's work in general on ancient Judaism, as essentially a Protestant one. While Weber has in many aspects of his work on Judaism received a remarkable degree of confirmation by later scholarship and research, Hahn comments, he did tend to overstress the free, independent, semi-nomadic, egalitarian, tribal, tradition of the confederacy in his analysis of Israelite prophecy and its role in the development of Judaism. This 'Protestant' view tended to exaggerate the role of the prophets as defenders of the old nomadic ideal against the corrupt urban civilisation of the Canaanites and the Canaanised Israelites. In relation to the development of moral individualism in Judaism, Kimbrough (1972, 1978) points out that Hahn's view is contradicted by the fact that Causse, who owed nothing to the Protestant tradition, came to similar conclusions.

Shmueli (1960, 1968), however, criticises Weber for being misled as a result of the typical liberal preoccupations of his time. It is this climate which led him to characterise, erroneously in Shmueli's view, the Jews of Biblical times as a pariah people and to attempt to uncover the social process that had produced this situation. Weber greatly exaggerated the degree to which the Jews promoted ritual self-segregation. It was largely imposed upon them, he argues. There was nothing unusual at the time in a people, living under foreign domination, preserving their distinctive religious beliefs and rituals.

Among those few specialists in Biblical and Old Testament studies who have taken a more sociological approach, Smith (1971) and Lang (1983) are the most prominent. Both have emphasised the fact that the upholders of Yahweh worship, the 'Yahweh alone party' as Smith calls them, were a minority group, probably not homogeneous in social make-up, who emerged in the northern Kingdom of Israel somewhere around the eighth or ninth centuries BC. Smith stresses that the worship of other gods by the Israelites at this time and later was in no way laxity or defection from the tenets of an earlier monotheistic faith but simply the normal polytheistic practice of peoples in the region, including the Israelites. The original polytheistic religion of the Israelites was, Lang claims, typical of the West-Semitic cults of Syro-Palestine which included those of the Ammonites, Moabites, Edomites and others. By the tenth century the Yahweh cult had become the predominant one in the region but the 'Yahweh aloners' demanded that *only* Yahweh be worshipped. The social conditions which promoted this monolatry according to Lang may have been (i) rivalry between the priests and prophets of Yahweh and those of other gods, (ii) opposition on the part of conservative nomads to Canaanite cults and culture, and (iii) the desire to prevent the ritual life of the nomadic conquerors of Canaan from being overwhelmed by that of Canaan. The monolatry of the 'Yahweh aloners' may have derived from the 'temporary monolatry' that emerged from time to time among many different peoples of the Middle East by which, during a time of crisis, worship was directed exclusively towards a single deity rather than the usual many in the hope that special help would be forthcoming. What distinguishes Israel is that crises were so frequent that it provided fertile soil for the emergence from 'temporary monolatry' of a permanent monolatry. 'Yahweh alone' worship would thus be a crisis cult preserved beyond any given immediate crisis because crisis is perceived as a permanent state. All this is, of course, very reminiscent of Weber as is Lang's analysis of how the succession of disasters which befell the nation, culminating in the destruction of the temple in 586 BC, enabled the monolatry of the 'Yahweh aloneists' to triumph completely. In the process, full monotheism emerged as a new doctrine within Israelite religion.

Monotheistic tendencies may not have been confined to the Israelites, Lang notes. They seem to have existed in Egypt and among other peoples in the area. Such ideas may have reached Palestine from Zoroastrian Persia. Kautsky (1925) argued that such ideas were absorbed during the period of the second exile in Babylonia. For whatever reason, however, the transition was made from the belief that Israel should worship only one god to the conviction that the God that Israel worshipped was the only God.

In contrast to the views of Smith and Lang, Zeitlin (1988) has recently argued that monotheism was prominent among the Israelites from an early period and not something that became significant only after the exile or even as a consequence of the activities of the prophets, as Weber suggests and which was the dominant view in his day. It was an integral aspect of the covenant from the start, Zeitlin argues, as was the ethical dimension of Judaism as expressed in the Decalogue. This cannot be understood as a creation of the prophets as the dominant school of Biblical criticism under the influence of Wellhausen has for so long accepted. It can only be understood, according to Zeitlin, in terms of the exigencies of the situation at the time of the covenant and the confederacy when the overriding need was to bind the various groups together and preserve their unity. The greatest threat to it was internal conflict over resources. The emphasis in the Decalogue is therefore against coveting what others have. As Zeitlin puts it, the greatest threat was envy. If it had been the product of the late monarchy, a time of great social inequality, the emphasis would have been upon the condemnation of oppression.

As for other criticism of Weber, most has been directed at his characterisation of the position of the Israelite prophets. Berger (1963) and Turner (1974) have questioned Weber's claim that they represent an entirely independent force based upon pure charismatic authority and motivated entirely by religious concerns. This Protestant interpretation was to a large extent, Turner claims, aimed at countering the Marxist approach of Karl Kautsky who, in *The Foundations of Christianity* (1925), had cast the Biblical prophets in the role of revolutionary leaders of an oppressed class. Recent research and scholarship, they claim, have established that they occupied official positions in the Yahweh cult. Their religious ideas were developed while acting in an official role. The implications of this for Turner are that charisma is not to be seen as an independent and autonomous force in society but one which arises from within central social institutions. This is perhaps too extreme. There do seem to have been temple prophets with an institutionalised role in the temple cult but while these may have been the majority of prophets those with which Weber was concerned were mostly not of this type but independent of the official cult.

Petersen (1979) has argued that Weber's equation of charismatic authority and the Biblical prophets is mistaken on the grounds that the former implies leadership of a group of followers while there is no evidence for such a following regarding the latter. Emmet (1956) argues that there are several different types of prophet. One is the institutional prophet who fulfils a traditional role and may live in a community of prophets. Secondly, and corresponding to Weber's charismatic prophecy, there is the prophetic leader of a radical movement seeking change. Thirdly, there is the independent critic and advocate of reform who provides moral leadership without attaching to himself a personal following. Petersen, therefore, questions whether the Israelite prophets could have provided the breakthrough that Weber attributes to them.

Other scholars are more supportive of Weber's view. Williams (1969), on the basis of a careful examination of the sources, concludes that many of the prophets, especially the classical prophets, were completely outside the cultic institutions. Wilson (1980) finds evidence that in the pre-monarchical period in the Ephraimite tradition of the North there were clear ideas about what constituted acceptable prophetic behaviour, that prophets used stereotypical speech patterns and exhibited standard behavioural patterns, all suggesting that they had a defined role and position in the society and the religious institutions. From the monarchical period, however, these prophets seem to have become peripheral to the established institutions of society and acted as the voice of certain groups which sought to bring about change. They used their prophetic authority to pronounce on social, political and religious issues and to advocate change in both the North and in Judah. In the Southern tradition of Judah rather different prophetic roles can be discerned depending upon political circumstances, alliances and so on. Peripheral prophets taking a critical stance or advocating change can be distinguished from those more supportive of the status quo. This would suggest that some prophets stood outside the established religious cult.

Long (1981) also reminds us in his analysis of Jeremiah that conflict between prophets is widespread in many cultures. In Israelite society prophetic conflicts are linked to political factions. In the case of Jeremiah the conflict were between the 'autonomists' who considered the best strategy to be resistance to Babylonian pressure and Jeremiah's party advocating coexistence. Carroll (1979), agreeing with Weber, argues that prophets tend to arise at times of political or military crises which call for a social critique, which the prophet provides. It is likely that some prophets given the sorts of conflict that Lang and Carroll refer to, would be more closely allied to the regime and would be more likely to hold some office within the cult, while others would be more peripheral and critical of the regime.

Lang (1983) shows that the prophets were largely from a landowning noble background which may have considerably constrained their activities. Lang sees the prophetic tradition as an institution belonging to the landowning nobility which provided a channel by which it could express its political views publicly. Prophets, it is true, were not chosen by any formal means; they simply emerged. In many cultures, Buss (1981) points out, prophets receive a call which they may accept only with great reluctance. This enables them to abrogate any personal responsibility for what they say or do. This is not untypical of tribal and preindustrial societies where, in small communities, personal qualities and authority are more important than formal procedures for recruitment. Prophecy also, Lang argues, had to be learned. It was part of a tradition with its own rules and established criteria of what constitutes valid action. This does not mean, Lang admits, that the prophets were wholly bound by convention. They belonged to Emmet's third type. They were 'neither lone wolves nor bearers of an anti-rational and anti-institutional charisma; rather charisma and tradition are bound to one another and permit no more than theoretical differentiation. The prophetic charisma is to be understood as a power of renewal which breaks out in the middle of traditional structures that are transcended without being destroyed' (Lang, 1983, p. 113).

Finally, Albrektson (1972) supports Weber in seeing the prophets as motivated primarily by religious concerns. Naturally, this often led to them making pronouncements with political implications but they were essentially utopian, idealistic and unpragmatic and not concerned with promoting social opposition.

The most clearly and self-consciously sociological approach to the rise of monotheistic Judaism in Palestine, and the most radically controversial, is that of Gottwald (1979). He challenges the most fundamental and long-established assumption that it was from a tradition of semi-nomadic pastoralism that the values of Judaism developed, denying that there was any nomadic conquest of Canaan. The alleged conquest, he claims, was in fact a revolutionary movement from within which reacted against and overthrew the emerging centralist, bureaucratic state systems, 'retribalising' the society in the process. Monotheistic Yahweh worship was the religious outcome and expression of this radical movement.

The picture we have of a migratory Israelite conquest of Canaan is the result, Gottwald argues, of a highly selective priestly synthesis of materials from a wide range of traditions, periods and social groupings designed to affirm their unity and cohesion as a single people. The Israelites from early times, he claims, were settled agriculturalists who practised some animal husbandry and among whom there may have been subsidiary specialised transhumant pastoralist groups. While a group of nomadic pastoralists, the Israelites of the Exodus, may have appeared in Palestine having migrated from Egypt sometime earlier, there is little evidence that they conquered the region from non-Israelite Canaanites. They may have joined a coalition of radical anti-statist peasants, pastoralists, outlaws and other factions opposed to the emergence of city–state rule. Their role may have been catalytic and exemplary and in some ways less material than symbolic in providing a useful myth – that of the victory of nomadic, pastoral egalitarianism over urban, centralised and hierarchical institutions. They may, also, have introduced pure Yahweh worship which came to be the ideological expression of the interests of the radicals binding their diverse coalition together under the leadership of the Levites. Important as this role was, its impact took effect upon an already existing situation of social tension and division within Canaan. It is a mistake, Gottwald argues, to see the Israelites as an entirely separate people from the Canaanites, emerging from the desert and bringing their new religion to the area. Israel and Judaism must be seen as emerging eclectically and synthetically from the vortex of Canaanite civilisation. Yahwism was an experimental conceptual–institutional alternative to the oppressive rule of city states. This experimentalism finds its expression in the notion of the covenant – a freely chosen contractual relationship with the deity. The Canaanite cults were undemanding upon their followers but sanctioned the heavy appropriation of resources by a small and privileged elite whereas the strict and demanding cult of Yahweh left human and natural resources for the enjoyment of the whole people.

Israel was faced with the contradictory aims of maintaining egalitarianism while securing its defence against external enemies. The latter tended to undermine the former. Mono-Yahwism (as Gottwald calls it in preference to monotheism or monolatry) was the reaction to the acute necessity of resolving this potentially destructive contradiction. It was 'a delicately balanced, innovative, cultic-ideological instrument for selectively strengthening both egalitarianism in social relations and an effective united front against enemies in minimally contradictory or antagonistic ways' (ibid., p. 618). Thus the belief in Yahweh stood for the power to establish and sustain social equality against counter pressures either external or internal. The notion of a 'chosen people' stands for the self-consciousness of an egalitarian society which demarcated itself from a surrounding world of centralised and stratified social systems. The notion of the covenant stood for the bonding of decentralised social groups in an egalitarian society based upon co-operation and without centralised authoritarian rule. Eschatological ideas stood for the confident and determined commitment to fellow tribesmen and an egalitarian society which would prevail against the odds.

Gottwald claims that the success of the anti-statist Yahweh worshippers which lasted for some two hundred years before the rise of the
monarchy was founded upon a material economic basis. There were a
number of technological developments underlying it – iron tools,
waterproof cisterns, terracing of hill slopes and so on. Peasants now
able to store water were freed from dependence upon natural springs
and able to disperse over a wider area of land which their new iron
technology allowed them to exploit. They were thus able to free themselves from the grasp of the city states of the plains and valleys. But
Gottwald does not rely upon a purely materialist explanation and
advocates what he calls a 'cultural–materialist' approach. This fully
acknowledges the crucial role that Yahwism played as a form of
cultural feedback – a symbolic facilitator which validated and motivated egalitarian relations acting as a servomechanism feeding back
information into social relations enabling the system to constantly
correct itself. In the last analysis, furthermore, it was the determination
of the Israelite people to win their economic and political autonomy
that led them to seize upon technological developments and whatever
means were available to them. In Gottwald's analysis, then, the main-
spring of change lies in values and preferences and not in economic
stimulus or determination.

Much of Gottwald's analysis is, of course, perfectly compatible with
Weber. Weber did see the Israelites, it is true, as a semi-nomadic,
conquering confederacy among whom the values of tribal egalitarianism and anti-statism were strong and expressed through pure Yahweh
worship. But it does not alter very much the substance of Weber's
analysis of the dynamics of Israelite society and political life in which
monotheistic Judaism was forced to say that those egalitarian forces
arose largely from within a peasant agricultural society. Where Gottwald does take issue with Weber is on the question of the military
function of Yahweh in Israelite belief which Gottwald believes Weber
overstated at the expense of its social–egalitarian function. This
weakens the social–structural dimension of his analysis. It also leads
him to see the prophets as lone innovators and critics cast adrift from
any coherent social location.

Critics of Gottwald have found it very difficult to give any credibility
to his peasant revolt theory. There is simply no evidence for it in the
historical record they argue. Lemche (1985), on the basis of a very
detailed examination of relevant anthropological literature (summarised by Rogerson, 1990), has argued that Gottwald's thesis rests
upon an incorrect view of the relationship between the peasants and

the cities. They did not necessarily stand in opposition to one another. Nor is it the case that a tribal or segmentary society is necessarily egalitarian. Brandfon (1981) has argued that the autonomy of the new village settlements of which Gottwald speaks was just as likely to have been the consequence of being cut off from the goods and services otherwise supplied by the urban centres as a result of their breakdown. Early Yahwism may thus have reflected necessity rather than any desire for egalitarian social forms. Gottwald is accused of introducing too great a degree of voluntarism into his analysis to the detriment of the materialist side.

An original interpretation of certain central aspects of Judaism and of Jewish mentality is that of Jacobson (1982), better known as a novelist than as a social scientist. Jacobson is concerned with the ambivalence surrounding the notion of the Jews as a people specially chosen and favoured by God and the emphasis in Judaism upon the law – the Torah. The notion of the Jews as a divinely chosen people served to legitimate their conquest and possession of the land of Canaan. However, the fact that God, according to Judaism, is an omnipotent being who chose Israel for special favour at the expense of others aroused the uncomfortable anxiety that he could also choose to reject Israel and allow it to suffer the fate of the Canaanites. Casting oneself in the role of the divinely chosen may have generated an underlying sense of moral unease but more significantly the very notion of being chosen seems to engender also that of divine retribution for holding such a belief at all. Scripture is full of accounts of divine retribution upon Israel ostensibly for the misdemeanours of the people or their rulers but, Jacobson suggests, expressing this underlying feeling that there is a terrible price to be paid for being chosen. It is this feeling also which promotes the Jewish emphasis upon the law, its elaboration and the keeping of it. This stems from a psychological process by which the anxiety induced by the sense that retribution is an ever-present threat is reduced by binding God to continued favourable treatment through scrupulous and meticulous observance of his laws – an attempt to preclude the possibility of God ever exercising his freedom to chose again. In lashing themselves to the covenant the Israelites sought to lash down God also. Precisely because God had arbitrarily chosen Israel every effort had to be made to ensure that relations with him went strictly according to the book.

Other writers have interpreted the Jewish emphasis on the law, particularly the dietary laws, as bound up with the question of identity. Weber argued that it was the experience of exile and the threat of absorption which led to an extreme emphasis upon the distinctive customs of the Israelites, an emphasis given equal stimulus as a result of the Diaspora. Douglas (1975) argues that the dietary laws of Leviticus and particularly the ban on pork became important symbols of group allegiance. This is in considerable contrast to her earlier work (Douglas, 1966) on the dietary laws which she qualifies substantially in acknowledgement of the points made by several of her critics admitting that it was an over-cognitive interpretation. She had argued that pork was banned to the Israelites because the pig was an anomalous animal in terms of their system of animal classification and categories. Animals which do not quite fit the major categories are tabooed and cannot be eaten. A major category is that of animals that chew the cud and have cloven hooves. The pig does not chew the cud but does have a cloven hoof; it is an anomaly not belonging to any category in this system of classification and so must be avoided. Such practices of tabooing anomalies are found in many societies, according to Douglas. Anomalous things are dangerous and must be avoided; they have a kind of power. Consequently they often come to be classed along with the sacred, which is also dangerous and powerful.

In our own society, while we do not assimilate the anomalous to the sacred, we practise avoidance of such things. Our concept of dirt is not really a product of fear of infection or of transmission of germs or diseases, according to Douglas. The idea of dirt is much older than our knowledge of the causes of disease and the mechanisms of their transmission. Ideas of dirt have, in fact, to do with notions of order and disorder. Dirt is simply 'matter out of place' (ibid., p. 35). Dirt is a by-product of a system of classification and ordering which inevitably produces anomalous things which have no clear place. In the Israelite system of classification the pig had no place and was consequently unclean and avoided.

These ideas were challenged on the grounds that they oversimplified and failed to explain the pattern of taboos found either in Leviticus or in contemporary tribal and other societies. While broadly supporting Douglas's basic contention that it is anomalous things which are taboo, Carroll (1978) argues that the fundamental distinction in the case of Leviticus between nature and culture is that which produces the anomaly. Human beings belong to the realm of culture and can eat meat but animals belong to the realm of nature and should eat only vegetable matter. Carnivores, therefore, are in an anomalous situation and are tabooed by the dietary laws. The pig is tabooed because it eats carrion. This approach, Carroll argues, can account for many more of the things mentioned in Leviticus than Douglas's theory including, for example, vermin, mold and mildew which belong to nature but invade the world of man and of culture. It also accounts for more than just the dietary regulations, he claims, including regulations relating to leprosy.

Yet, Carroll himself admits, his theory cannot account for all the taboo prescriptions of Leviticus. Other attempts to understand the logic of Jewish laws of mixture uncover quite different oppositions. Cooper (1987) examines the laws forbidding the mixture of meat and milk, wool and linen, grape and wheat/barley. The fundamental principle he finds to be an opposition between life and death. Blood represents life whereas flesh with the blood drained from it represents death. Milk represents life so cannot be mixed with meat from which the life aspect has been removed. Harvesting flax destroys the plant (death) but taking wool from a sheep leaves it alive. A problem with structuralist analyses such as these is that different readings of the data yield different results as do different choices of data to examine.

Bulmer (1967) and Tambiah (1969) argue that it is not possible to account for such taboos in entirely taxonomic terms. While polluting things may be things out of place there are many different ways in which things can be out of place. Taxonomic systems relating to animals, for example, are closely linked to social classifications and as a result come to be charged with a variety of affective connotations.

In the light of such criticisms Douglas has modified her analysis of the Jewish dietary laws (1975).[1] Central to this later analysis is the fact that the Jews maintained very strict social boundaries. Marriage with outsiders of certain categories was strictly forbidden whereas marriage within the group between fairly close relatives, such as first parallel cousins, was allowed. The ban on eating pork was not simply due to its anomalous position in the taxonomic system but also because pigs were reared as food by outsiders, that is non-Israelites. This dietary rule also expressed the theme of purity versus impurity – the pig eats carrion and is unclean. Among an African people whom Douglas studied early in her career, the Lele (Douglas, 1963), the opposite circumstances prevail. Boundaries here are weak and the crossing and confounding of boundaries considered a good thing. The pangolin, an animal quite as anomalous in the taxonomic system of the Lele as was the pig in that of the Israelites, is considered sacred by the Lele rather than polluting. In short, the social situation has a profound influence upon how anomalous things are treated. The social situation of the Israelites was such as to place a premium on the treatment of anomalies as polluting. During the exile this was reinforced by the threat of absorption and loss of identity. The refusal of commensality entailed by the Jewish dietary laws was a clear, visible and public statement of distinctiveness.

This is a view supported by the work of Smith (1989) on the exilic development of the Jewish law and religion. It was a strategy of resistance. An examination of the levitical literature shows an exaggerated concern with purity and fear of transfer of pollution which is the expression of a concern with the maintenance of boundaries. The dissolution of mixed marriages after the return to Palestine can be seen as an example of this. The rise to prominence of the priests is clearly related to their role in preserving the collective solidarity of a minority people and maintaining boundaries between themselves and others through carefully elaborated notions of purity and impurity. What is particularly distinctive now is the emphasis upon the transfer of impurity and pollution and the association of purity and holiness with separation.

Another prominent feature of Judaism is its apocalypticism explained by Weber as a reaction to the continuing failure of the Israelites to overcome or resist their enemies by normal military means. More recent studies of Jewish apocalypticism have set it more clearly within the context of internal divisions and conflicts within Jewish society in the post-exilic period. Hanson (1975) rejects the view that it was imported from other cultures such as Greece or Persia. He sees it as a development of a deeply rooted internal tradition extending from pre-exilic times and linked to the prophetic tradition. This development occurred in a situation of crisis in which the community was attempting to adjust to the loss of nationhood and was facing internal division between the proponents of a hierocratic and a visionary ideal. The group which can be identified as the main carriers of the apocalyptic tradition translated the earlier prophetic this-worldly ethos of Judaism, which anticipated a material, political and social transformation of the world order, into a cosmic vision remote from the realm of everyday political and social affairs.

The circumstances which promoted this outlook in post-exilic conditions were ones that promoted disillusionment and pessimism on the part of those groups in the society, followers of the Second Isaiah according to Hanson, which saw their opponents prosper and themselves lose control over the central political and religious institutions of the society. At the core of these disaffected groups was the priesthood who were displaced by the Zadokites after the restoration, a group they regarded as illegitimate and defiled. They were joined by disenfranchised Levite factions. The Zadokites stood for the preservation of the pre-exilic structures as far as possible and for compromise with the ruling Persians in order to achieve this and to preserve a position of supremacy for themselves within the regime and the cult. They thus became committed to the maintenance of peace and to suppression of oppositional and dissident views.

In the face of the contradiction between the promises that the restoration seemed to hold out for them but which did not seem to be realisable within the political structures and realities that actually prevailed, these groups in society sought to respiritualise the religion and to project the vision of restoration to the cosmic plane of myth. The current order was defined as inherently evil and rejected. Fulfilment was sought on a different plane and in a manner which rendered mundane realities irrelevant. It is significant that the Zadokite priests ultimately took up this apocalyptic vision when displaced in their turn by the Hasmoneans in the second century. Hanson, then, firmly places his analysis of Jewish apocalypticism within the framework of the sociological analysis of millennial movements[2] although Grabbe (1989) has accused Hanson of blatant misuse of such models. The established priesthood in Persian-controlled Palestine is presented by Hanson, Grabbe claims, as occupying far too secure and powerful a position. They were, in the political circumstances, as marginal and vulnerable as any group in the society in Grabbe's view.

Post-Diaspora Judaism and Identity

The question of identity is one which inevitably asserts itself as fundamental in sociological studies of post-Diaspora Judaism, which are, however, hardly abundant. The survival of a distinct Jewish community resistant to absorption is something that is puzzling according to Eisenstadt (1992) and can only be understood if one recognises the Jews to be not just a religious community as Weber had argued, nor even a political community, a people or a nation but as a distinct civilisation on a par with Christianity and Islam encompassing all of these aspects and others. Jewish civilisation was for a long time, according to Eisenstadt, in competition with Christianity and Islam and was, consequently, seen as a threat and a rival.

The systematic regulation of the daily lives of Jews during the Middle Ages and especially the dietary laws served to preserve this distinct civilisation and maintain boundaries with the surrounding world and society while justifying the practices in religious and ethical terms. By this means the Jewish people were held together and the continuity of their national and cultural identity upheld. The tradition preserved a national and political and not just religious dimension to the Jews' perception of their identity even though they were unable to compete with other nations and were compelled to channel their energies into the maintenance of their distinctive religion and culture. Hope of political redemption was projected into a distant Messianic future which would be enjoyed if they demonstrated conformity to the law. In this sense they saw themselves as a civilisation as being outside of history. The Messianic vision became bound up with an identification with the land of Israel which acquired a metaphysical and religious meaning.

While this vision of redemption was normally seen in such terms, at certain times, usually times of disorder, persecution and expulsions, it found expression in social movements of a messianic form. Sharot (1982) has applied sociological insights stemming from the study of millennial and messianic movements worldwide to the understanding of Jewish movements of this type from the time of Crusades up to the modern era. Millennial movements, he points out, have frequently been explained in terms of a revolt against social or economic oppression directed against ruling or dominant groups or against the wealthy and propertied classes. In the Jewish context this would mean either a protest against the wealthier sections of the Jewish community or against powerful and dominant gentile oppressors.

There is little evidence that Jewish millennial outburst were directed against fellow but wealthier Jews. Many movements attracted adherents from the wealthier sections of the community and none showed any antagonism towards the Jewish upper class. They were generally directed against gentile society exhibiting a strong desire for political and national independence. Their timing and location cannot be explained, however, in terms of either political or economic subordination. While suffering various forms of discrimination during the Middle Ages, Jews enjoyed a considerable measure of freedom, autonomy and protection. They were no worse off than the general population and often somewhat better off. Sharot turns to explanations in terms of disaster and relative deprivation to explain the particular occurrences.

Many millennial outbursts and similar types of movement followed periods of persecution and or expulsion. Such was the case, for example with those expelled from Spain in 1492, among the conversos in Spain and Portugal, and in Poland at the time of the rise of Frankism and Hassidism. The Zionist movement grew up after the pogroms in

Eastern Europe and Gush Emunim can be seen as a response to the losses of the Yom Kippur war. Persecution was not always a factor. Since other circumstances could stimulate an outburst and persecution was not always followed by one, it cannot, therefore, be seen as a necessary condition. A factor which helps to account for variations in this respect is the predominant experience regarding integration into the surrounding society. The Ashkenazim were never integrated into the wider society to the extent that the Sephardim had been in Iberia. The expulsion of the Jews from Spain thus came as a deep shock tending to promote millennial hopes, whereas the Ashkenazim were much less prone to react to setbacks in this way. They were more inclined to attribute such things to punishment from God for their own wrongdoings. Each group thus tended to interpret events in different ways in the light of their experience of their relationships with the wider society and general conditions of life.

The very different circumstances of Jews in Poland may help to explain why Hassidism, although in may ways a response to persecution and disaster, did not take on a revolutionary or millennial character. Hassidism arose against a background of adversity and social dislocation in Jewish communities. With the decline of the Polish state in the eighteenth century the Jewish community suffered a series of calamities. There were attacks and massacres perpetrated by Cossack and peasant marauders from the Ukraine. The number of ritual murder trials increased. There was widespread impoverishment among certain sections of the Jewish community. Many Jews were forced out of the towns placing heavy burdens upon the communities to which they fled. The *kehillot*, the semi-autonomous community organisations, were greatly weakened and impaired in their role of providing regulation of community affairs. Tensions and conflicts arose within the communities and the legitimacy of the kehillot was much reduced. Central and regional Jewish organisations were abolished in 1765. Opposition to the official rabbis became widespread as a result of a fall in their status due to the practice of purchase of office, growing distance between them and the people due to their intellectual and scholastic preoccupations remote from everyday practical concerns, and their disparaging attitude to the ordinary population's slackness in observance. Religious leadership, consequently, became ineffectual.

The ecstatic character of Hassidism and its emphasis on joy can be seen, according to Sharot, as providing an emotional outlet against a background of insecurity and poverty. It provided a sense of identification with the divine through prayer or the spiritual mediation of the zaddik. To a considerable extent, Hassidism can be seen as a reaction on the part of unscholarly, ordinary Jews who rejected the status claims of the educated. Direct relationship to God rather than scholarly accomplishment was upheld as spiritually superior.

Hassidism, unlike millenarian movements which stress collective salvation, placed the emphasis on individual salvation. Although it did level certain criticisms at society it was a movement that kept millenarian tendencies in check focusing instead on redemption of the individual.

Hassidism spread widely in Eastern Europe but not beyond. It had little appeal in Western Europe where the position of Jews in society was beginning to undergo radical change. Hassidism succeeded in the East through its revitalisation of the traditional culture in its distinctiveness and separation from the surrounding society which corresponded to the actual situation of the Jewish communities there, namely stability and absence of change.

As the movement spread through Eastern Europe its social base, Sharot points out, widened, ultimately encompassing every class of Jewish society. The forces which brought it into being, impoverishment and insecurity, cannot, of course, explain this spread. Sharot draws here upon Weberian notions of routinisation of charisma to explain this phenomenon. The leaders of the Hassidic communities, the zaddikim, were, Sharot argues, charismatic mystagogues. The mystagogue unlike the charismatic prophet derives his charisma from magical powers rather than a divine source but unlike the magician has a congregation around him. The zaddik offered redemption and protection from both evil and material threat. This thaumaturgical role met a widespread need among Jews in Eastern Europe subject as they were to persecution, impoverishment and pauperisation. The movement never became centralised and uniform, however, and a wide range of varieties of Hassidism developed particularly with regard to the role and character of zaddikim and the manner of the succession to this position. The result of this diversity was that it was able to appeal to a wide range of groups in the society.

Messianic, millennial and similar movements were, of course, relatively ephemeral phenomena within Judaism. For the most part, the preoccupation of Judaism has been with the ultimate possibility of redemption as a nation and people but in the meantime the preservation of identity and culture and consequent relations with the non-Jewish community. Sharot (1976) has posed and attempted to answer the question why Jewish communities have been acculturated and assimilated to differing degrees in different societies and at different historical periods. Broadly speaking, his findings are that Jewish acculturation was greatest in those cultures where the dominant religion was syncretic such as China and India than in those where it was insular such as Islam and Christianity. Also important was the strength of the dominant group's disposition to demand allegiance to its religion within a given territory. The syncretistic religious traditions tended also to be pluralist and the insular to be monopolistic. The consequence of attempts to coerce Jews into acceptance of the dominant religion was generally to provoke a determination to preserve and emphasise cultural and religious distinctiveness on their part. Social segregation of Jews was also a significant factor promoting the retention of distinctive customs. Thus in Eastern and Central Europe, where the majority was largely intolerant, Jewish communities developed and retained until quite recent times a markedly distinct culture whereas in Western Europe, where from the eighteenth century an increasingly pluralistic and less intolerant environment prevailed, Jews tended to accept more of the surrounding culture although, of course, the extent of tolerance and patterns of acculturation varied markedly from place to place. Reinforcing factors were the existence of estate systems in Eastern and Central Europe with the accompanying legal restrictions and their absence in England and North America. Also significant was the existence of craft and merchant guilds. Where they were replaced by free contract and economic universalism, as in cities such as Hamburg, Amsterdam, Bordeaux and London and in North America, it was possible for Jews to enter the social circles of the gentile bourgeoisie. A marked form of cultural distinctiveness accompanied Hassidism which rose to prominence only in Eastern Europe, however, despite the segregation of the Jews in Central Europe.

Whatever the impact of the prevailing circumstances upon the degree of acculturation of Jews they have universally retained some degree of traditional religious affiliation and observance even though this has varied enormously. For many this can be seen as much as, if not more than, a means of preserving a distinct identity as an expression of religiosity. The overwhelming emphasis in Judaism on the law and on observance (*halakha*) is in part the product of a history and experience of dispersion, threat of assimilation and loss of identity but in turn lends itself to the use of observance as a means of expressing and retaining identity. For the more orthodox it lends itself to the maintenance of boundaries and distinctiveness. For the great majority of non-orthodox Jews 'religious' observance has become greatly attenuated and, it is often claimed, is largely a means of affirming identity. Williams (1987) expresses the emphasis on observance characteristic of all forms of Juduaism in saying it carries an 'empty ritual load' (ibid., p. 276); that is to say that what is important for most Jews is not belief but custom, ritual and observance. A number of studies have shown this to be the case but have shown also that the pattern can vary considerably.[3]

Many Jews in Britain and Israel, Williams shows, while rejecting the official belief content of Judaism, or aspects of it, nevertheless participate considerably or fully in certain traditional customs and rituals. Many traditional symbols of Jewish faith such as abstinence from pork, the use of Hebrew in prayer, the bar mitzvah, and so on, have lost any cognitive credibility, according to Williams, but a considerable affective aspect remains which is bound up with their importance for identity. Others have found a similar pattern for the United States where there has been a retention of those traditions most congruent with the prevailing culture (Goldstein and Goldscheider, 1968; Sklare, 1971).

Important everywhere is the celebration of Hannukah and of Passover. Participation in the Seder meal is interpreted by Freedman (1981) as an expression of the situation of Jews throughout history in all its contradictions as a community in exile, in galut. As a re-enactment of the Exodus it celebrates Jewish identity and distinctiveness and echoes on the domestic level the expression of identity as a people in place of the long since defunct central cult associated with the most potent symbol of national, cultural and religious identity, the temple in Jerusalem (Bokser, 1984).

To the extent, of course, that Jewish identity becomes less a matter of concern or something to be preserved then religion and observance may become less significant as a means of preserving that identity. This process has affected non-orthodox Jewish communities to a very considerable extent in the contemporary world. Again the pattern varies from community to community and over time according to the degree of religiosity. In Israel there was a tendency for the non-religious young to demonstrate a markedly lower propensity to see their identity in ethnic terms than the religious young. They saw themselves as Israeli rather than Jewish (Zuckerman-Bareli, 1975). Today this distinction has probably become less significant. Steinberg (1975) considers that in the United States, while religion has played its role in maintaining identity, acculturation means that the decline in religion has only been prolonged. Sharot (1991), on the other hand, on the basis of more recent studies and data, presents a pattern of decline followed by relative stability among non-orthodox Jews. Fourth-generation American Jews are showing signs neither of loss nor of revival of religious affiliation and practice. More religious and orthodox groups, however, which are also growing in size, demonstrate a marked intensification of traditionalism, more rigorous observation and greater segregation resulting in an overall polarisation between different Jewish communities.

7 Christianity

ORIGINS

Despite a paucity of sources, a great deal has been written about the origins and early development of Christianity. While numerous New Testament scholars have recently attempted to apply sociological models to this question, few sociologists have attempted to apply their skills and insights to it. Among the classic theorists it has been Marxist writers, and then largely only nineteenth-century ones, who have given the subject their attention. Marxist theorists emphasised the link between Christianity and class oppression which, they argued, explained its millennial character. But though were not agreed as to which elements of the oppressed classes were the main social carriers. Weber made many relevant if scattered observations in his writings in which he emphasised the millennial character of early Christianity but saw it largely as a lower middle-class movement lacking any element of class antagonism. Recent approaches have differed markedly in their estimation of the character of the social base of Christianity but have attempted to apply the insights of sociological and anthropological studies of the forces which generate millennial and sectarian movements as well as related theoretical ideas to the understanding of early Christianity.

Engels examined the background to the emergence of Christianity in a number of writings including 'Bruno Bauer and Early Christianity,' 'The Book of Revelation', and 'On the History of Early Christianity' (Marx and Engels, 1957). In these three works Engels characterises the prevailing social and political conditions at a time when the Roman Empire was in decline. He attempts to show that Christianity was the response of various groups of oppressed and alienated people – slaves, national groups, the poor, and so on.

In his article 'Bruno Bauer and Early Christianity', Engels sets out to provide an interpretation of the origins of Christianity that is more acceptable, in his view, than those which were common among atheists and free thinkers at the time, namely that Christianity was simply the work of deceivers, charlatans and the product of fraud; there must have been more to it than that.

A religion that brought the Roman world empire into subjection and dominated by far the larger part of civilized humanity for 1,800

166

years cannot be disposed of merely by declaring it to be nonsense gleaned together by frauds. (Marx and Engels, 1957, p. 174)

What is required, Engels explains, is an interpretation based on a sound analysis of the prevailing conditions under which Christianity arose. He first acknowledges the contribution made by the German Biblical scholar Bruno Bauer who established a more scientific object-ive approach to the analysis of the scriptures and in whose honour the article is written. Bauer's analysis of early Christianity is, however, marred by philosophical idealism and Engels offers, therefore, his own interpretation.

The social, economic and political circumstances prevailing in the Roman Empire at the time can be characterised by (i) the domination of Rome and the dissolution of all former political and social condi-tions after conquest, (ii) oppressive taxation, and (iii) imposition of Roman law whenever local or native law was incompatible with it.

This had a levelling effect, reducing all areas of the Empire to similar circumstances. The population became divided into three classes made up of varying groups and nationalities – the rich and the landowners, the free urban propertyless and the slaves. All felt their situation to be unsatisfactory. Even the rich were in a precarious position in relation to the state and the Emperor and could easily find themselves accused of some disloyalty, often as an excuse to seize their property. In the provinces the free class were usually poor and had to compete with slave labour. On the whole slaves were treated badly and severely oppressed.

Roman domination had destroyed the old religious traditions of many of the peoples under Roman rule. Nevertheless, in all classes men sought some kind of salvation or spiritual compensation for material and moral despair. But because of the destruction of old beliefs this new religious movement became a world religion. 'By thus rejecting all national religions and their common ceremonies and addressing itself to all peoples without distinction it [Christianity] becomes the first possible world religion' (ibid., p. 181). Hence the power of expansion of Christianity. (He seems to have overlooked Buddhism). It had a powerful appeal for another reason according to Engels – the idea of sin, of moral responsibility for the general unsat-isfactory conditions and the acceptance of this as a precondition for salvation. This was an idea easily understood by the masses. Also the belief that a saviour had through his own sacrifice taken on the burden of that sin so that all might achieve salvation had enormous appeal. It was these factors that enabled Christianity to win out over the rival movements that proliferated throughout the Empire at the time.

In another article, 'On the History of Early Christianity', Engels says more about what gave Christianity its appeal. He goes on to draw many comparisons between early Christianity and the socialist movements. To some extent Christianity was the socialism of its time. But unlike socialism early Christianity did not, of course, promise a solution to suffering in this world but in the world beyond. 'Christianity, as was bound to be the case in the historical conditions, did not want to accomplish the social transformation in this world, but beyond it, in heaven, in eternal life after death, in the impending millennium' (ibid., p. 282).

A true picture of the character of early Christianity can be found in the Book of Revelation which Engels claims is the oldest authentic source relating to the early Christians and he makes a great deal of it. It reveals just what sort of millenarian, ecstatic, fantasy-prone movement early Christianity must have been, characterised by 'wild confused fanaticism' and 'a multitude of visions and prophecies' (ibid., p. 176).

Interpretations of the Book of Revelation reveal it to be a cryptic statement concerning the manner in which the last judgement and the destruction of the present world would come about followed by the millennium. The Emperor Nero (the anti-Christ) would return to establish a reign of terror lasting 42 months, after which God would arise and defeat him and establish the millennium.

With this kind of approach and also his interpretation of the peasant movements that occurred in the middle ages in Germany, Engels established a continuing tradition of interpretation which sees such movements as essentially revolutionary protest movements which are doomed to failure since they are before their time. Modern interpretations of third-world millennial movements see them as incipient political movements which through their failures confront participants with the realities of the situation, eventually becoming fully-fledged political movements.

Another early Marxist study of the origins of Christianity was that of Karl Kautsky (1925). At the heart of Kautsky's study is an analysis of the social and economic structure of the Roman Empire centred on the institution of slavery and the reasons for its decline. With the expansion of the Empire and its victories over other peoples a system of production grew up based upon large scale cultivation on estates (latifundia) using slave labour. In the early period of Rome's expansion slaves had been employed mainly in domestic service where they were not harshly treated. Later they were used extensively in industrial enterprises, particularly in mining, where they were ruthlessly exploited. Life expectancy was short, which did not matter since they were plentiful and cheap while Rome was expanding. This expansion also placed large areas of land in the hands of important Roman families who used slave labour to cultivate it on a commercial basis providing food for the growing urban market.

Competition from the latifundia tended to impoverish small land-owners who relied on selling part of their produce in the market. As sources of income dried up they often fell into debt, their land being swallowed up by the latifundia. They would join the free, propertyless citizenry of the towns, an urban proletarian class supported by the generosity of nobles seeking office and, therefore, the support of the city mobs, by providing them with bread and circuses.

Independent artisans and craftsmen were similarly often put out of business by competition from slave labour. During the slack season the large slave owners put their slaves to work making tools and equip-ment and commodities for the market, undermining the position of the free artisans.

One sees here again the development of the three classes to which Engels refers. But slave labour was not efficient, Kautsky claims. Slaves could not be trusted with decent equipment and methods of cultivation were crude. Slaves could only be induced to work effect-ively by threats and had to be constantly policed. None of this mat-tered as long as the Empire was expanding and they were cheap. Productivity per unit was, however, declining as a greater and greater area of land and size of workforce was brought under slave cultivation. Once expansion slowed and ceased this had serious consequences. The vast size of the Empire meant that expansion had to come to an end. It also became increasingly costly to maintain and to defend its frontiers. The army became recruited mostly from foreign, barbarian, mercen-aries. Romans became interested only in luxury and their circuses. The whole enterprise became extremely expensive requiring heavy taxation of the populace. The state had to buy its security from barbarians with large payments which further impoverished its peoples.

In this climate, intellectual ideas and attitudes towards life took a characteristic turn. Originally Romans were not much concerned with the life beyond or any kind of salvation. They were content with their earthly existence and the knowledge that in some way they would continue to exist in their offspring and in the continued domination of the Roman state. With economic decline, however, the state became

a matter of indifference and even of hostility. Ideas that a better
existence could be had in the hereafter began to grow up. It is at this
time and in this climate that one sees the emergence of Stoicism, ideas
of the soul, immortality and the life hereafter. Many fundamental ideas
similar to those of Christianity prepared the way before it really took
hold within the Empire. Kautsky traces the development of these ideas
and sums up in the following way:

> The picture that we are recording is not a pleasant one . . . as society
> sank deeper into bondage, submission became the supreme virtue,
> and from it were derived all the noble qualities to which we have
> devoted our attention: aversion to the common weal and concentra-
> tion on individual interests, cowardice and lack of self-confidence,
> longing for redemption by an emperor or a God, not by one's own
> strength or the strength of one's class; self-debasement before the
> powerful, priestly impudence toward inferiors; blasé indifference
> and disgust with life, yielding to a yearning for sensations, for
> marvels, hysteria and ecstasy, together with hypocrisy, lying and
> forgery. Such is the picture afforded us by the Imperial era, and its
> traits are reflected in the product of the era, which is Christianity.
> (Kautsky, 1925, pp. 47–8)

Some of the characteristics that can be seen in the ideas of the time are:
the abandonment of the investigation of the nature of the world, which
had begun with the Greeks, and its replacement with moralising and
the drawing up of demands upon the individual, that is to say the
replacement of science by ethics; the growth of priestly rule; the belief
in a redeemer or saviour; and the readiness to accept any kind of
nonsense and fantasy or the cheap tricks of charlatans. It was a
common idea among Roman ladies, Kautsky reports, that they could
be impregnated by a god and give birth to a saviour.

Is it not true, however, Kautsky asks, that Christianity preached
charity and humanitarianism? Was its morality not above all the
prevailing ideas? The extolment of charity, he points out, implies the
existence of poverty on a large scale. It is not surprising that the notion
of charity should only really come to prominence at the time of the
Roman Empire. Thus it was not the exclusive property of the early
Christians but a general product of the times. Here Kautsky is trying to
combat the idea that Christian morality was the product of an innovative religious genius, an extraordinary and superior individual. He is
defending the materialist conception of history which requires that

Christian morality be seen as a product of prevailing social and economic conditions.

He goes on to look at the way in which Roman domination tended to internationalise the peoples under its rule, to break up traditional forms of organisation, national grouping, tribal structures, and so on. In these conditions there was a natural tendency for people to establish new groups, associations and organisations. These were generally seen by the state as a threat and were suppressed. To survive they had to go underground. Because the penalties for involvement in such organisations were severe, only those could survive which were motivated by some high ideal or general class interest rather than by purely personal interests. At this time such idealism could only take a religious form. Their religious orientation, because of the levelling effects of the Empire, was not nationalistic but for the first time tended to address the whole of humanity.

There was a proliferation of religious movements at the time which embodied elements of older religious cults – the idea of redemption by a divinity, for example. This was a feature not only of Christianity but of the cult of Isis and of Mithraism, Christianity's chief rival.

One of the most notable features of Christianity was its monotheism which it derived from Judaism. Kautsky traces the history and development of the Jews and their religion to the point where Christianity emerges, a time when Palestine is under Roman occupation and in a state of ferment and rebellion. Three main religious orientations are prominent which are at the same time political positions and which, according to Kautsky, represented different class situations – that of the Sadducees, the Pharisees and the Essenes. One could add the rather more purely political stance of the Zealots.

The Sadducees represented the priestly nobility and the group which controlled the Jewish state. They were the masters of the temple and of the taxes paid to it. They were aristocrats who aped the opulent style of life of the Roman aristocracy and who adopted the basically Greek culture of the Romans. They did not suffer from Roman rule but were often able to benefit from it. Their policy was to further their interests by astute diplomacy. The Sadducees did not always conform to the Jewish law and denied the doctrine of resurrection.

The masses, on the other hand, ignorant of the true strength of Rome, favoured the use of force against Roman rule and were bitterly opposed to the aristocracy and their style of life. It was the Pharisaic party which captured their allegiance. The Pharisees were traditionalists and upheld the Jewish law. They retained and promoted the idea of the ultimate deliverance of Israel by a superhuman hero and military leader, the Messiah, who would overthrow all enemies. Part of their messianic, millenarian hopes involved the idea of past heroes and saints being resurrected from death to enjoy the millennium.

A third group that existed in Palestine at this time was the Zealots, a sect whose members did not believe, as the Pharisees did, that the Messiah should be passively awaited but advocated insurrection and guerrilla tactics against the Romans. They were drawn largely from groups with little to lose – the impoverished herdsmen of Galilee some of whom had turned to banditry, and the destitute proletariat of Jerusalem who were frequently given to rioting. Rebellions and insurrections occurred several times up to the destruction of the temple in 70 AD. It was at such a time that Jesus was born and in which Christianity emerged.

Not all sects and movements in Palestine were violent or overtly political. The Essenes, probably authors of the Dead Sea Scrolls discovered in caves near their monastery at Qumran, were, like the Zealots Kautsky argues, of proletarian origin. They were established around 150 BC and existed at least up to the time of the destruction of the temple. The Essenes were not interested in merely waiting for the millennium or in transforming the world by force or diplomacy. They attempted to set up an ideal society in the midst of the existing one based upon communistic principles. But, Kautsky points out, it was a communism of consumption and not of production. This way of life is not easy to reconcile with marriage and family ties, according to Kautsky. True Essenes did not, therefore, marry and were celibate. The communities often recruited new members by adopting children. Such communities could not survive anywhere but outside of the cities where they would not have been tolerated by the authorities.

In the cities a rather different type of organisation grew up which was to have far more importance than any of the groups so far mentioned. This was the Christian congregation. The early Christians were largely urban proletarians according to Kautsky. Like all groups recruited from this class they shared certain attitudes towards the state and towards other groups and they shared the basic beliefs and assumptions about the ultimate deliverance of the Jews and the coming of the Messiah.

Originally, the Christians were characterised by savage class hatred, Kautsky tells us. There is much denunciation of wealth and the rich in the teachings of Jesus. But revisionism soon softened this and eventually wiped out all trace of it. The Christian congregation was also a communal form of organisation, again of consumption. New members were originally required to donate all of their property to the community, which in most cases was not very much. These communities were based around the provision of a communal meal and of aid and charity for those in need.

Kautsky does not believe the early Christians were non-violent like the Essenes. Their aim, he speculates, was not armed mass insurrection but to stage some kind of *coup d'état*.[1] This he deduces from a gleaning of certain statements in the gospels. The true story, he claims, was covered up by the Church much later, after Christianity had changed its nature in accommodating itself to the real world, politics and the state. Jesus is presented by the later Church as meek and mild and pacifist. It preached a doctrine of acceptance of and submission to authority and faith in a better life hereafter. Elements and traces of the original character of Christianity, too deeply rooted to expunge entirely, remained, however, and from them we can get some idea of its true character. There is reference in the gospels, for example, to the disciples being armed in the Garden of Gethsemane.

Figures like that of Jesus commonly appeared in Palestine from time to time and were usually abandoned after their death at the hands of the authorities. The unique feature of Christianity was that after the death of Jesus his followers did not abandon him or his message but continued to believe that he was the Messiah. This was possible because of the idea of his resurrection and ultimate return which the Christians innovatively adapted from the common idea of the resurrection of the holy dead at the day of judgement.

There was another reason, however, for the survival of the Christians as a group which was of great importance, namely the Christian congregation. Jesus left behind him, Kautsky argues '... an organisation with elements that were excellently calculated to hold together his adherents and attract increasing numbers of new adherents' (Kautsky, 1925, p. 376). It was not primarily faith in the resurrection which enabled the Christians to survive as a group but the strength and vigour of their congregations.

A further important factor accounting for the appeal of Christianity was the fact that it did not only preach liberation for Jews but for all the poor and the oppressed. It was thus able to attract adherents among non-Jews. Christianity did not believe in a national Messiah but a universal one. This and its established base outside of Palestine enabled it to survive the catastrophe that befell the Jewish people at the time of the destruction of the temple and devastation of the land.

Christianity was not, however, to achieve its aim of transforming the world but was to become instead 'the most tremendous instrument of domination and exploitation in the world' (ibid., p. 381). This began with its spread among non-Jews, largely due to the missionary activities of Paul. In order to be successful it had to rid itself of its Jewish peculiarities – the distinctive Jewish law including circumcision and the dietary rules. This caused for a time a good deal of controversy among the congregations. The outcome was that Christianity became essentially a non-Jewish doctrine and even hostile to Judaism. The Jewish Christian community sank into insignificance and obscurity and the spread of the new religion among Jews ceased. The Jewish Messiah was transformed into the Greek Christ.

Christianity took on its familiar peaceful and submissive, even servile, character. All hope of rebellion had been extinguished with the destruction of Jerusalem and now the whole character of Christianity changes. The millennium is now interpreted as far off. Deliverance is now seen to occur not here in this world but in heaven. The resurrection of the flesh was transformed into the immortality of the soul. Slavery is condoned and the slave is told to obey his master as a moral duty. Here Kautsky differs markedly from Engels. Christianity, after its very early phase, ceased to have any attraction for slaves. It had always been a religion of the free proletariat and despite the early rapprochement between the latter and the slaves they remained different classes with different interests.

With these changes in its character Christianity became more concerned with acquiring property and money to be able to further its charitable activities, an aspect which now receives particular emphasis in its teachings. More and more effort was put into recruiting wealthier members which again altered its character. The duty to donate all one's property was relaxed; small gifts were considered to be sufficient. Communal consumption diminished in importance and the communal meal became a formality. Status distinctions appeared within the congregations and this was intensified as a bureaucratic structure and organisation began to emerge.

Kautsky examines the apostles, the prophets and teachers and the new elite of bishops and deacons that arose with the expansion of the Church. Democratic organisation disappeared and a distinction between clergy and laity emerged. With such developments Roman and Byzantine rulers saw in the Church a means of strengthening and legitimating their rule. In any case it was no longer possible to suppress Christianity; the alternative was to incorporate it.

Weber agrees with a number of points in the work of Engels and Kautsky. He did not contribute an analysis of early Christianity as such but there are many scattered observation throughout that section of *Economy and Society* which has been translated and published separately as *The Sociology of Religion* (1965).

Weber very much agrees with Engels and Kautsky that Christianity began in the cities. In his view it is a feature of doctrines that grow up in an urban setting that they are anti-magical and anti-ritualistic, which early Christianity was, being essentially an ethical religion of salvation. But its anti-magical character should not be over emphasised; it was only relatively so. The early Christians practised miraculous cures and the charisma of Jesus was based to some extent on the belief in his power to work miracles.

Weber differs from Engels and Kautsky, however, in his emphasis on Christianity as a religion of the lower middle classes. It was a religion of artisans he asserts. Jesus came from an artisan family and his missionaries were wandering apprentices. Weber thought that salvation doctrines were strongly associated with this type of social location. He includes some slaves in this category. They were often working as independent craftsmen paying tribute to their masters and hoping eventually to buy their freedom. Mithraism, he observes, was another religion which attracted this group.

Among free artisans attracted to Christianity were a number of self-educated intellectuals, Paul being an example, who were influential in the development of Christianity. Christianity, however, remained an anti-intellectualist doctrine opposed to the ritualistic, legalistic, elitist scholarship of Judaism and to the kind of intellectual elitism that could be found in other sects. It remained a layman's religion appealing to the ordinary lower-middle-class artisan.

Weber mentions one other category for whom Christianity had much appeal – women. One reason for the failure of Mithraism as opposed to Christianity, he argues, was that it was an extremely masculine cult which excluded women. Middle-class and even upper-class women, one might add, were in an ambivalent and contradictory status position – a fact which, it has been argued, often predisposes people to take up beliefs and join movements of an unorthodox kind. To a large extent women took the class position of their husbands and enjoyed the benefits and status associated with it but as women they were lower in status than men and debarred from the more important roles in the society that only men could undertake. Roman women converts, furthermore, would have brought up their children as

Christians and in this way men who were Roman citizens and of some social standing may have been brought into the congregations.

Weber, then, does not see early Christianity primarily as a religion of the poor, even though it directed its promises at the poor and contained elements of a compensatory doctrine. There were no 'proletarian instincts' in the teaching of Jesus. Rather than being the product of resentment as Nietzsche had argued, it eliminated, in fact, feelings of resentment among those Jews who espoused it. What Jesus taught was brotherly love. Christianity was a congregational religion which set the co-religionist in the place of fellow kinsmen and clansmen. As we shall see, Islam was to do the same thing some five hundred years later. Weber interprets the statement of Jesus that whoever does not leave his own mother and father cannot become a follower of Jesus as not so much implying hostility to the family but expressing the idea that the brotherhood of Christians comes before all other ties. The emphasis on charity was natural in a congregational religion such as this.

The only 'class' element in Christianity, according to Weber, was the rejection of scholarly arrogance and aristocratic intellectualism. Yet Jesus' own teaching contained an elitist element. Only those who really renounced all worldly things could be saved. He taught a kind of religious heroism.

Early Christianity, Weber agrees, was certainly millennial in character. Jesus taught that the new order was to come about very soon and was in fact already coming about. Hence indifference to this world was more easily acceptable. Such an attitude cannot last long, Weber states. After the death of Jesus millennial expectations became associated with the idea of his resurrection. Weber's unfinished section of *Economy and Society* breaks off at this point. It is reasonable to suppose that he would have agreed that the millennial character of early Christianity would have progressively weakened as hopes for the millennium were repeatedly postponed. In an earlier passage he shows how the original hostility to the Roman Empire was transformed into either complete indifference to the state or the view that the state's authority was somehow desired and ordained by God.

A final point to note about Weber's treatment of Christianity is his emphasis on the role of the charismatic[2] prophet, Jesus, in bringing about a religious innovation. Christianity was, for Weber, more than a religion which took up prevailing ideas of the time or simply the product of social and political circumstances but must have been shaped to a considerable extent by the personality, ideas and insights of Jesus.

Recent scholarship has tended to undermine the more traditional view of the social position of early Christians which believed that they were from the poorest and most oppressed of the Roman Empire in favour of a view closer to that of Weber. That the early Christians were diverse in social status and not all from the poorer groups was a view expressed by Judge (1960). The Gallilean followers of Jesus, he acknowledged, were of humble background but others, many of them originating from other parts of the Empire, were able to provide support and funds for the movement. Missionary activities outside Palestine presuppose, also, a level of support for travel, sustenance and shelter which only better-off households and communities could supply. There is much in Paul's letters and the Acts of the Apostles, Judge, suggests, to support the view that there were many people of substance in the very early Christian congregations. Humbler members may have been dependants of these people; household servants, dependent relatives and so on. That there was considerable diversity among the early Christians is supported by Malherbe (1977) who points out that Paul was educated and a Roman citizen who mixed with and was supported in the homes of his equals who were his first converts. Only later, at places such as Corinth, did larger numbers of poorer people join the Christian congregations. Theissen (1978, 1992) argues that many of the early Christians were marginal middle class; marginal either because they had been upwardly mobile in conditions of change or because they were under pressure of debt. Conditions of life had become precarious for many independent craftsmen, fishermen, tax collectors and landowning peasants, all of whom must be considered as enjoying middle-class status in this sort of society, in contrast to landless peasants, agricultural labourers, slaves and servants. Smith (1983) agrees that there were many such people among the early Christians. Meeks (1983) finds evidence that people of most types of social background, barring only the very top and the very bottom of the hierarchy, are represented among Christians.

Not all New Testament scholars influenced by sociological approaches abandon the view that early Christians were recruited from among the downtrodden and oppressed poorer groups, however. One of the pioneers, John Gager (1975), argues that the majority were of such a background but acknowledges that there seem to have been downwardly mobile persons of originally higher social status among them who felt relatively deprived as a consequence. The character of the movement was, however, determined by the majority who were from the poor and low status groups. Scroggs (1980) questions the soundness of the methodologies and the selectivity regarding evidence and sources of those who have contributed to the 'new consensus' on the social location of the early Christians. It tends to produce an overstatement of the degree of higher-status membership of the early Christian communities. He questions whether, echoing Gager, the presence in any case of some persons of higher status should cause us to abandon the traditional view of Christianity as a movement of the poor and oppressed. Methodological worries have also been expressed by Rohrbaugh (1984, 1987). The definitions of class, status position, or social location generally have been somewhat vague in the work of sociologically oriented New Testament scholars, he argues (1984). He favours a concept defined in terms of power relations which would have more applicability to the type of society in which Christianity emerged where wealth and status tended to follow power. A second difficulty with the work on the social level of early Christians is that it is to a large extent based upon the writings of a single person, and in particular Paul's letters (Mack, 1988). It cannot be assumed that what is said in these sources reflects the actual social constitution of the early Christian congregations as groups and the type of social location that the majority of their members came from. A further difficulty lies in the fact that New Testament materials, rather than reflecting actual conditions, may well have been written with specific purposes in mind, a point Mack (1988) makes with respect the Gospel of Mark. It was, he argues, a reaction to the failure of some of the early Christian groups in their campaign to reform the local Diaspora synagogues from which they had not yet entirely separated. The Gospel provided a mythical charter for their final break with the synagogues and the establishment of the in distinct and separate identity.

Despite these difficulties and the paucity of hard evidence a recent detailed review and assessment of the extensive literature on the subject (Holmberg, 1990) is firmly of the view that something has been achieved. 'Romantic proletarian notions' (ibid., p. 75) must be relinquished. A great deal of careful work has been carried out on New Testament materials by the scholars discussed above, relating particularly to prosopographical evidence, the overall thrust of which, Holmberg argues, suggests that first-century Christianity was not a movement confined to the poorer strata of society anywhere in the Roman Empire.

If Christianity was not primarily a movement of the poor and oppressed, what factors account for its emergence? On this question New Testament scholars have turned to sociological concepts such as anomie, relative deprivation, status inconsistency and cognitive dissonance. They have applied theories of millennial and sectarian movements developed by sociologists and anthropologists.

Gager, in *Kingdom and Community* (1975), was the first to make extensive use of the sociological and anthropological literature. He draws out the parallels between early Christianity and the millennial movements studied by anthropologists in Melanesia, Africa and among North American native peoples. Five main characteristics of the millennial movement have been identified by writers such as Talmon (1966) and Cohn (1970) upon whom Gager bases his analysis. Millennial movements are, according to Talmon, 'religious movements that expect imminent, total, ultimate, this-worldly, collective salvation' (1966, p. 166). In place of 'ultimate' Cohn (1970) adds that this salvation will be brought about by miraculous means. Examination of a wide range of such movements shows them to be characterised typically by an expected transformation of the world order which may be thought to be only days, weeks or months away. The new world will be a material one, essentially like the one it replaces but without its flaws and faults. Peace, justice and plenty will prevail while evil and unhappiness will be banished. Millennialism expects a this-worldly salvation, not an otherworldly one. Since the world to come will be perfect no further development is possible; it marks an end to history. Salvation is usually seen in collective terms, applying to a whole society or group within it rather than in terms of individual salvation. Early Christianity, according to Gager, meets these criteria closely.

Such movements are promoted by conditions in which oppression and social disprivilege is experienced but this alone is insufficient, Gager argues. A charismatic prophetic leader is required to spark off the movement. A common, if not universal, feature of millennial movements has indeed been found to be the central role of a prophet or leader who may have experienced revelations concerning the imminence of the millennium and who may believe that he has been specially selected for his mission. Sometimes this prophet is seen as a cultural hero returned from the dead or a supernatural figure in human form. In this case, the movement can be said to be messianic. It was, of course, Jesus that filled this role in early Christianity.

Early Christians were, however, not all from the deprived and oppressed classes of society. To account for the better-off converts to the movement Gager brings in the notion of relative deprivation which, he argues, was the situation of a section of the Jewish population of Palestine who had experienced a degree of downward mobility.

Millennial movements are generally ephemeral and short-lived affairs. They may develop into small millennial sects which remain rather marginal (Worsley, 1970) but generally vanish as rapidly as they emerge. This was not, of course, the case with Christianity. In order to explain this Gager utilises the theory of cognitive dissonance. This states essentially that we are discomforted by contradiction in our perceptions of and beliefs about the world and have to do something to remove this contradiction or dissonance when it occurs. We resort to a variety of strategies to achieve consonance in our cognitions but broadly speaking they involve either altering one or other of the cognitions or taking courses of action that deny or mask the dissonance. An example of dissonance might be the belief that a major catastrophic end to the world is to happen at a certain time, and the perception that it has not in fact happened though the time is well past. The theory of cognitive dissonance was developed by Festinger (1956) as a result of encountering a situation like this in which the response was surprising. In the course of his investigation of a flying saucer cult Festinger observed that when the prophecy of a major catastrophe and rescue by the flying saucers of the believers did not occur at the appointed time the reaction was not abandonment of the beliefs but intensification of them and of the proselytising effort. By such activity the cognitive dissonance generated by the discrepancy between commitment to the beliefs and reality was removed or reduced. A disconfirming event, the non-appearance of the flying saucers at the appointed time, was overcome by reaffirmation of belief through intense proselytising.

Applying this to early Christianity, Gager argues that the disconfirming events were the death of the prophet and the failure of the millennium to transpire. The response to the resulting dissonance was again intense missionary activity which ultimately led to the transformation of the movement into a non-millennial missionary one. A second strategy for reducing dissonance is to affirm belief through attacking rival beliefs. This explains the antagonism expressed by Christianity towards Judaism and paganism laying the foundations for Christian attitudes towards heresy. Drawing upon functionalist theory and the idea that conflict can serve social functions Gager goes on to argue that this focus upon heresy promoted internal solidarity within the early Church. A third response that Gager might have identified is the belief in the resurrection of Jesus. Jackson (1975) points out that the death of Jesus must have generated an extreme cognitive dissonance given his followers' intense expectation of the imminent coming of the Kingdom. Instead of the expected triumph they experienced, with the death of Jesus, a humiliation. Dissonance theory states that a response to a situation such as this is to deny or seek disconfirmation of one of the cognitions but retaining that in which most emotion is invested. The response of the followers of Jesus was to refuse to believe that he had died, hence the doctrine of the resurrection.

The success of Christianity was bound up with the success of the missionary endeavour which Gager emphasises. The conditions prevailing in the Roman Empire were favourable to this missionary project. The Empire from the time of Augustus had created a unified, ordered and peaceful context in which to work. Travel was relatively easy. This promoted the spread and universalisation of Hellenistic culture with widespread knowledge and use of Greek as a common language. There was a high degree of tolerance of religious movements for most of the time. Persecution of Christians was very sporadic and the result of its exclusivism and uncompromising attitude to such things as honouring the divinity of the Emperor which, in the long run, proved to be great strengths of Christianity. Tolerance was stimulated by the prevailing diversity in the Empire and its cosmopolitan and international character and there was no single state religion or priestly caste that felt unduly threatened by new religious movements. The early church was able to follow the model of the synagogue which had spread throughout the Empire. On this basis the Christian congregations were able to establish a strong sense of community among their members.

Gager's work has attracted stringent criticism, much of it on methodological grounds. The relevance of models based on third-world millennial movements for understanding early Christianity has been questioned by critics. Best (1984) and Rowland (1985) believe them to be too distant to be appropriate. Smith (1978) considers them to be too close. He points out that despite Gager's insistence that being based upon anthropological models his account is formulated independently of Christian evidence, these models were in fact themselves heavily based upon Christian history. According to Smith this makes Gager's account a self-fulfilling prophecy. Of course early Christianity will look like a millennial movement if the model of a millennial movement is taken in the first place from Christianity. While Gager may not have used a model that is derived independently from the Christian context this would not necessarily, however, invalidate his account. The point is pertinent only at the level of description. The description of millennial movements in diverse parts of the world may well reflect assumptions of what is relevant that derive from Christian models. Having established that these movements are of the same type as early Christianity an understanding of the social, economic and political conditions associated with their emergence can then be applied to early Christianity itself. Their conditions of emergence are much easier to establish in the case of movements that are recent and contemporary and examination of a range of them enables us to establish what the relevant conditions are. This knowledge can then direct us to look for relevant evidence in the case of early Christianity in order to assess whether it does in fact fit the model. Gager did not need a model that was established independently of Christianity; he is not guilty of circular reasoning.

The characterisation of early Christianity as essentially millennial might be questioned, however, on empirical grounds (Tidball, 1985). Millennial movements, as pointed out above, are ephemeral affairs and cannot sustain long continued enthusiasm. They seem generally to fade away or may settle into small millennial sects. Not denying, however, the millennial tendencies of Christianity, Tidball considers that they have tended to be overstated to the neglect of the role of Jesus not so much as prophet but as Rabbi and teacher. To this extent Judge's (1960–1) characterisation of early Christianity as a scholastic community might be acknowledged as of value. Early Christianity would thus appear as a somewhat hybrid movement in Tidball's view.

Gager's use of cognitive dissonance has also been questioned by these critics and others (Richter, 1984) since it is a theory which suffers from a number of unresolved questions and about which there is considerable disagreement within the disciplines of sociology and social psychology. Richter points out that the missionary timescale we are dealing with in the case of Christianity is very much longer than that involved in cognitive dissonance studies. Could it account for the lifelong endeavours of the Christian missionaries? Tidball (1985) considers that the early millennial expectations of the followers of Jesus were a misunderstanding of his teaching which did envisage an extensive missionary endeavour on a long timescale. Such misunderstandings and the cognitive dissonance stemming from them were, however, soon dispelled – at the time of Pentecostal revelation. The missionary programme was thus not an attempt to overcome cognitive dissonance but simply the fulfillment of the task that Jesus had set them.

Finally, relative deprivation theory has been subjected to much criticism. In order for it to work as an explanatory factor it must be shown that a sense of deprivation was actually felt by those involved. This is rarely achieved; usually it is inferred from what is known about their prevailing conditions and circumstances rendering the argument circular (Beckford, 1975). Felt deprivation is probably impossible to demonstrate in the case of early Christianity.

Relative deprivation is a concept that might have been utilised by Theissen (1978, 1982, 1992) in his treatment of early Christianity. It is certainly implicit in his characterisation of the social level of the Christians in the early church, as we have seen. The fact that many of them were lower-middle-class artisans under pressure of debt suggests they might have felt a sense of deprivation relative to expectations. Theissen relies rather upon Durkheim's notion of anomie, a confusion of norms and standards or a discrepancy between legitimate or established expectations and the realities prevailing in times of rapid change and social dislocation. Early Christianity is seen as a response to such dislocation which sought to reintegrate followers once again into normative patterns of relationships and life and met, therefore, a functional need.

The response of some to conditions of anomie was to abandon normal patterns of life to become wandering charismatic figures who relinquished home, family and property to live a life of poverty supported by sympathisers in local communities they passed through. Jesus and the disciples were a small band of ethically radical itinerant preachers who rejected worldly and material goals, condemned the rich and the pursuit of riches and the ties of family and possessions. They disseminated millenarian ideas of an imminent end to the present world order. They relied upon supporters who lived normal lives but who accepted the ultimate truth of their teachings and their authority.

This movement emerged in a situation of social, economic and political malaise. Palestine had suffered famines and overpopulation. There was growing inequality and heavy taxation imposed by the Roman rulers and at the same time taxation imposed by the Jewish religious elite centred in Jerusalem. This exacerbated urban–rural tensions especially with respect to the Galilean periphery. The policy of the aristocracy and high-priestly families of accomodation to Roman rule undermined Jewish conceptions of an ideal theocratic state. Jewish values and culture seemed to have been rejected by the Jewish traditional elite. There was a deep urge for renewal. Judaism had long reacted to adversity and threats to identity by what Theissen calls an 'intensification of norms' or stringent reaffirmation and enforcement of the law. This had, however, produced schism. Different groups interpreted this in different ways. Christianity sought to intensify norms relating to social relations but tended to relax norms relating to aspects of religious observance. The central doctrines of Christianity sought to overcome aggression through emphasis upon brotherly love. Theissen draws upon psychoanalytical theory to argue that aggressive impulses were reversed or introjected by emphasis on guilt and sinfulness which had to be overcome through Christ's teachings. The relaxation of some of the peculiarly Jewish religious norms aided Christianity in universalising these beliefs. Ultimately these ideas lent themselves in the wider context of the Roman Empire to the role of integration of the society and support for the regime.

Theissen's work has been subjected to extensive criticism particularly by Horsley (1989) who takes him to task for his functionalism.[3] Rather than the logical and theoretical deficiencies of this approach, however, Horsley appears to be more unhappy with its conservatism and Theissen's emphasis on the integrative role of Christianity. On the question of the itinerant radicalism of the wandering charismatics, however, Horsley's point is that there is precious little evidence for it. It cannot be documented from the sayings-tradition that Theissen uses as the basis for his claims. Similarly, there is no textual basis, Horsley claims, for the process of introjection of aggression that Theissen postulates.

To the concepts of relative deprivation, cognitive dissonance, and anomie Meeks (1982, 1983) adds status inconsistency. Socioeconomic position can be described in terms of a number of dimensions; class, status, education, ethnicity and so on. Individuals can be consistent on all dimensions (status crystallisation) or inconsistent (status inconsistency). They may, for example, have a high economic position in terms of wealth or income but have a low social standing because of very recent acquisition or source of the wealth. There can be counter pressures on such people and dissatisfaction of expectations as a result. Some research has shown that those who are status inconsistent are more likely to join social movements in response to these dissatisfactions. Many of the most prominent among the early Christians, Meeks argues, were socially mobile and consequently status inconsistent. Their status inconsistency was experienced in conditions likely to produce a millenarian response. Meeks notes from anthropological sources on millenarianism, and particularly the work of Burridge (1960, 1969), that a prominent aspect is the desire for an explanation of a situation that seems incomprehensible and senseless. The millenarian myth meets cognitive needs and thereby helps to resolve the cognitive dissonance experienced as a result of the gap between expectations and reality.

Meeks' use of the notion of status inconsistency might have been fruitful if it had been possible to measure accurately the various positions of early Christians on a number of dimensions. As we have seen, however, it is extremely difficult to ascertain even in the crudest terms their overall gross position from the sparse and unreliable data that is available. Another aspect that Meeks ignores is that the relevance of status inconsistency as a factor which is associated with involvement in social movements is contentious in sociology. While some studies have found a connection others have not. Also suspect is the linkage of status inconsistency with cognitive dissonance. The latter generally refers to rather concrete and specific discrepancies between cognitions. Status inconsistency would imply a very complex and indeterminate set of potential discrepancies.

The fact that the concept of status inconsistency was developed in the context of twentieth-century American or Western society worries Stowers (1985), and he would generalise the point to most of the sociological concepts that have been applied to New Testament times. There is an illegitimate assumption in these approaches, in Stowers' view, that past and present societies are commensurable and that what applies to one will apply to another. We have no way of knowing whether reactions to status inconsistency in the first century Roman world would have been anything like that typical of twentieth-century America, or that there would have been any reaction to it at all. These things have to be demonstrated before contemporary sociological approaches can usefully be applied. The question might be posed, however, as to how past or how different a society must be before concepts such as status discrepancy or relative deprivation become suspect in their applicability. Would they apply to eighteenth-or seventeenth-century America, or Europe, or to Medieval Europe or contemporary Japan? They are part of general models of human behaviour and society intended to have universal application.

What is also somewhat dubious about Meeks' use of the concept, however, is the assumption that status inconsistency could be a central factor in stimulating a full-blown millennial movement. Most studies that have made use of the idea have been concerned with a propensity to support or join social, political or sectarian movements of a much less radical or dramatic kind.

On the other hand, we might question the relevance of anthropological models of millennialism for early Christianity, and this point would apply equally to Gager's approach, on the grounds that the millennial movements documented and studied by anthropologists exhibit a number of important features that seem absent from Christianity. A common feature of these movements is the intense emotion experienced by or induced in their followers. They are often ecstatic and sometimes hysterical. They can spread at an alarming rate and totally dominate the lives of those who fall under their influence. Millennial expectations promote a complete break with normal ways of life, social and moral rules, norms and customs. Very often the millennial expectation is so strong that people abandon normal productive activities. They may abandon homes and fields and in some cases have destroyed property and livestock convinced that they will have no further need of such things. Some of these features are particularly strong in the movements studied by Burridge (1960, 1969) whose work Gager pinpoints as particularly influential on him. He does seem to ignore these aspects of third-world movements, however. On the other hand, we should not expect all such movements to be identical. They will inevitably manifest a range of differences of detail which may reflect very particular local and historical conditions.

An alternative to the model of the millennial movement is that of a 'social revolution' which Horsley favours (1987, 1989). On the basis of a detailed and extensive critique of Theissen's work, Horsley develops his own interpretation of early Christianity. The crucial background factor was the tension and conflict in Palestine between the rulers and ruled. The 'rulers' includes both Roman and Jewish elites. Both levied heavy taxes on the population. The consequence was widespread indebtedness and despair on the part of badly affected individuals and groups. The frequent references to the theme of contrast between rich and poor in the Gospels reflects this economic situation. There was much more than this to the resentments and dissatisfaction among ordinary Jews, however. The situation was an affront to their conception and traditional ideal of Jewish society as a just and egalitarian one. It is significant in this respect that the triggers of major protests were often threats to traditional religious symbols or practice. The movement centred on Jesus sought to restore justice by instituting a new social order. The Christians constituted a new 'family' the members of which were exhorted to behave towards one another as members of a family but with the patriarchal element removed. The new social order would be accomplished through the renewal of local community based upon the familial model interpreted in terms of a brotherhood with no distinctions of rank, power or prestige. This necessitated the intensification of norms that Theissen speaks of. The traditional peasant emphasis upon reciprocal generosity was to be restored as the foundation upon which new communities were to be based. Against Theissen, Horsley argues that far from helping to integrate society and overcome aggression, Christianity probably exacerbated tension between rulers and ruled. Rather than introjection of aggressive impulses manifested in self-blame and guilt, Christianity relieved tensions and anxieties stemming from such impulses by transferring them to God's judgement. Christianity represented an overcoming of aggression through a vision of love and reconciliation which even as they attempted to practice it sharpened the Christians' rejection of the ruling elites and dominant institutions.

It is perhaps the differences outlined above between early Christianity and the millennial outburst documented by anthropologists that have made, for some New Testament scholars, the sociological model of the sect more attractive. Despite his characterisation of early Christianity as a millenarian movement Meeks, for example, also refers to it as a sect. This is especially so in his later work (1987). While sectarianism is by no means incompatible with millenarianism the millenarian movement has generally been seen as a different sort of animal to the sect. Use of the sociological model of the sect has been quite common in sociologically-oriented New Testament scholarship (Scroggs, 1975; Elliot, 1981, Rowland, 1985; Watson, 1986; Esler, 1987; MacDonald, 1988). These writers have looked to the work of Bryan Wilson (1961, 1967, 1970, 1975) who defines the sect as a voluntary institution with a strong sense of distinct identity and separateness. Membership requires proof of eligibility in the form of evidence of acceptance and knowledge of doctrine, or of genuine religious experience. Sects consider themselves to be in sole possession of truth and reject the claims of other religious groups. They separate themselves from such groups and from the wider society. They generally enforce standards of behaviour of members and often have procedures for expulsion of those who do not live by these standards. Commitment is high and membership tends to define identity in the eyes of sect members and of others. Wilson identifies a number of clearly different types of sect on the basis of their 'response to the world'. Generally, those who have applied this model to early Christian groups have found Wilson's conversionist type of sect to fit early Christianity closely. Wilson (1970) characterises the conversionist type of sect as emphasising evangelism which seeks to induce a religious awakening and genuine experience of conversion. By maximising conversion and bringing about a 'change of heart' in as many people as possible a better world can be created. The conversion experience is necessary for salvation and evidence of it constitutes the main test of eligibility for membership. Conversion experience is more important than ritual and ceremonial and it is frequently very intense and emotional. Conversionist sects embody a contradiction between the desire to remain separate and distinct from the rest of the world and yet actively to proselytise which necessitates close contact with the surrounding social world. This tension is usually resolved in favour of a reduction in sectarian radicalism and closer integration with the wider society, a fate which, of course, Christianity was to experience (MacDonald, 1988).

The term 'sect', however, is by no means used uniformly by sociologists. There are broadly two schools of thought. Wilson's use of the term is an example of the first though there is a considerable range of variation in the details of what characteristics are crucial. Broadly it is the exclusivity and rejection of the validity of others' interpretations that lies at the heart of this use of the term. Stark and Bainbridge (1980), on the other hand, define sects or sect movements as essentially breakaway groups from established religious traditions which seek to rescue the tradition from what it regards as corruption and distortion of true belief and practice and restore the religion to its proper state. Innovative movements which add a major new dimension or direction to the religion or entirely new movements unrelated to the prevailing tradition are defined as cults or cult movements.

Stark (1986) considers that early Christianity must be considered to be a cult movement and not a sect or sect movement. It was the belief in the resurrection of Jesus that transformed it from a sect within Judaism, led by Jesus, into a cult movement. The resurrection belief added a dimension that was sufficiently new and innovative that it took Christianity outside the Jewish context. It was no longer a movement within Judaism but a new and distinct religion in its own right.

These typological considerations are enlightening to some extent but do not add a great deal to our understanding of the reasons for the emergence of Christianity. Esler (1987) goes somewhat further than most in relating the conversionist character of early Christian groups to processes of schism. He bases his analysis of Luke–Acts on the work of Barrett (1968) who analyses the bewildering proclivity towards schism and fragmentation of African Christian Churches. Central to Barrett's analysis is the role of a prophetic leader who is able to channel disaffection within Churches and offer a new and more vital interpretation of the faith or style of worship. Paul clearly fits this pattern and his opposition to the Jerusalem Christians and to the law is the factor that established Christianity as a sect outside of Judaism.

This view of Paul is shared by Watson (1986) who applies insights from sociological studies of sectarianism that show that reform movements within a religious tradition which meet with insurmountable opposition (which they often do) tend to become transformed into a breakaway sect. This, he believes, is what happened to early Christianity.

Watson challenges the 'Reformation' interpretation of Paul's theology, namely that salvation cannot be earned by 'works' (conformity to the law) but only by faith. God cannot be obligated to save even the most pious by their actions but will save whosoever he chooses to save – the elect – and in accordance with his own inscrutable purposes. Salvation is predetermined and no action can alter it. This interpretation of Paul's theology ignored the social context in which he was operating. Only a sociological perspective can make sense of Paul's statements in his various letters, Watson argues; '...the origins of Paul's theology of the law are to be found in a specific social situation, and not in his conversion experience, his psychological problems or his insight into the existential plight of humanity' (ibid., p. 28).

When Paul began his mission he, like the other Christian missionaries, preached among fellow Jews but found them on the whole unresponsive to his message. Gentiles seemed more responsive so the early Christian missionaries agreed to turn their attention towards them. Paul and other Christians at Antioch, however, found that it was easier to proselytise among gentiles if they were not required to conform to the Jewish law, especially circumcision. They began to teach that it was not necessary to obey the law and thereby aroused the opposition of the Jewish Christians in Jerusalem. At this point some of his supporters at Antioch abandoned him and reverted to the position of defending the Jewish law. Paul's rejection of salvation through the law, then, was not a rejection of salvation through works and an affirmation of salvation by faith alone for the elect but a rejection specifically of the idea of salvation through the *Jewish* law. Since this was quite unacceptable to fellow Jews, Paul accepted that he would have to seek converts only among gentiles. The Church had to separate itself from the synagogue.

Schonfield (1974) points out that Paul, the leading missionary in the gentile world outside Palestine, stood to gain by seeking converts among gentiles many of whom were in the habit of attending synagogue service although they had to remain outside the boundaries of the synagogue. Paganism did not satisfy the religious aspirations of many in the Empire at this time. Paul taught that the old law had been abrogated by a new covenant between God and all mankind. The implications of this were very favourable, of course, for recruitment of gentiles since they could avoid circumcision and ignore the Jewish dietary laws.

The Palestinian Christians are seen by Schonfield as essentially a Jewish nationalistic and anti-Roman party who hoped to restore the position of the Jews by re-establishing piety and the truly religious way of life. The creed of Jesus and his early followers was thus pre-Christian. Christianity developed only later. Jesus was arrested largely because of the mass support he received in Jerusalem which looked as if it might get out of control and lead to an insurrection. Jesus and his followers were a disturbing influence at a time when the city was seething with discontent and millennial expectations.

The spread of the ideas of this group, the Nazoreans – a Jewish messianic sect hoping for an immanent end to Roman domination of Palestine and the Jewish millennium – occurred, Schonfield agues, firstly as a result of the conversion, often with Zealot assistance (elements of the Zealot movement were won over to the Nazorean cause), of hellenised, Greek-speaking Jews living in various parts of the Empire. Eventually the Nazoreans were isolated and became insignificant. Meanwhile the gentile Church developed a quite distinct set of doctrines suited to the needs and circumstances of its adherents and became firmly established in the Empire.

The general conditions which account for the success of the gentile Church and the transformation of Christianity from a Jewish sect or movement to a non-Jewish world religion are little touched upon by most New Testament scholars who, very much in accordance with the tradition of New Testament scholarship, have been rather specifically focused upon the detailed interpretation of texts in the light of sociological concepts and theories (Nielsen, 1990). They have taken particular concepts and 'employed them in an ad hoc fashion to illuminate particular corners of the historical landscape' (ibid., p. 101). Nielsen points out that in this they depart, with the possible exception of Gager, from the perspective of Engels and Kautsky, and of course Weber, who set their interpretations in the broad context of an analysis of Roman and Hellenistic society and culture. We cannot understand either the emergence of Christianity or its success if we do not adopt the broader perspective of encounters between civilisations and particularly between Judaism and Hellenism. It is significant that the period was one of great change. The Greek city–state structures had broken down, new political units had been established and above all there was unprecedented exchange of ideas, intercivilisational communication and exposure to diverse perspectives. The encounter between Judaism and Hellenism produced a religious conception of greater abstraction and generality than had previously been available. Crucial to the spread of Christianity was the existence throughout the Empire of Jewish communities whose thought and intellectual habits embodied this new religious outlook. A key role was played by the synagogues which provided a receptive audience for new religious ideas such as those of the Christian missionaries.

CATHOLICISM AND PROTESTANTISM

Remarkably little attention has been paid by sociologists to medieval Christianity. Sociologically oriented historical work, also, is not nearly so abundant as sociologically-informed New Testament scholarship. Weber made a number of observations in the course of the section on religion in *Economy and Society*. Christianity, he believed, carried over from Judaism a relatively rational and ethical orientation. Its anti-magical, monotheistic, and inner-worldly, ascetic tendencies were more internally consistent than oriental religions. This rationality was to reach its most developed state in Calvinistic Protestantism. Catholic Christianity was relatively less rational. It did not divest itself quite so completely of magical ideas. This can be seen in its emphasis on the sacraments. For example Weber says:

> Of an essentially magical nature is the view that one may incorporate divine power into himself by the physical ingestion of some divine substance, some sacred totemic animal in which a mighty spirit is incarnated, or some host that has been magically transformed into the body of a God. (Weber, 1965, p. 186)

Weber considers that a characteristic of magic is that it attempts to coerce gods and spirits whereas the truly religious attitude to them is to worship them. In the Catholic Communion, he argues, there is an essentially magical attempt to coerce God to enter the host and so the communicant. Weber speaks of the Catholic priest exercising coercive power in executing the miracle of the mass.

Similarly he considered the practice of confession and absolution to be largely magical and derived from primitive divination which often seeks to diagnose the cause of troubles in terms of possession by spirits and to treat the afflicted by pacifying the possessing spirit.

As for monotheism, Weber considered Catholicism to be less mono-theistic than either Judaism or Islam, which he thought was perhaps the most strictly monotheistic religion of all. It is the doctrine of the Trinity and the cult of the Virgin Mary and the saints which makes Catholic Christianity less than wholly monotheistic. Weber regarded monotheism as to a large extent an evolutionary development and the most rational conception of the deity possible. The idea of the Trinity, while perhaps monotheistic to a considerable extent, fell somewhat short of pure monotheism, he argued. Similarly the cult of the saints qualifies Catholic monotheism. 'In practice the Roman Catholic cult of masses and saints actually comes fairly close to polytheism' (ibid., p. 138).

Catholicism represents for Weber, then, a somewhat 'backward' development in the history of the Judeo-Christian tradition. It was less rational than what had gone before. The rationalising tendencies of the tradition were only fully realised in Protestantism and particularly in Calvinistic Protestantism.

It may be thought that these views are very much Protestant influenced rather than detached and disinterested sociological views of Catholicism even though we must remember that by 'rational' Weber did *not* mean 'better', more true, admirable, desirable, and so on. Whatever position one takes on this question, however, it is clear that Weber thought the emergence of this highly rational form of Christianity, namely Calvinistic Protestantism, had very significant consequences for the development of European culture and for economic development. This is not at all to say that Catholicism and particularly the Catholic Church was not itself without significance for European development. As a relatively rationally organised bureaucratic structure it was itself an important force, Weber argues, for the rationalisation of European culture. Equally important was the ascetic tradition of the monasteries. Monastic asceticism remained, however, otherworldly and it was not until asceticism was carried out of the monasteries by Protestantism into everyday life that a fully innerworldly ascetic ethic exercised its rationalising and transforming influence.

Recent sociologically oriented work on aspects of medieval and Catholic Christianity has tended to focus on such features as the cult of saints and of the Virgin Mary and the institution of confession. Brown (1981) takes the view that the traditional picture of the cult of saints, that it represents a popularised form of Christianity which in meeting the needs of the vulgar masses deviates from the understandings of the more sophisticated and enlightened elite, is misleading. This traditional view is, of course, somewhat reminiscent of the contrast Weber frequently makes between elite and popular religion, between Mandelbaum's pragmatic and transcendental dimensions and perhaps between Redfield's great and little traditions. Thus, historians, Brown argues, have tended to explain the rise of the cult of saints in terms of 'dramatic moments of "democratisation of culture"' and consequent '"landslips" in the relation between elites and the masses' (p. 17). Again, this is all very reminiscent of Weber's analyses, in his studies of the world religions, of popular ecstatic and magical forms of religiosity being encouraged or tolerated by religious elites in order to promote quiescence, retain the support of the masses against rival creeds or simply to accommodate their religious needs. Against such a view Brown argues that the rise of the cult of saints reflects changes in the outlook of the Christian religious elite itself and was congruent with changing patterns of human relationship in late-Roman society. The attitude of the religious elite to cults of saints was in no way one of 'grudging or politic accommodation to a growing "popular" form of religion' nor 'designed to absorb leaderless pagan "masses" by a homeopathic dose of "superstition"' (ibid., p. 36). Brown sees the emergence of the cult of saints as a creative response to a new social situation and a restructuring of established beliefs to give them a 'heavier "charge" of public meaning' (ibid., p. 48). This response was in large measure the creation of upper-class culture including religious leadership. The cult of saints involved dealings with dead persons who act as intermediaries with God. Unlike angels and other spiritual intermediaries, saints had particular attributes which made them more appropriate and appealing in this role given the conditions of the time. Their popularity reflects the centrality of patron-client relationships in late-Roman society. Like a patron, the saint, although dead, was a fellow human being with whom one could identify and who acted as a protector. Augustine, in his *City of God*, had spoken of the superior ability of martyred saints above that of angels to link men to God. Augustine thus laid the foundations for a replacement of spiritual entities as the intermediaries with the divine by human intermediaries. An added attraction of saints above spiritual beings was that they were quite unlike the religious entities of paganism and offered a means by which pagan converts could distance themselves from their pagan past.

The pantheon of saints soon came to reflect, however, the status hierarchy of society. George and George (1953–5) examined the social background of the saints as recorded in Butler's *Lives of the Saints*. They note that 78 per cent were of upper-class origin – Roman Catholic sainthood, contrary to the way it might wish to present itself, is far from having been 'spiritual democracy in action' (p. 97). Focusing on the period from the fifth through the twelfth centuries, for which the same figure is rarely lower than 90 per cent, they analyse the reasons for this pattern. The disintegration of the social order during the fifth and sixth centuries left the Church and senior Church officials very often in the position of having to fill the gaps of a weak and fragmented secular authority. The Church tended to maintain this position of authority long after such conditions had been replaced by a fully functioning secular administration. The Church worked closely and intimately with secular rulers and authorities in bringing newly conquered territories under regular administration and in converting the populations to Christianity. There was little division of labour between Church and state in this respect. The senior personnel of the Church, as a consequence, came to be recruited from the same class as the secular elites and dominant social groups. Saints were predominantly those who gave service to the Church and those who exercised leadership within it. About half of the saints of this period held high office in the Church. Many others were of noble origin and therefore well placed in terms of power and wealth to aid substantially the Church in its work. Sainthood could be earned by combatting paganism and heresy by force of arms, by endowing churches and monasteries and by using position to guide subjects in the ways of orthodox Christian teaching. In this we observe a transformation of the character of sainthood. As Turner (1974) points out, sainthood in the earliest period was earned largely through martyrdom reflecting the situation of a persecuted and oppositional religious movement. In the early period, also, saints often became so by popular acclaim whereas once Christianity became the official state religion sainthood is conferred only through Papally controlled procedures of canonisation. This was the inevitable consequence, Turner argues, of the needs of an established faith and bureaucratically organised Church.

Common also, George and George point out, was the granting of sainthood to those who relinquished wealth and position in order to live the religious life. This sort of sacrifice in favour of devotion to religion was sure to earn the award of sainthood, again ensuring that saints were almost entirely drawn from the ranks of the nobility. Here again we observe a shift from the heroism of martyrdom to the dramatic but still heroic virtues of ascetic self-denial (Turner, 1974).

From the thirteenth century an increasing proportion of saints are persons of middle-class origin, the figure reaching a high level during the sixteenth and seventeenth centuries and finally accounting for the majority by the nineteenth century, reflecting the great social changes that occurred throughout this period. It was a period in which the Church was anxious to counter the threat of heresy and new religious currents and movements which were attractive to the rising middle classes. By the nineteenth century it is social services to the community of a largely secular nature that earn someone sainthood.

Alongside the cult of saints the cult of the Virgin Mary has played a central role in medieval and Catholic Christianity. It has been strongest, however, Carroll (1986) points out, in the Mediterranean region and particularly in Italy and Spain. Only these two regions experienced no anti-Marian movements at any time and also retain the cult up to the present day.

The cult appears around the fifth century and reaches its peak around the eleventh to twelfth centuries. What is particularly distinctive about it is the total disassociation of Mary from all sexuality and in this it differs from earlier cults of mother goddesses. Mary, in Church doctrine, not only conceived and gave birth as a virgin but remained permanently a virgin thereafter.

Carroll links the prominence of the Marian cult to the existence of what he calls the father-ineffective family. In this type of family authority is vested in the wife and mother. It tends to occur in circumstances in which males are economically marginal. The consequence of this type of family situation for male children is a conflict of identity and identification between mother and father. Initially male children will identify with the mother who is the strong figure and the person who exercises authority. Yet later in life they must identify with and act like males. As a result they experience a deep insecurity relating to their masculinity the response to which is an exaggerated demonstration of it giving rise to the *machismo* complex. It is significant that the geographical spread of this complex matches closely the geographical strength, intensity and persistence of the cult of Mary.

Following Freudian influenced theorists, Carroll argues that close early identification with the mother produces an intensified Oedipal desire for sexual contact with her which must be repressed.

Devotion to the mother figure of Mary on the part of males allows them to dissipate in an acceptable way the tensions built up from the repressed sexual desire for the mother. The fact that Mary is totally disassociated from sexual intercourse reflects the need to disguise the sexual content of this devotion thereby generating what is most distinctive about Mary as a mother goddess. Female devotion to Mary is similarly explained in terms of Freudian theory, penis envy and the wish for a baby from the father in compensation for not being able to acquire a penis. Desire for sexual contact with the father is reflected in the particular characteristics of Mary who received a baby from God the Father. The cult allows females the vicarious fulfilment of their Oedipal desires in an acceptable form.

This approach, Carroll maintains, helps us to understand several other features of Catholic Christianity, particularly in these regions. The emphasis on the passion of Christ, so graphically represented in images of the crucifixion, expresses and testifies to a need for punishment. This desire for punishment arises from the repressed desire for the mother. It is significant that Jesus is the son of God sent to earth in order to undergo suffering so that humankind can be redeemed from its sins. The image of the suffering son of God the Father is one which expresses the feelings of the devotees and their own desire for redemption of their sinfulness through punishment. It is also significant that the cult of self-flagellation has been prominent in Spain at various times.

As for the timing of the appearance of the cult of the Virgin Mary, Carroll argues that it was the transformation of Christianity from a minority religion, frequently subject to persecutions, to the officially recognised and dominant religion of the Empire that explains it. With this transformation of the position of Christianity after Constantine, the Roman proletariat, during the fourth and fifth centuries, was incorporated into the Church. It was this social stratum where one finds the father-ineffective family most clearly represented. It was in this period also that images of the crucifixion, as well as the cult of the Virgin Mary, became popular. It is also significant that it was at this time that celibacy of the clergy was imposed by the Church. Before the end of the fourth century various attempts had been made to make this Church policy but had failed. From the end of the fourth century through the fifth century celibacy of the clergy became established as policy.

Whatever the merit of such interpretations it is clear that penance for sins was and is a prominent feature of Catholic Christianity and is closely associated with the confession of sins. Sociological approaches to confession have, naturally, tended to emphasise its role in social control. Turner (1977), however, argues that there is more to it than that. Comparative analysis of confession and penance in the case of witchcraft and in primitive societies which shows that they serve certain social functions suggests that they did so also in medieval Catholicism. We have noted that Weber considers confession and penance to be derived ultimately from divination procedures in cases of sickness and affliction attributed to transgressions of some kind. Frequently, such transgressions involved breach of taboos and notions of pollution. Sin in such cultures was often thought to bring about affliction since it was conceived as involving pollution of the body. The affliction can be removed by removing the pollution through rites of purification which often involve confession. What is distinctive about the Christian conception of sin is that it became a pollution of the inner self rather than of the body, to be removed not by purification rites but by the cure of souls (Hepworth and Turner, 1982).

Confession and penance seemed to serve four functions according to Turner (1977). Firstly confession is therapeutic and cathartic; secondly confession and penance reconciles the sinner with the Church and thereby the community; thirdly the process of confession and undergoing penance serves to uphold social values and legitimate concepts of proper behaviour and of orthodox teaching; finally, through the expression of remorse and repentance confession allows the sinner to demonstrate a fundamental humanity and worth justifying reintegration into society.

This functionalist view, insightful as it may be, suffers from the universal fault of functional explanations in that it is only alert to one side of the picture. Confession can also play a part in disrupting human relationships. Where no common set of social values is well established, as is the case in situations of social conflict, confession can exacerbate tensions. This occurred, Turner claims, with the collapse of the feudal system in France. Turner interprets the conflict between the Jansenists and the Jesuits over confession in the eighteenth and nineteenth centuries in France in this light.

The view of confession as an instrument of social control can also be given a less functionalist interpretation and a more Marxist spin in that the control involved is that of the dominant class over subordinate classes. Turner observes that the status differential between priest and laity, confessor and penitent mirrors the hierarchy of honour and personal worth within the wider society. The priest is an authority figure and, at least in theory, a knowledgeable and qualified expert. The confessional played a role not only in upholding moral principles as defined by Christian teaching and in defending orthodoxy but also served to uphold the existing social order of dominance and subordination. It did so through internalised private guilt, the 'court of conscience'. Drawing upon Tentler's analysis (1974), Turner argues that confession occupied the central position in a system of social control and a culture of guilt.

It is a mistake, however, to take too one-sided a view in this respect, Turner concedes. Nobles and even kings had to confess their sins. Confession was more than simply a means of controlling subordinate classes but was a comprehensive system for the surveillance of conscience which operated within as well as between social classes. It was also, as Nielsen puts it, 'the great conduit for the mediation of doctrine and a central point of contact with wider currents of European civilization' (Nielsen, 1990, p. 117).

THE PROTESTANT REFORMATION

Protestantism has interested sociologists more from the point of view of its connections with modernity than from a concern to understand its causes. Weber in particular, through his famous Protestant Ethic thesis, steered sociological interest in this direction. We shall examine Weber's thesis and the enormous amount of debate and writing it has generated in the next section. First though, sociological theories of the Reformation will be reviewed.

Engels, in various writings, made a number of observations and claims concerning the Reformation.[4] He derives the essential ideas and teachings of Protestantism from the social and economic changes which were occurring during the late medieval and early modern period. He criticised the view common in his day that the events which closed the middle ages, the religious wars, were really struggles over theological matters. Engels claimed that these so-called religious wars cannot be understood apart from the structure of the society of that time and apart, specifically, from the class structure.

In the struggle against the Roman Catholic Church the class most directly interested was the rising bourgeoisie. In pursuing its interests it was bound to come into conflict with the Church and its struggle consequently became a religious struggle. The Church was a leading supporter of the feudal order against the restrictiveness of which the rising bourgeoisie had to struggle in order to remove barriers to their new activities and enterprises. Any struggle against feudal constraint was bound to take on a religious dimension at the time, Engels argued. The halo of sanctity surrounding existing social arrangements had to be stripped away before they could be attacked.

He traced the beginnings of anti-Catholic religious movements to certain heretical movements of the late middle ages such as that of the Albigenses, a religious sect which had become established in the towns of southern France and northern Italy during the twelfth and thirteenth centuries. The Albigenses or Cathars opposed the ritualism of the Catholic Church and the power, wealth and privilege of the clergy and priestly hierarchy and were ultimately the victims of severe repression by the Church. Frequently, the lesser nobility joined such movements hoping to profit from the changes they would have brought about if successful.

Many of the attitudes and demands of the Albigenses and other groups were to re-emerge later, however, in the central ideas of the Reformation: a return to the simple constitution of the early Christian Church, the abolition of an exclusive clergy and an end to the celibacy of the clergy. Just as the earlier movements, stimulated by the aspirations of the growing bourgeoisie, often attracted the lesser nobility so also did the movements unleashed by Luther and Calvin. The appeal of Luther's ideas, Engels argues, was mainly for the propertied classes and the bourgeoisie in particular. In its early stages, however, it also appealed to the masses who saw in these ideas a signal for rebellion. Early on, Luther, according to Engels, spoke in quite revolutionary terms but this was soon moderated. He quickly dropped the popular elements of his programme when he realised that he needed the support of the lesser nobility and prominent townsmen whose side he took against the peasants who rose in revolt sporadically in many parts of Germany at this time.

The nobility and the princes found in Lutheranism a useful means of freeing themselves from dependence upon the Catholic Church and acquired an excuse for confiscating Church lands and property. Luther eventually established through negotiation a religious creed acceptable to these princes and one which was well adapted, according to Engels, to absolute monarchy as a system of government.

The peasants fought on, deserted by the bourgeoisie of the towns and were eventually defeated and brutally repressed by the armies of the princes, cheered on by Luther himself who advocated that no mercy should be shown to them. Luther wrote a tract entitled *Against the Murderous and Plundering Peasant Hordes* in which he said that 'they must be knocked to pieces, strangled and stabbed, covertly and overtly, by everyone who can, just as one must kill a mad dog' (quoted in Engels, 1965, p. 52).

The result of the Lutheran Reformation was that in the long run only the princes and nobility benefited. Neither the bourgeoisie nor the peasantry gained anything. The bourgeoisie certainly did not achieve the kinds of social and political changes they had wanted.

Where Luther had failed Calvin succeeded. Calvin, according to Engels, placed the bourgeois character of the Reformation at the forefront. Calvinism was the 'true religious disguise of the bourgeoisie' (Marx and Engels, 1957, p. 236). 'The doctrine of predestination was the religious expression of the fact that in the commercial world of competition success or failure does not depend upon a man's activity or cleverness, but upon circumstances uncontrollable by him' (Marx and Engels, 1957, p. 268) – circumstances dictated by the market place.

But if the first great bourgeois upheaval, the Reformation, had taken place in Germany, the second took place in England. Its occasion was the Civil War which was brought about, Engels argues, by the middle classes of the towns but fought out by the yeomanry whose victory only ensured, in fact, their own economic ruin as a result of the consequences which followed.

This great upheaval found its appropriate doctrines in the teachings of Calvin. Once victorious, however, the compromise that the bourgeoisie made with the old nobility produced Anglicanism – a sort of Calvinised State Church. Religion now ceased to have any revolutionary importance but became a tool in the hands of the dominant class which they used to control and keep the lower classes submissive.

For Engels then, Protestantism and especially its Calvinistic forms was a set of doctrines which largely expressed and promoted the interests of the emerging bourgeoisie – a bourgeoisie which was not necessarily yet, however, a class of capitalist entrepreneurs. Engels' fellow Marxist, Karl Kautsky (1988), analysed Protestantism in a similar way as more recently has the Marxist historian Christopher Hill (1961, 1963 and 1966).

They have pointed out that the actions of artisans, petty traders and early capitalist employers in the new and growing towns in the later middle ages and early modern period may well have been determined by the exigencies of the market conditions in which they operated. We might perhaps characterise their situation along the following lines. Credit institutions and capital markets were non-existent or little developed. Rates of interest were high. Small businessmen were subject to the vagaries of the market and would have difficulty during lean times. A larger market share was one way of providing a measure of security since it gave some extra capacity that could be cut back in times of recession. To achieve this it was, of course, necessary to invest and the only feasible source of investment funds was from profits earned through hard work. Those with a predisposition for personal frugality, thrift, elimination of waste and idleness and a deprecation of self-indulgence would have been more likely to succeed. In this way the values of the spirit of capitalism might have become prevalent. Calvinistic Protestantism provided a religious expression and legitimation of such values. The position of the artisan and small business class can be contrasted against that of the nobility and landed gentry who scorned commerce. The landowner had a more secure and regular income from rents. If inflation had been a periodic threat in the feudal era, when dues tended to be fixed in amount, this was less so in the early modern period when rents had become more a matter of short-term contract. In any case, saving and thrift are no safeguard against inflation which eats away cash reserves alarmingly. There would have been little incentive for such a class to save and therefore to limit consumption. Ostentatious consumption at least earned prestige and social standing and accumulation of valuables was a hedge against inflation. These values were diametrically opposed to those of the rising bourgeoisie and anathema to them. The lifestyle of the gentleman was, however, upheld generally as the most prestigious. The values of ascetic Protestantism not only legitimated the lifestyle of the bourgeoisie but held it up to be superior to that of the dissolute aristocrat. It was precisely the *religious* backing for these values perhaps that enabled them to be held as superior to those of the still dominant class in society.

Engels and Kautsky, however, went rather too far in seeing ascetic Protestantism as entirely the product of material developments, namely the emergence of a capitalist class whose interests it expressed and legitimated. Hill is a little more sophisticated. While it was to some extent a rationalisation of the systematic pursuit of profit, the values stemmed naturally from Protestant theology. Fischoff (1944), commenting on Weber's Protestant Ethic Thesis, also saw ascetic Protestantism as nourishing the development of capitalism through its legitimation of capitalist aims, methods and modes of conduct. The capitalist could pursue his activities the more enthusiastically knowing that he was doing God's work.

There are, furthermore, empirical problems with the Marxist account of the Reformation. Andreski (1964), for example, has pointed out that it fails to explain the spread of Calvinism in Scotland or among the Hungarian nobility. Scotland especially was a country in which prevailing attitudes were quite incompatible with those of small traders and businessmen. It acquired, however, a very different set of attitudes in a relatively short time under the influence of Calvinism which 'turned the dissolute Scots into perfect examples of the worldly ascetic' (ibid., p. 192).

Somewhat different, although sharing some points of similarity, to Marxists accounts of the Reformation is the Durkheimian approach of Swanson (1967) who sees it not as the product of a rising bourgeoisie struggling against feudalism in order to further their own interests but as a reflection of certain political conditions. In such an interpretation Swanson follows the Durkheimian thesis and its implication that religious beliefs reflect the social order. This can be seen, Swanson argues, in the pattern of religious and social change at the time. Why, he asks, did some states become Protestant while others remained Catholic and why did Lutheranism prevail exclusively in some while in others Calvinism was a major influence? A crucial aspect of this pattern, according to Swanson, is the differing beliefs concerning the immanence of God in the world as opposed to a more transcendent conception of God.

The Catholic view was that God was immanent in this world to a high degree. The Church was seen as the body of God in a mystical sense – the real, concrete representation of God in the world. The Eucharist was in reality, yet mystically, the body of Christ and the sacramental wine was his blood.

The Protestants, on the other hand, saw God as absolutely transcendental, having created the world and then having withdrawn from it and being in no sense immanent in it in any way. The communion for many Protestants was simply a commemoration of the last supper and all mystical elements were removed from it.

These ideas, Swanson argues, were reflective of certain political situations. Those states which accepted Protestantism were those in which there was more than one single decision-making source, that is where the political regime did not have exclusive control of decision-making but in which certain independent or autonomous sources of power were incorporated into the decision-making process. Whenever central governments were penetrated by purposes relating to specific interest groups, that is where they became concerned with purposes other than those relating to the government itself, then Protestantism resulted. The greater was this penetration the more likely was the state to adopt Calvinism rather than Lutheranism.

The specific interest groups to which Swanson refers were the merchants and artisans. Consequently, Protestantism was a means by which they legitimated their interests and their way of life. This does not mean, however, that the Reformation was simply a product of economic changes or developments; it was the product of a very general change in the social structure which occurred at this time. What this seems to amount to, however, is the claim that Protestantism flourished in those states where merchants and businessmen were more numerous and influential and where as a consequence there would have been greater opposition to the Church, to feudalism and to all those restrictions associated with it, which is a view not that different from Engels'.

Another more important factor, however, than the strength of the mercantile class, according to Wuthnow (1985), was the relationship between the central state bureaucracy and the landed nobility. Wuthnow subjects Swanson's analysis to trenchant criticism. Swanson only establishes, or alleges to establish, correlations between social structures and religious ideas. The mechanism by which people's experience of social structures become translated into theological conceptions and religious ideology remains vague in Swanson's account. The possibilities are that people generally were more receptive to the ideas of Protestantism in circumstances where they had experienced decentralised political structures or that the ideas of the religious reformers were shaped as a result of their experience of authority patterns.

The first suggestion suffers from the problem that most people at the time were remote from the relevant political authorities and structures and had little knowledge of them. The actual experience of government was, according to Davis (1971), quite diverse in many of these regimes and would not have supported a uniform religious expression. Ozment (1975), while acknowledging that the nature of regimes may have played a significant part in the success or otherwise of the Reformation, does not believe that it explains the general appeal of Protestantism. Centralised regimes tended to be closed to religious change and to remain Catholic while decentralised regimes were more tolerant of change and more susceptible to the Reformation. This accounts for Swanson's correlations but it does not follow that the adoption of the new Protestant ideas were an expression of regime structure.

The second suggestion that Wuthnow identifies places undue emphasis upon psychological dispositions of individuals to the neglect of the social processes which govern the emergence and entrenchment of ideas and ideologies.

Another major set of weaknesses of Swanson's study that Wuthnow points out concern his methodology. He leaves out of account a great number of cases that could have been included: minor principalities are given the same weight as large states; the cases are not by any means all independent of one another; the classification procedures are, in many instances, very dubious. Davis (1971) has also questioned the basis upon which the regimes were classified; some of those classified as centralist manifested in her opinion quite a diversity of relatively autonomous local decision-making bodies and centres of authority.

Wuthnow offers an alternative explanation based upon a more focused examination of just two instances, England and France. Why did the Reformation succeed in England but not in France? Wuthnow's answer is that in England the state was more autonomous relative to the landed nobility which gave it great flexibility in determining religious policies and in promoting religious change. In France the state was far more dependent upon the landed elites whose interests were bound up with the preservation of Catholicism and the Church.

Such an approach, Wuthnow argues, allows us to see ideologies, and he would include religious and theological ideas in this, not as subjective beliefs but as constitutive of social orders. Ideologies must be maintained and promoted and this requires resources and organisational structures. His approach stresses the embeddedness of ideology in social arrangements and the consequent necessity of appropriate social conditions for ideological change to take place. In the case of the Reformation, the crucial social circumstances which determined success were the relationships between state bureaucracies and landed nobility.

Wuthnow's view has been challenged by Moaddel (1989) who points out that his theory rests upon the assumption that the state has an interest in the Reformation and religious change. Nowhere does Wuthnow establish this fact. To argue that a weak French state was unable to further the Reformation because of its dependence on the landed nobility one has to show that the French state wished to further the Reformation in the first place. But Wuthnow's aim, as Garrett (1990) points out, is rather more limited than that of Swanson. Swanson sought to demonstrate why certain states adopted Protestant ideas while Wuthnow is only concerned to show how it was possible for them to succeed in adopting Protestantism should they have an interest in doing so. Even so, Wuthnow's concentration on just two cases does not help his argument in this respect. In order to show that it was not possible where the state was weak he needed to show that Protestantism failed in such circumstances despite the desire of the state to foster it or at least where it would have been in the interests of the state to have adopted it.

A further criticism of Wuthnow that Moadell makes is that the state in England was certainly not autonomous relative to mercantile interests. He suggests that a straightforward class theory of the Reformation is preferable to Wuthnow's, reflecting the view of Engels. Wuthnow, in his reply to this, acknowledges that the class factor is an important one but considers that it explains very little; only the propensity of the merchants to support the religious reformers and that of the landed nobility to oppose them. It fails, on the other hand, to answer a whole host of other questions such as why did rulers in England, Saxony, Denmark and Hesse, who derived as landowners much income from their land, side nevertheless with the reformers, and why did landowners who were moving to more capitalistic methods of exploiting it and who were channelling their profits into new commercial ventures, nevertheless support the Church?

An interpretation which places rather more emphasis upon psychological variables in the Reformation is that of Walzer (1963). During a period of rapid and far-reaching social change and disruption, he argues, individuals suffer psychological pressures. Walzer stresses what he regards as among the most fundamental aspects of the mentality of the time, and which can be seen most clearly in Puritanism, namely its 'nervous lust for systematic repression and control' (ibid., p. 111). This derived from a basic psychological insecurity and deep fear of disorder and chaos. Puritanism flourished during a period of instability and social change. There had been a breakdown of the habitual system of conventions and routines. In conditions like this many tend to panic and to suffer extreme anxiety.

Puritanism was one response to the disorder and fear – a way of organising to overcome the sense of chaos – whereas others, of a different personality, thrived in the fluid situation. The Puritan response was one of self-discipline, the repression of desires and an attempt to bring everything under rigid control; not only all instincts and passions but all aspects of life and society. And they sought to impose such regulation on other men. This made them political activists who sought to transform the social order. This reaction was largely directed at the old order which they saw as lax and corrupt and which had to be swept away before a properly regulated society and way of life could be achieved.

The repressive attitudes of the Puritan mentality can be seen clearly in its attitude to the family, Walzer argues.

The insistence upon the absolute sovereignty of the father and upon the family as an institution for repressing and disciplining naturally wicked, licentious and rebellious children derives in both cases from an extraordinary fear of disorder and anarchy. (ibid., p. 126)

Another manifestation of this was the prevalence of witchcraft beliefs in many Puritan communities. Such beliefs tended to rise dramatically during the period when Puritanism was flourishing.

In the long run Puritanism was to decline. The Puritans failed to establish their Holy Commonwealth. This was because, Walzer argues, the circumstances which caused so much anxiety tended to stabilise. People became used to a new way of life. 'When men stopped being afraid, or became less afraid, then Puritanism was suddenly irrelevant' (ibid., p. 128).

To a considerable degree Walzer's characterisation of Puritanism is aimed at Weber's famous Protestant Ethic Thesis and its claim that the mentality of Calvinistic Protestantism was conducive to the growth of rational capitalism in the West. It is to this thesis that we now turn.

THE PROTESTANT ETHIC DEBATE

Whatever the causes of the Reformation its impact upon European society was profound. In his celebrated thesis, Weber argued that certain forms of Protestantism had, in fact, a dramatic impact in promoting a distinctive type of capitalism, rational capitalism, characterised by an enormously dynamic and thrusting potential for expansion. Capitalism of this type was exported from Europe worldwide and has now come to dominate the global economy.

It is vital to note that religion of a certain type was, according to Weber, a necessary but not a sufficient condition for the emergence of this type of capitalism. A number of other material factors were crucial to this outcome. He is very cautious in *The Protestant Ethic and the Spirit of Capitalism* and indeed somewhat tentative and it is easy to overstate his claim. Interpretations of what, precisely, this claim is vary but the view taken here is that broadly his thesis is that certain forms of Protestant religion may have been a necessary condition for the vigour and expansive potential of capitalism, not for its original appearance.

Protestantism, or more accurately ascetic forms of Protestantism best exemplified by Calvinism, did not stimulate capitalism directly, Weber argued, but through the medium of the 'spirit of capitalism'.

This spirit of modern capitalism is thus itself an ethos rather than a set of actual practices but which informed practice and the way early capitalists went about their business. It had, Weber argues, a close affinity with the ethos and values of Calvinistic and related forms of Protestantism, 'the Protestant ethic'. This ethic of ascetic Protestantism was entirely compatible with modern rational capitalism. It did not inhibit the pursuit of profit or its maximisation. Capitalists could go about the business of profit-making with an easy conscience, vigour and enthusiasm in the knowledge that they were carrying out God's wishes (Fischoff, 1944). More than this, ascetic Protestantism actually enjoined the capitalist to pursue and maximise profits as a duty.

At the outset of his essay Weber notes that certain religious affiliations are frequently associated with business success, capital wealth, and so on. It has frequently been commented, he points out, that those who have been economically successful seem often to have been Protestant. Economic development occurred first and to a greater extent in Protestant than in Catholic countries and regions. Some connection thus seemed to exist between Protestantism and capitalism.

In making such observations Weber makes it clear that he is concerned with *rational capitalism* or 'the rational capitalistic organisation of (formally) free labour' (1930, p. 21) which he clearly distinguishes from other types of capitalism which have existed throughout history and in many cultures. Adventure and political capitalism have not been uncommon in the past. Rational capitalism has been much less common and has flourished only in the modern era beginning in parts of Northern Europe.

Underlying this modern European rational capitalism is the spirit of capitalism the character of which can be seen particularly clearly in the writings of Benjamin Franklin. Weber uses the words of Franklin in his study in order to portray this spirit in its purest, that is to say ideal–typical, form. Significantly, Franklin came from a society which was still largely agrarian and was not himself a Puritan of any description. One might consider that this allows Weber to imply that the spirit of capitalism as an ethos could exist independently of capitalism itself as an economic system and consequently as a causal factor which promoted it.

Central to the spirit of capitalism is the work ethic; time spent in idleness rather than devoted to increasing income was wasted. Time is money as Franklin put it. Not only this but since the income that could have been earned during the period of idleness was clearly not necessary for survival and since it could have therefore been saved and a further return on it earned, time spent in idleness is wasted many times over.

The spirit of capitalism further enjoins the maximisation of profit through continuous and optimal use of resources; not simply because it is prudent to do so but as a duty. More than this, the pursuit of ever renewed profit through reinvestment of the maximum available resources above modest and customary levels of consumption was upheld as an ideal. Profits were often dissipated in the pre-modern era through lavish living and extravagance. The spirit of capitalism regards such consumption and dissipation of capital as almost morally reprehensible. Again, money spent on luxuries was lost many times over, Franklin said, because once spent it could not be multiplied.

Systematic, rational pursuit of profit for its own sake required, further, that all waste be eliminated, costs cut wherever possible and all available resources fully utilised and in a manner which would earn the maximum return on them. Careful calculation of cost in relation to returns and accurate book-keeping were essential to such endeavours.

All this was, however, more than just good business sense and practice or a set of sound principles for ensuring success; it was, Weber states, a true ethic. 'The earning of money within the modern economic order, is, so long as it is done legally, the result and the expression of virtue and proficiency in a calling...' (ibid., pp. 53–4).

This ethos was one which was peculiar to Western capitalism. While the desire to make money was natural enough and universal in human society and history the requirements of the spirit of capitalism were not ones which came naturally to human beings. The patterns of economic conduct typically found in pre-modern societies Weber terms traditionalism. In such societies the tendency has always been to work only as long as is necessary to satisfy customary needs and expectations. Such is the situation still in many Third World countries today. Also no man *by nature* wishes to earn more and more for its own sake, according to Weber. In itself this would be a pointless pattern of conduct and it must, therefore, rest upon some other basis.

If the careful and systematic pursuit of money accompanied by an emphasis upon restraint in its use in consumption was neither a mode of conduct that is common nor one which people readily adopt then it had to be the product of very particular conditions. In fact, Weber says, the desire to make money when divorced from such an ethic is correlated with an absence of rational capitalist development. 'The universal reign of absolute unscrupulousness in the pursuit of selfish interests by the making of money has been a specific characteristic of precisely those countries where bourgeois–capitalistic development, measured according to Occidental standards, has remained backward' (ibid., p. 57).

The spirit of capitalism, then, was a new, distinctive and powerful force which transformed those societies in which it came to prevail. It was characteristic of the rising stratum of the lower industrial middle class who upheld the ideal of the expression of virtue and proficiency in a calling, an ideal which had its roots ultimately in religious sources.

The notion of the calling, while not entirely absent from Catholic thought, was in certain aspects and emphases essentially a product of the Reformation. In its Protestant interpretation it became something distinctive in Weber's view: '... the valuation of the fulfilment of duty in worldly affairs as the highest form which the moral activity of the individual could assume' (ibid., p. 80). It imparted a religious significance to mundane activity which Weber contrasts with that of Catholicism. The only acceptable way of life from the point of view of ascetic Protestantism was one which did not look always to a world beyond but rather to express one's faith in and through the obligations imposed by one's existence in this world. Such an ethos was in stark contrast to both Catholic and Lutheran attitudes, according to Weber.

The notion of the calling was one which had, in fact, been emphasised by Luther but in his interpretation it had, on the whole, rather conservative and traditionalistic implications. The individual, according to Luther, 'should remain once and for all in the station and calling in which God had placed him and should restrain his worldly activity within the limits imposed by his established station in life' (ibid., p. 85). Obedience to authority and acceptance of the way things were was central to the Lutheran outlook which did not contribute in any direct way to the development of the spirit of capitalism according to Weber.

The impact of the notion of the calling, then, only fostered the spirit of capitalism in its Calvinistic interpretation even though there was no intention whatever on Calvin's part that it should do so. The impact of Calvin's teachings and those of his followers was entirely unintended and unforeseen. Other groups with strong Calvinistic influences in their theologies that were significant in promoting the more radical idea of the calling included the Pietists, the Baptist sects and Methodism.

It was the specifically Calvinist emphasis upon predestination and *sola fide* (salvation by faith alone and not by works) which combined with the idea of the calling gave it such a radical impact. The doctrine that no one can earn or do anything to ensure salvation which is absolutely and entirely the predetermined gift of God generated extreme anxiety in the individual believer. Feelings of helplessness and uncertainty motivated intense desire to be reassured of salvation. It was not sufficient simply to trust in God as Calvin himself had taught. Consequently, Calvinist pastoral preachers developed the teaching that the devout could seek a sign that they were among the chosen, the elect. The sign they might be given was that of worldly success in their calling. They were enjoined, also, to attain a state of self-confidence in their elect status by engaging in intense worldly activity which would help to dispel doubt and anxiety. Although the official doctrine maintained that salvation could not be earned and that worldly success was merely a sign and hard work merely a means of dispelling doubt, in effect Calvinists came to believe that they had to prove themselves before God in their daily work and vocation in life. Combined with the belief that God had placed us in this world not for our own benefit and pleasure but solely to carry out his commandments, this led to a complete rationalisation of life conduct. 'The moral conduct of the average man was thus deprived of its planless and unsystematic character and subjected to a consistent method for conduct as a whole' (ibid., p. 117).

Catholicism, in Weber's view, could never have had the kind of impact that ascetic Protestantism had since central to it were ideas of atonement and remission of sin through confession and penance. No psychological tensions were generated in the believer by such an emphasis; there was no necessity of proof before God, as there was for Calvinists, through unceasing devotion to one's worldly calling. The nature, also, of some of the Protestant sects influenced by Calvinism fostered a similar attitude to worldly duty in that members of them felt a strong pressure to prove themselves before other members as well as before God. This was a theme which Weber developed further in a slightly later essay on the Protestant sects.[5] These sects were exclusive in outlook limiting membership to those who were religiously qualified or eligible. Within the sect behaviour was more strictly regulated than in the churches. Being small, the regulation of conduct and appraisal of qualification for membership was the mutual responsibility of members. Sect members thus had to prove their virtue in order to be accepted within the group and to maintain their membership. An emphasis upon asceticism and the proof of worth through devotion to worldly calling, combined with this constant watching over one another, produced very similar consequences to those of the Calvinistic churches with respect to the promotion of a spirit of capitalism.

Ascetic Protestantism, then, focused religious attention towards the everyday world in contrast to the ethos of medieval Catholicism the asceticism of which tended to retreat from the everyday world into the monasteries. 'Now it strode into the market place and slammed the monastery door behind it' (ibid., p. 154). The implications of this transformation were greater than any other major development in European culture in Weber's view. 'Such a powerful, unconsciously refined organisation for the production of capitalistic individuals has never existed in any other church or religion, and in comparison with it what the Renaissance did for capitalism shrinks into insignificance' (1961, p. 270). Accumulation of wealth and capital was inevitable given such an emphasis upon hard work and profit maximisation, but ascetic Protestantism was opposed to the over-enjoyment of wealth and luxury; this would mean a life of idleness and temptation. Puritanism held sensual indulgence to be both sinful and irrational since it was not devoted to the sole end of glorifying God and fulfilling his commandments.

Profits above a modest level, then, had to be reinvested; the inevitable result was a growing accumulation of capital which is the key to economic breakthrough to continuous growth and the driving force of the modern economic system.

> When the limitation of consumption is combined with this release of acquisitive activity, the inevitable practical result is obvious: accumulation of capital through ascetic compulsion to save. The restraints which were imposed upon the consumption of wealth served to increase it by making possible the productive investment of capital. (Weber, 1930, p. 172)

> ... when asceticism was carried out of monastic cells into everyday life, and began to dominate worldly morality, it did its part in building the tremendous cosmos of the modern economic order. (ibid., p. 181)

Once an economy has made the breakthrough to continuous growth it no longer needs the stimulus of a Protestant ethic or, for that matter, a spirit of capitalism. It continues to exist and to flourish under its own dynamic. Ascetic Protestantism helped to create a creature, if unintentionally, which had no further need of its creator and in the process sowed the seeds, also, of its own demise in promoting the forces of secularisation through its promotion of worldly activity and concern. Once this had generated economic prosperity, continuous expansion of wealth and enhancement of material wellbeing, concerns turned increasingly away from God and religion. Calvinistic Protestantism was in many respects its own gravedigger.

Critics and Defenders of the Protestant Ethic Thesis

It is perhaps the boldness of Weber's thesis that has inspired such long running debate and unflagging interest. More words have been printed on this issue than almost any other in sociology. Other theses, however, may have been as bold but have not retained such intense interest. Another factor has been that the issue is one which goes to the very heart of the endeavour to understand society and social life. It addresses an issue of general and fundamental importance, namely the role of ideas in history and in shaping human society. Weber seemed to be providing a counter to the materialist conception of history and thereby to Marx in emphasising a religious factor in the process of historical development and change. However, Marshall (1982) has shown that it was not so much Marx that Weber had in mind but rather Sombart who had argued that capitalism owed its development to the Jews.

Whatever the truth of Marshall's claim, it is clear that Weber certainly did not hold a view that ideas alone could shape the course of history nor did he deny 'the influence of economic development on the fate of religious ideas' and was concerned to show how while 'religious ideas themselves simply cannot be deduced from economic circumstances... a mutual adaptation of the two took place' (Weber, 1930, pp. 277–8). His thesis is far from being an idealist explanation of the origins of modern capitalism:

> we have no intention whatever of maintaining such a foolish and doctrinaire thesis as that the spirit of capitalism could only have arisen as the result of certain effects of the Reformation, or even that capitalism as an economic system is a creation of the Reformation ... On the contrary, we only wish to ascertain whether and to what extent religious forces have taken part in the qualitative formation and the quantitative expansion of that spirit over the world... In view of the tremendous confusion of interdependent influences between the material basis, the forms of social and political organisation, and the ideas current in the time of the Reformation, we can

only proceed by investigating whether and at what points certain correlations between forms of religious belief and practical ethics can be worked out. At the same time we shall as far as possible clarify the manner and the general *direction* in which, by virtue of those relationships, the religious movements have influenced the development of modern culture. (ibid., p. 91).

Weber's emphasis upon both a set of material conditions necessary for the emergence of a vigorous rational capitalism and also the motivational factors provided by the Protestant ethic and its offspring, the spirit of capitalism, allows him to sidestep many potential criticisms. This has not prevented many of his critics from misunderstanding him and as a consequence, citing evidence against the thesis which does not in fact count against it. In some ways Weber's caution and emphasis on multiple factors in the emergence of modern rational capitalism makes it very difficult to falsify his thesis, as MacKinnon (1993) implies in speaking of his causal pluralism. Consequently, arguments that point out, for example, that while the first capitalist countries may have been Protestant not all Protestant countries were capitalist, that there is no simple relationship between Protestantism and capitalism nor any clear pattern in the relationship between them, that the Protestant countries show considerable variation in the extent of their development and not all Puritan communities were economically advanced (Samuelsson, 1961), can all be easily dismissed as missing the point. They neglect the fact that Weber quite clearly and explicitly states that it was not only Calvinistic Protestantism that was important for the development of rational capitalism but that many other factors were also important. Variations in the occurrence of these other factors account for variations in the strength and the pattern of development of capitalism in different regions at different times. Reference to a spirit of enterprise and innovation associated with economic enterprise and advance in Renaissance Italy or the Hanseatic towns, which pre-dated the Reformation (Samuelsson, 1961; Tawney, 1938) is thus ruled out of court as no refutation of Weber. The fact that in Calvinistic Scotland capitalism did not develop until relatively late is similarly an irrelevant observation.

Much of the power of Weber's thesis lies in its plausibility. But plausibility is no substitute for verification. Plausibility, in any case, it has been argued, may well be an artefact of Weber's method which relies heavily on the use of ideal types (Robertson, 1970, pp. 172–3). Weber's notions of the spirit of capitalism and the Protestant ethic are distillations or essences which he does not claim actually to have existed in reality in this pure form. The ideal-type method which Weber uses throughout his work removes, it is claimed, all factors extraneous to the hypothesis to be tested. Any relationship between the ideal types which can be shown to exist will also hold in reality *to the extent that* reality approaches these types. Use of this method is a way of overcoming the fact that controlled experiment is usually impossible in sociology but it entails the problem that selectivity creeps in when defining the types in the first place. An unconscious selection of elements is made such that the two concepts are in effect the same thing, thereby rendering empirical claims tautologous (Marshall, 1982).

This need not necessarily be fatal for Weber's thesis, however, since its claim is that it is rational capitalism that has been promoted by the Protestant ethic/spirit of capitalism complex. The spirit of capitalism as the practical expression in the context of business activity of the religious ethic of ascetic Protestantism could still have provided an independent motivational complex which stimulated the development of capitalism as a system of action.

Perhaps a more telling criticism of Weber is that nowhere does he offer any concrete evidence of the kind that would provide a test of the thesis. Also, despite it attracting so much interest there have been remarkably few attempts to verify or refute it empirically. An exception is that of Marshall (1980) who sets out to ascertain whether (a) Calvinistic and ascetic Protestants did in general behave in accordance with the Protestant ethic, (b) non-Protestants behaved differently, (c) early capitalistic entrepreneurs were predominantly Calvinistic Protestants, (d) such people were indeed imbued with the spirit of capitalism, (e) this spirit did indeed derive from ascetic Protestantism, and (f) they did in fact conduct their businesses in accordance with the spirit of capitalism. Marshall attempts to answer these questions in the context of sixteenth- and seventeenth-century North Eastern Scotland. Calvinist pastoral teaching during this period in Scotland, he reports, was very much as Weber had portrayed it. Capitalists in this part of Scotland at the time did conduct their business in accordance with the spirit of capitalism. There is also evidence, he claims, though not sufficient to establish the point firmly, that the attitudes of capitalists to the conduct of business did stem from their Calvinist faith.[6] On balance, Marshall considers this case does provide fairly good grounds for supporting the general thrust of Weber's thesis at least as far as the business class is concerned. This cannot be said, however, for the attitudes and conduct of the labouring classes, since there is very little available evidence relating to these things.

In a later study, on the other hand, Marshall (1982) questions many of the assumptions upon which Weber's thesis is founded. A central weakness of Weber's procedure, he argues, is that it attributes motives and understandings to the actions of rational capitalist businessmen not on the basis of sound evidence but through inference on the basis of an examination of their behaviour. This is not a legitimate procedure, Marshall points out; it is necessary to provide evidence which is independent of observed actions. In the absence of such evidence we cannot be sure that it was the Protestant ethic or the spirit of capitalism which guided behaviour rather than the exigencies of the situation faced by those in question. Neither can we assume anything concerning the alleged traditionalism of medieval businessmen from the way they acted (ibid., pp. 108–19). Conspicuous consumption, luxury and acquisition of valuable possessions might, for example, have been the most rational use of wealth given the prevailing conditions of market and political uncertainty rather than being motivated by status considerations or a desire for self aggrandisement. Investment in gold, jewellery, fine houses, and so on may have been the best way to preserve wealth in an uncertain world in which opportunities for other forms of investment were limited. We cannot conclude from their actions that those who led such a lifestyle were any the less imbued with a spirit of enterprise than the most frugal and diligent Calvinist Protestant.

Much the same could be said with respect to the 'traditionalism' of labour in pre-capitalist economies (ibid., pp. 126–31). Motives are here again imputed on the basis of observed behaviour. But in a situation of scarcity of consumer goods upon which to spend earnings there is not much point in earning more than needed for basic and customary standards of life. In such circumstances leisure will be chosen in preference to greater income.

Walzer (1963) has similarly questioned Weber's characterisation of the values of Protestantism. What is striking about ascetic Protestantism, he argues, is its stress upon control and regulation of conduct. Protestants seem to manifest a need to bring passions and desires under rigid control. It is significant that Protestantism arose at a time of change and disorder which tended to generate anxieties and fears of potential disorder and threats to the stability of life. The values of Protestantism were in this respect quite unlike those that Weber attributes to it and would not be particularly conducive to rational capitalistic behaviour. There is more mileage in Weber's essay on the sects than in the Protestant ethic in Walzer's view. Because members of the sects were always being watched by one another for probity in all aspects of life, businessmen often preferred to do business with them as they could rely upon their scrupulous honesty. This character of Puritan congregations again testifies to the desire to impose order stimulated by feelings of constant suspicion and distrust which led to collective vigilance against temptation. Control and regulation of desire was, then, not so much motivated by the conviction that one must live daily life in accordance with God's intentions but rather by fear and insecurity. Puritans and ascetic Protestants were, as a consequence, rather conservative in outlook.

One might argue against Walzer that insecurity and anxiety are not necessarily inhibitive of hard work in the pursuit of a calling. In some ways they might be seen as simply the other side of the coin in contrast to the values of Protestantism that Walzer emphasises. It must be remembered that Weber does acknowledge the psychological insecurity that the doctrine of predestination tended to induce which hard work in the pursuit of one's calling could help to dispel according to the pastoral teachings of Calvinist preachers.

Other critics of Weber have argued that it was not so much Protestantism as a set of religious doctrines that contributed to the development of rational capitalism so much as the marginal position of some Protestants, particularly Calvinists, who were minorities in their societies (Tawney, 1938; Trevor-Roper, 1967). This position of marginality, it is argued, encouraged innovation and individualism – values which were congruent with rational capitalist activity – while exclusion from traditional occupations stimulated the development of new types of economic activity. The fact that Catholic minorities did not succeed in business or acquire the values of the spirit of capitalism, which Weber himself had pointed out, would seem to work against this view. Luethy (1964) points out, however, that Catholic minorities, despite their position, were not actually in dissent against a long dominant tradition as were Protestants. For Luethy it was the dissenting nature of Protestantism, especially where it was a minority faith, that gave it its dynamism, not any specific set of religious or theological views. He points out that Protestants were not only successful in commerce and business but in many spheres of life. It was not the Protestant Reformation *per se* that accounted for the dynamism, innovative capacity and new outlook upon life of many Protestants. Throughout much of Catholic Europe a new ethos, new attitudes and innovative ideas were blossoming even before the Reformation. In those parts of Europe which remained Catholic, however, this new spirit was eclipsed by the Counter Reformation which stifled initiative and enthusiasm for change. This ethos of change survived in many places where the Protestant Reformation had been successful and which remained, therefore, immune to the effects of the Counter Reformation. Areas which before the Counter Reformation had, in fact, been among the most progressive and dynamic, such as northern Italy, stagnated as a result of the restrictions imposed under its regime.

It was the relative autonomy and independence of the rising bour-geoisie which enabled them to resist the pressures of the Counter Reformation in many Catholic areas, according to Luethy. Other, more dependent, groups were unable to stick to the new faith. The Huguenots in France offer an example of a minority group that was able to hold out against the Catholic Church and state. Their bour-geois character gave them not only the independence to do this but combined with their minority position made such people a great force for change. 'The significance of Calvinism in world history lies in the fact that it failed to win political power and thereby remained almost free of political-opportunistic considerations and princely usurpations' (Luethy, 1964, pp. 102–3). Luethy, therefore, agrees with Weber that ascetic Protestants did indeed have a new mentality but this was the product not of their theology but of their social location. They answered only to God and their conscience and bowed to no human authority. They were a 'yeast in the Western world, the most active agents of the development towards a modern Western society in which "capitalism" is but one strand among many' (Luethy, 1964, p.103).

Also sceptical of Weber's characterisation of the impact of the doctrines of Calvinism in generating the spirit of capitalism is the work of MacKinnon (1988a, 1988b, 1993). For MacKinnon, not only was Calvinist theology not the source of the spirit of capitalism but it could not be since it was not what Weber claimed it to be. Calvinism, as opposed to the ideas of Calvin, effectively abandoned the doctrines of predestination and *sola fide* except in only the most formal sense and could not therefore have induced the psychological tension and anxiety that Weber claims required Calvinist preachers to provide a means of resolving through the notion of signs of proof of salvation and immersion in the duties of the calling. This was not just a feature of pastoral teaching but also of theologically authoritative doctrine. The adoption of covenant theology in the Calvinist commu-nities offered, by the time of the Westminster synod, in effect infallible assurance of salvation to all who sincerely and earnestly sought it. This divested Calvinism of any crisis of proof of election. The believer is no longer a passive and helpless recipient of God's grace but holds responsibility for his or her salvation in his or her own hands. The essential requisite is the will for salvation.

MacKinnon further argues that the dominant emphasis in Calvinism was not upon this-worldly works but upon other-worldly, that is to say spiritual and religious, works in the form of acts of piety, devotion, humility and so on. In these respects Calvinism became indistinguishable from Catholicism and Lutheranism. In his characterisation of Calvinism, Weber slides over these facts, MacKinnon argues, and accuses him of considerable sleight of hand amounting almost to intellectual dishonesty.

MacKinnon has himself been severely criticised for gross selectivity in the use of documents. Zaret (1993) charges him with failure to observe any of the rules that should govern the use of documentary evidence; ensuring unbiased sampling of passages, highlighting crucial passages that conflict with the interpretation being offered, finding independent corroborative evidence for judgements relating to the behavioural and psychological impact of beliefs and giving due attention to the context in which and the purposes for which the document was produced. Care of this kind in examining the relevant texts reveals that MacKinnon's characterisation of Calvinist teaching is disastrously one-sided. Zaret readily admits, however, that the sources are quite contradictory containing both deterministic and voluntaristic elements. MacKinnon, he feels, was wrong to focus only on the voluntaristic dimension to the neglect of the deterministic which Zaret considers to be predominant.

Lessnoff (1994) also finds a high degree of ambiguity and contradiction in Calvinist teaching using much the same sources as MacKinnon and Zaret. Lessnof distinguishes between the work ethic and the profit ethic within the spirit of capitalism, conceptualising the former extremely broadly to include a general self-denying asceticism, desire for freedom from sin, particularly the sin of idleness, and moral conduct. Contradiction was inherent in Calvinism, according to Lessnoff. If salvation really is by faith alone and not by works how can moral conduct be ensured? Calvinism found itself in the position where it had to simultaneously uphold the dogma of *sola fide* and deny it through its emphasis on good works and worldly success as a sign of election.

What the Calvinist preachers taught in this predicament was that although all are equally sinners and God will choose those he will save, a sign of election can be found not so much in actual worldly success, as Weber stated, but in the striving against sin, including the sins of idleness and waste. The elect were not those without sin but those who constantly struggled to overcome it. This would, according to Lessnoff, have provided just as strong a motivation for hard work as Weber's criterion of success.

As for the injunction to maximise profits, Lessnoff finds less evidence. Calvinist teaching was equally contradictory on this subject because it faced a similar dilemma to that posed by the doctrine of predestination and salvation by faith. Clearly those who prospered did not always do so through upright conduct and vice versa. A variety of attempts were made to resolve this contradiction; for example, that the sinner may prosper for a while but not in the long run or that poverty was the way God sometimes tests our faith and so on. All of these attempted resolutions worked only at the cost of undermining the link between prosperity and election which was nevertheless reasserted in other contexts. Calvinism was simply unable to provide any consistent answer to these dilemmas.

What is important for the development of rational capitalism, however, is not so much the link between prosperity and election as the direct emphasis upon the duty to seek worldly profit. Was there such an emphasis in Calvinist teaching, Lessnoff asks? Again we find inconsistency. What tends to predominate is the notion of 'stewardship' – the use of God's gifts wisely. While very different from medieval attitudes in that it approved of the pursuit of wealth if done for the right reasons, this does not really amount to a full-blown profit ethic. It allows the pursuit of wealth but does not enjoin it. Also, the aim of wealth seeking in Calvinist teaching is clearly to be able to carry out works of charity, other-worldly works as MacKinnon expresses it. In other words it encourages the dissipation of wealth rather than its accumulation. There was, also, a marked anti-profit ethic in Calvinist teaching which was even more prominent, in Lessnoff's view, than any positive profit ethic. Calvinism was strongly opposed to wealth seeking since this would lead to idleness, temptation and immorality. Despite this emphasis in the works of theology and pastoral preaching Lessnoff turns to a source not much utilised previously, namely catechisms, to see if there is any evidence there of a profit ethic in Calvinism. Many reveal no such ethic but the most common one in use, the Westminster Assembly shorter catechism, does provide a gloss on the eighth commandment which forbids the coveting of the wealth of others. This takes the form of an injunction to further one's own estate. On this basis he concludes that it is possible that Calvinist teaching could have induced, albeit unintentionally, a profit ethic through the widespread use of this catechism the relevant part of which tended to be interpreted and understood by believers in a certain way.

This is unconvincing. Why should it be interpreted in this way against the intentions of its authors and against all the other sources and teaching which stressed an anti-profit ethic. It could, of course, have been a rationalisation of a motive and attitude which already existed but if this were so then the motive underlying capitalist accumulation would not derive from ascetic Protestantism.

Theological treatises, pastoral texts and even catechisms tell us about a particular section of the Calvinist communities, namely the religious leadership. They tell us little about the way these ideas were received, understood and interpreted by ordinary believers or the practical impact they had upon the conduct of such people. For such information, Greyerz (1993) points out, we need to turn to autobiographies and diaries. From a study of materials of this kind Greyerz reports that the dominant outlook of ordinary Calvinists was one which emphasised God's providence and readiness to intervene to assist the devout in mundane concerns and problems. This modifies significantly the picture of the remote and inscrutable God that other Calvinist sources have given us.

Whether this undermines the claims of Weber's Protestant ethic thesis Greyerz declines to say but his work clearly adds to doubts that other recent scholarship has raised concerning the nature of Calvinist thought or its interpretation by relevant actors. The debate over the Protestant ethic thesis seems, in any case, set to run and run for some time to come.

8 Islam

WEBER ON ISLAM

Weber always intended to carry out a study of Islam to complete his set
of studies of the major non-Christian religions but never managed to
do so. There are, however, scattered throughout his writings, many
observations and references to Islam. From these fragmented materials
Bryan Turner (1974), has attempted to reconstruct Weber's analysis of
Islam to comment on its theoretical implications and significance and
to subject it to critical appraisal.

As in his other studies, Turner points out, Weber was careful to
analyse in his work on Islam the degree to which political, economic,
and military factors tended to inhibit the development of industrial
capitalism and the attitudes that go with it rather than simply explore
the impact of the religious ethic. He was also concerned with the way in
which the dominant attitudes associated with a particular religious
ethic themselves arise out of a specific set of social circumstances;
even more concerned than he was to assess the extent to which
these attitudes would have inhibited the development of rational capitalism.

Weber's position on Islam, according to Turner, was that a certain
set of attitudes, such as hedonism, fatalism, conservatism, and so on,
were incompatible with rational capitalism but that these attitudes
were dominant because of the character of Islamic society. They were
predominant because of the existence of a patrimonial bureaucracy
and because of the interests of an Arabic warrior group which was the
social carrier of the world view of this society.

Weber was concerned mostly with these political and social factors
and treated values and attitudes as secondary and dependent upon
Islamic social conditions. In this, Turner argues, Weber does not differ
dramatically from the position of Marx and Engels on the Asiatic
mode of production.

In attempting to show all this Turner covers a number of aspects of
Weber's approach to religion in general, and Islam in particular, from
a critical perspective. In enables him to raise a series of theoretical
issues relating to Weber's sociology and the sociology of Islam. The
greater part of the book is, in fact, devoted to these broader theoretical
concerns and wider issues which arise out of a critical appreciation of

222   *Sociology and the World's Religions*

Weber's work. We are concerned here, however, with Turner's recon-
struction of Weber's analysis of Islam.

The essence of Weber's position, as Turner sees it, is that Weber
considered Islam to be initially the product of pure charismatic prophecy exemplified in Muhammad. But to win support for his vision
Muhammad needed to link it to a set of material interests of a particular group in the society. All prophetic inspiration has to give proof of
its insights and this proof has to be in a form which convinces potential
followers that there is some benefit to them in the message. They must
be convinced that the prophet has some definite power. While Jesus
had to perform miracles to give proof of his charisma, Muhammad
had to provide rewards for his warrior supporters – booty, land and
power. Muhammad's charisma depended upon and grew out of his
military and political supremacy. He depended upon the support of
warrior groups whom Weber saw as the specific social carriers of the
new religion.

The fact that it was military success and its material rewards which
lay behind the success of Islam meant that the religious message came
to serve military and warrior interests. The original message was
reinterpreted to suit the needs and interests of the nomadic warrior
Bedouin supporters. Sufi reaction to the resulting worldliness of mainstream and elite Islam produced a mass religion characterised by
ecstatic and orgiastic mysticism. In the case of both the Islam of the
elites and of the masses there was no force which directed conduct
towards methodical regulation of life characteristic of ascetic Protestantism and Puritanism.

Turner disagrees with Weber's assessment of Islam as we see in the
following section. Here it remains to conclude that clearly, in Weber's
view, the ethic of a warrior stratum motivated by the expectation of
war booty and the taxation of the conquered population, was hardly
likely to have provided any stimulus for the careful, abstemious,
frugal, rational pursuit of profit through hard work and reinvestment
rather than consumption which ascetic forms of Protestantism produced in Europe.

RECENT SOCIOLOGY OF ISLAM

Sociological and anthropological studies of Islam while more extensive
than those concerned with Hinduism or Chinese religion are still dis-
appointingly scarce. Turner (1974) has taken up the issues raised by

Weber's comments on Islam. Having reconstructed Weber's views on Islam from the latter's scattered observations on the subject Turner finds these views to be heavily by a typically European (we would say Western today) Christian, indeed Protestant influenced negative bias, towards Islamic religion, culture and society.

Turner disagrees with Weber's analysis of the character of Islam as the product of the need to accommodate the material interests of the Bedouin warrior following. Islam, he points out, grew up in an urban and commercial context which is reflected in its ethic. It did incorporate much of the ethic of the nomadic tribal ideal. But it was not that the original message was reconstituted to suit the warrior group. Rather Islam took over the major values of the tribal society – generosity, courage, loyalty, veracity, and so on – and gave them a new religious content. Islam also promoted a universalism which cut across tribal distinctions. It established a religious community the *umma*, in the place of the purely political alliances that had previously come into being from time to time.

Weber, then, did not explain the character of Islam primarily in terms of the charismatic leadership of the prophet but in terms of the material interests of a warrior group. Turner accused Weber of giving a very one-sided and predominantly economic explanation of the character of Islam.

One area in which Weber's European bias can be seen, Turner argues, is in his treatment of the attitude of Islam, stemming from its warrior carrier group, to sensuality and the enjoyment of sensual pleasure and luxury in comparison with Puritanism. While the latter treated sexual intercourse as a necessary evil, Islam regarded women as objects of sexual exploitation. Weber refers to the gross sensuality of Muhammad and the way in which he even bent the liberal rules of Islam to allow himself as the prophet more than the normal maximum number of wives. Weber, furthermore, comments that in Islam 'even the world beyond is pictured as a soldier's sensual paradise' (1963, p. 264).

In Islam, also, Weber points out, the conspicuous consumption of wealth and the enjoyment of personal luxury as a means of indicating status was accepted. Capital tended to be dissipated in this way. In contrast, the Puritan was abstemious and reinvested accumulated capital. The enjoyment of personal luxury was considered irrational in ascetic Protestantism as well as sinful.

This is a typically nineteenth-century European view of Islam according to Turner, which manifests all the accumulated prejudices

of the Christian world against the Islamic world which had long been
seen as a major rival and threat. Christianity attempted to account for
the success of Islam in terms of its propensity for violence, deceitful-
ness and dishonesty. At the time Weber wrote Islam had also become
associated in the European mind with the exotic, erotic, bizarre and
fantastic. Weber is influenced by all this, giving a one-sided and selective view of Islam.

From the beginning, however, Turner points out, Islam was just as
much influenced by the values and outlook of a mercantile class as it
was by its Bedouin warrior following. Islam in the early period was a
fusion of elements of a merchant mentality and those of the Bedouin
warriors. As Islam developed the merchant class became more significant and dominant than the warrior group and its attitudes became
more entrenched within the religion. With the growth of the patrimonial, bureaucratic Islamic states the importance of the merchant class
declined relative to that of the bureaucratic officials. A new emphasis
was placed upon obedience and conformity. It was such developments
that led to Islam being characterised as slavish and fatalistic.

Although mercantile interests were very important in the rise of
Islam it did not provide a stimulus for the development of rational
capitalism and therefore for economic development. However, this
failure was not due, according to Zubaida (1972), to attitudes or values
inherent in Islam but to the fact that the merchant classes in Islamic
states did not enjoy the autonomy that they did in medieval Europe
nor did they develop class-based organisations. It was the relative lack
of political power of the mercantile class in relation to the patrimonial
state and the military–bureaucratic elite that propelled Islamic societies
in a different economic direction to that of the West. Zubaida rejects
the notion that religions have inherent tendencies towards the promotion or inhibition of specific forms of action or behaviour. The notion
of inherent-implications-for-action approach fails to take cognisance
of the fact that the ideas of any religious tradition will change in their
interpretation and emphasis over time in reflection of changing experience and will vary along with the social position of different groups.
These varying and changing understandings are the way people
attempt to make sense of their world and deal with it. While ideas
are not just reflections of material and social reality but also play their
part in shaping action and therefore reality, they are, nevertheless,
never isolated influences upon social reality but must always be understood in the context of a concrete social reality of which they are also a
part. Islam has gone through various stages of development that have

reflected the interests and concerns of dominant social groups and which have had varying implications for action.

There have been, then, a wide range of influences upon Islam and its world orientation has been diverse and changing. Weber oversimplified matters in greatly exaggerating the contribution of the warrior group and ethos and was unaware of the contribution of the mercantile ethos. We must remember also the very different circumstances in which Islam originated compared with Christianity which go a considerable way towards explaining the differences between the ethos of Islam and of Christianity especially with respect to attitudes to wealth, pleasure, asceticism and so on (Turner, 1976). Christianity began as a deviant and frequently oppressed sect whereas Islam achieved early and rapid military and political dominance. There was thus no tendency in Islam to extol suffering and self-denial. The manner in which Islam arose and became dominant in its social environments, also, meant that no distinction between the religious and political sphere developed. No distinct notions of religious values associated with otherworldliness, spirituality or asceticism, at least outside of Sufism, were likely to develop. The religious found its expression in and through the law governing, at least in theory, all aspects of life and existence. This lack of distinction between religious and secular spheres meant that no separate priesthood developed in Islam, such as developed in the case of Christianity, to uphold otherworldliness. The 'religious' virtuoso in Islam is an expert and scholar in the law and has no sacerdotal functions. Islamic saints are not martyrs who have sacrificed all for their faith as in the case of Christianity.

A similar emphasis to Turner's on the mercantile contribution to Islam is found in an earlier study of its origins and development than Turner's. Watt (1961) also sees Islam as a fusion of warrior and mercantile values. His study is, he makes clear at the outset, a deliberately selective attempt to assess the positive, that is to say integrative, achievement of Islam. While this is admittedly only one side of the picture, Islam did achieve a measure of harmony and integration. Watt is concerned to show the interaction of social and political circumstances in the environment in which Islam appeared, on the one hand, and what he calls 'ideational' factors, on the other. In fact, the study is as much a general treatment of the relationship between ideal and material factors in history as it is of Islam *per se*, using Islam as a case study.

Watt begins by noting the fundamental transition from nomadic pastoralism to settled urban commercialism on the part of the

Quraysh, the tribe of the area around Mecca. Mecca had established a monopoly of the caravan trade which passed north and south along the western side of the Arabian peninsula. The bulk of this rich trade was in the hands of a few clans of the Quraysh. The transition from nomadism to urban life was a rapid one taking place over only a single generation or so.

As a result of this transition Meccan society was in a state of some disarray, according to Watt. The values of the society were still those of tribal pastoral nomadism which emphasised loyalty to the tribe and clan and to one's own immediate kinsmen – above all, bravery, generosity, hospitality, acceptance of the obligation to revenge any harm to one's kin, the blood feud, and so on. These were hardly appropriate in the new urban context. The richer clans were now more concerned with amassing personal wealth than with fulfilling their kinship obligations. The old nomadic ideal was one of generosity towards kinsmen in need. A wealthy man was expected to provide for and help fellow clansmen at times of need. A man's status and prestige depended upon his generosity and readiness to use his resources in this way. Now, in the urban, commercial situation this tribal solidarity had broken down. A much greater degree of stratification had emerged. Commercial priorities had weakened the sense of obligation to kinsmen and the opportunities for investment provided by trade were proving too tempting to be passed over in order to aid others. As a result of these changes in values and attitudes social cohesion in Mecca had been undermined. Wolf (1951) points out that Islam represented the emergence and centralisation of worship under a deity associated with non-kin relations.

The new doctrines that Muhammad began to preach fully reflected this urban and commercial background and at the same time can be seen as a response to the social malaise that had set in. Muhammad's ideas came, of course, in the form of revelations which were received, he claimed, directly from God. Set down in the Koran they fully accept the legitimacy of commerce and are in no way opposed, Watt says, to 'big business'.

There was a close intermingling of religious and business concerns in Muhammad's life and activities, Watt points out. He came from a mercantile group himself – from a clan, the Hashim, which had, in fact, enjoyed in the past some prominence in the caravan trade but which had lost this position and had become largely excluded from the more important and lucrative side of the trade. Muhammad's commercial interests can be seen, Watt claims, in the fact that once at

Medina he set about raiding the Meccan caravans in order to break its monopoly and power.

Muhammad's success in this lay partly in the ability of his new ideas to unite diverse groups under the banner of Islam by fusing together the nomadic virtues with the ethic of the new mercantile class. This ethic of Islam was essentially an individualistic one reflecting Muhammad's commercial background. The ethical commandments of the Koran are sanctioned by the promise of reward or punishment after the day of judgement. Men are judged as individuals according to their conduct in life.

Through a synthesis of tribal and commercial values Muhammad was able to strengthen the declining clan solidarity and promote mutual support. In place of the clan, a group united by kinship, Islam introduced the community of believers, the *umma*, a group united by religious conviction. It is significant, as Eickelman (1967) points out, that Muhammad's movement was not the only one present at the time. A number of radical religious movements mushroomed in the Arabian peninsula at the time the most important of which, that led by Musaylima, posed a major threat to Islam itself until its armies were defeated by the Muslims. It is significant that none of these movements succeeded probably because they seemed to lack the ability to transcend tribalism and kinship. In many ways Musaylima's movement could be seen as a form of tribalistic resistance to Islam.

The creation of the umma was the eventual achievement of Muhammad but at first he met with little success in Mecca attracting only a small number of followers, many of them his own kin and associates, and much opposition from the more influential families in the city. So intense and dangerous did the opposition become that he and his followers were forced to migrate to Yathrib (Medina) to the north. Here, where Muhammad was a stranger, the Muslims had much greater success. How can we account for this, Watt asks.

One factor which may have played a part was that there were a number of Jewish tribes in Medina. While they rejected Muhammad's overtures and his religious message the pagan population of Medina had been exposed to their monotheistic religious ideas to an extent that the Meccans had not. This may have made the Medinans more receptive to Muhammad's teaching.

More important was the social situation at Medina. The Medinans, like the Meccans, had also recently undergone a fundamental transition from pastoral nomadism – but here to settled agriculture rather than commerce. They too retained much of the tribal ethos and here also it was largely inappropriate to the new conditions. Agricultural communities are highly susceptible to disputes over land and boundaries. In the nomadic situation there are no precise territorial boundaries. Disputes occur over grazing rights, water holes, and so on and if injury or death results it frequently leads to blood feud. The threat of blood feud was the only way of controlling the actions of others, and, for the most part, of keeping a reasonable degree or order. The fact that clans and sub-clans were widely dispersed, population density low and occasions and opportunities for conflict limited and infrequent enabled this system to work reasonably effectively. Feuds occurred relatively infrequently and when they did the incidence of attack and of killing or injury was not very high. In the settled situation in which population density was much greater and occasion for dispute and opportunity for revenge attack far more frequent, resort to revenge and blood feud was disastrous for social order. Feuding had become intense in Medina and the situation was becoming intolerable.

In this situation Muhammad, being an outsider and having no particular biases towards one faction or another, took on the role of arbitrator. His own skills and the fact that he claimed to be the mouthpiece of God enabled him to fulfil this role very successfully. He was able to undertake a vital role in Medina and rapidly established a position of prominence. Many of the Medinans became convinced of his special charismatic qualities and accepted, as a consequence, his religious message and joined the umma. Muhammad established himself as a major leader with a sufficiently strong power base that he was able to drive out or exterminate those groups who opposed him, including the Jews, and to establish himself as undisputed leader of the Medinans.

From his base at Medina Muhammad was then in a position to raid the Meccan caravans and to attract the surrounding Bedouin tribes to his cause who were lured by the lucrative booty that could be taken. Eventually, of course, Mecca was itself taken after a struggle in which Muhammad demonstrated that he also had considerable military skills and great boldness, decision and courage. He quickly united the whole Arabian peninsula. He was extremely fortunate, Watt points out, that political conditions at the time were very much in his favour. Both the Persian and Byzantine Empires had exhausted themselves in mutual conflict. The Arabs were able to mount raids against the rich lands of Iraq and Syria. Aswad (1970) places considerable emphasis, also, on this factor of the weakness of the neighbouring states. It was to a large extent these external factors that promoted the rise of Islam, according to Aswad. The Bedouin tribes had for long gathered in temporary alliances for this purpose but these were never able to sustain their solidarity for any length of time. The organisation that Muhammad set up, the new and revolutionary basis of unity that he created, now enabled the Arabs to form a permanent confederacy under his leadership. There was a strong incentive to join this confederacy. To remain outside it was dangerous while on the other hand the spoils available to those who did join were very considerable. Membership of the confederacy, however, meant conversion to Islam.

Watt considers that the Bedouin tribes that joined the umma, probably had no great religious conviction but were prepared to accept the religious message in order to enjoy the material benefits of membership. Muhammad's military successes, on the other hand, would also have given a considerable authority to the religious message. In any case, whether genuinely committed to the message or not the support of the Bedouin warrior tribes suited Muhammad's purposes.

Such were the social, economic and political circumstances against which, according to Watt, we have to understand the emergence of Islam. He in no way wishes, however, to suggest that these circumstances directly produced Islam. It may well have been the case that without such conditions Muhammad would not have arrived at his particular convictions and that had things been different in Medina his ideas might not have been accepted there. But these conditions did not in any automatic way produce Islam. They might have been necessary conditions but they were not sufficient. Ideas *per se* were just as important.

Watt uses the term 'ideation' in preference to 'ideology' because of the latter's connotation of departure from the truth in order to promote a specific interest. Watt makes no judgements of this kind in relation to Islam. The ideational content of Islam was, he argues, to some extent a reaction against the attitudes and individualism of the new mercantile class at Mecca. The message that Muhammad preached was in part an attempt to reinstate some of the traditional values while acknowledging the climate of individualism. If religious ideas are an attempt to make sense of the world rooted in an emotional need to see life and the world as meaningful, Islam, Watt argues, can be interpreted as an attempt to give a new significance to existence in dramatically altered circumstances. In its early teachings it sought to show that a significant and meaningful life was characterised by uprightness in conduct, generosity towards others, avoidance of oppression of the weak and of undue reliance upon human powers.

This ethic was supported by a doctrine of divine justice and reward or punishment at the day of judgement. This is a very powerful doctrine, Watt points out. Not only does it place life on a meaningful basis; also claims that to live such a life pays off with real benefits. This new outlook retains the individualism of the new commercial situation. It is no longer the tribe or clan as a whole whose conduct is significant but that of the individual. A materialistic individualism could not be a satisfying creed for the whole community, however, since most were excluded from wealth and power – the fruits of that way of life with which individualism was associated. Islam replaced this materialistic individualism with an ethical individualism. It promoted, thereby, not just sectional interests, but was to some extent conducive to the welfare of the community as a whole and allowed a successful adjustment to the new conditions.

As in all the great religious traditions it was not long before rifts and divisions appeared. What was the economic or social basis of these, if any, Watt asks? Two major divisions emerged in the early period of Islamic history. These were the Kharijites and the Shi'ites. The divisions were not merely to do with doctrine but were bound up with political questions relating to the succession to the caliphate.

The Kharijites were initially supporters of Ali and his faction against Mu'awiya in the civil war that broke out over the succession after the murder of Uthman, an Ummayad and less close to Muhammad in descent than Ali, a cousin of Muhammad and husband of Muhammad's daughter, Fatima. Ali was forced to accept arbitration and the decision went against him. The Kharijites would not agree to arbitration, deserted Ali for agreeing to submit to it, and withdrew from the Muslim community. The Kharijites stood for the resolution of such disputes by the free choice of the whole community which would be in effect, in their eyes, the decision of God. For them it was the charismatic community rather than the charismatic leader that was the basis of legitimacy. They also favoured a very strict interpretation of the Islamic code any major departure from which had to be punished by death in their view. Theirs was a pious and puritanical yet fiercely democratic ethos. Watt interprets their secession as the product of a feeling of insecurity on the part of those who had felt a loss of freedom and spontaneity with the transformation of the tribal system, the emergence of the Islamic state and growing bureaucratic administration. These new ways meant that life was too worldly and no longer virtuous in their eyes. It is significant, Watt notes, that the Kharijite sect found most of its support among the nomadic tribes of northern Arabia. Watt says of them:

> The Kharijite movement is first and foremost an attempt to mould the Islamic community in such a way that membership in it gave to the life of the individual something of the significance formerly given to it by membership in the tribe. (1961, p. 103)

The other major break-away group, the Shi'ites were the followers of Ali who had accepted the principle of arbitration but rejected the decision on the grounds that it was fixed and considered that Ali had been tricked. When Ali died they accused Mu'awiya of poisoning him. Ali's brother, Husayn rebelled against Mu'awiya's successor, Yazid but was defeated and killed. The Shia remained, nevertheless, a distinct faction attracting support mainly among the non-Arab Muslims who were not as well treated as Arabs and who were consequently discontented. This political faction began to acquire distinctive religious beliefs with strong messianic character. Unlike the Kharijites they rejected the idea of the charismatic community in favour of that of the charismatic leader. The belief grew up in an infallible leader or Imam specially chosen by God and having superhuman qualities. A whole variety of sects emerged within Shia Islam. Some came to believe that there had been seven great leaders of the Shia community, the last of which did not die but went into hiding to emerge when the time was right to establish the dominance of the Shia throughout the Muslim world. Others believe that there were twelve great Imams the last of whom will one day return.

The Kharijite and Shi'ite responses, then, were quite different. Watt considers that they owed a great deal to the different traditions found in the region. The Kharijites represent the nomadic tradition of northern Arabia while the Shi'ites draw upon the southern Arabian tradition of kingship and charismatic leadership.

Crone (1987) subjects Watt's thesis that Islam was a reaction to the anomic conditions brought on by the transition from tribal nomadism to commerce at Mecca to trenchant criticism. The period of commercial life experienced before the rise of Islam was far too brief to have had a sufficiently disruptive effect upon tribal institutions to have stimulated the Islamic reaction, according to Crone. There was no major uprooting or displacement of population nor did the adoption of commerce of the kind characteristic of the caravan trade necessitate or produce any major reorganisation of the social order. Crone finds little evidence of any general malaise in Mecca in the sources. In so far as there is some, Watt's use of them to establish the fact of such malaise forgets that being early Muslim sources they had an interest in or a bias towards portraying the Meccans, opponents of Islam at the outset, as having produced an unsatisfactory social situation characterised by cynicism, disintegration and malaise. The fact is that not only was Meccan society far from having broken down but that the successful Meccans were sufficiently content with things that they were quite unresponsive to Islam. They did not convert until conquered. It was in Medina that Muhammad enjoyed his first major successes, a fact which circumstances in Mecca do not explain. Muhammad was also successful among the Bedouin tribes, again not something that can be explained in terms of circumstances peculiar to Mecca. We should look then, in seeking to explain the rise of Islam, according to Crone, for factors common to the various communities of Arabia at that time and not to the very particular and special conditions prevailing in one small corner of the peninsula. It is hardly credible that a response to the peculiar problems arising in this small corner, namely Mecca, could prove to be a powerful attraction to diverse groups throughout Arabia.

This is a telling but not necessarily fatal point. It may well be that it took the specific experience and conditions arising from the transformation of patterns of life that occurred in Mecca to generate the vision of Muhammad and the conceptions of community, law, justice and morality that formed the roots of Islam. It could have been that once such a vision was in existence it lent itself to application elsewhere, such as in Medina. Other features of the prevailing circumstances, the opportunity for enrichment and power in particular, might then have enabled Muhammad and the Muslims to attach the Bedouin tribes to the umma, at first nominally but in the longer term more sincerely. In short, it is not entirely incredible that an extraordinary concatenation of events and combination of circumstances produced a historical result at the inception of which was the Meccan experience as described by Watt.

More difficult to answer is Crone's challenge to Watt's characterisation of Medina as in a pathological state of social disarray. Tensions and feuds there may well have been but there is nothing unusual about this in Arabia at the time as is true in many other stateless societies in which small settled communities have to manage conflicts in characteristically tribal ways. Feud and conflict was a constant in the situation, not a new factor and could thus not explain Muhammad's success there according to Crone.

This point does not, perhaps, give sufficient weight to the fact that a transition from tribal nomadism, in which blood feud is a normal part of the management of tension and conflict, to settled agriculture is likely to be particularly problematic. How many settled communities were there in Arabia at the time? How long had they been settled? Crone presents little evidence to show that Medina was not untypical.

The emergence and success of Islam in Arabia was, then, in Crone's view, not due to any social or spiritual crisis faced by the people but to the fact that Muhammad had something unique to offer, namely a programme of state formation and conquest. Muhammad's political and military ambitions were central to his mission not some by-product of his religious vision and the circumstances it led him into. His programme proved attractive to many because it offered power and wealth through conquest. Islam 'elevated tribal militance and rapaciousness into supreme religious virtues' (Crone, 1987, p. 245). We need look no further than the material interests of Muhammad's followers to account for their support and conversion. There are more than echoes of Weber in this position. What Muhammad was able to do was to put together an alliance based on transkinship principles. In this Crone agrees with Watt. Muhammad put monotheism to political use.

This suggests that someone with Muhammad's vision and programme could have united the Arabs at any time in their history. Crone certainly believes that the potential was always there. It occurred only in the seventh century because it was at this time that Arabia suffered serious foreign penetration. The Persians had established colonies in Eastern Arabia, the Najd and the Yemen and exercised influence over a wide area. The Byzantines had client kings in the Syrian desert region and were allied with the Ethiopian rulers of the Yemen until they were expelled by the Persians. Byzantine influence was felt throughout the western part of Arabia. Crone interprets Islam as an Arab nativistic movement. Such movements are common in circumstances of foreign pressure among people who have never had much political organisation or unity. They invariably take a religious form, are usually millennial and often messianic. The leader frequently claims to be a prophet or messenger of God and the message is couched in terms of the religious language of the foreigners but in such a way as to affirm the values, worth and identity of the native people. The early phases of the movement are always military and designed to oust the foreigners. The movements tend to throw up new political organisations even if highly embryonic. In the case of Islam,

Muhammad mobilised Jewish monotheism against Christianity and turned it to use in the furtherance of the interests of the Arabs.

Crone is well aware of the obvious objections to this analysis. The Arabs were far from being subjected to foreign domination to the extent that many peoples have been by powers who have established complete domination and rule over an area. Their way of life was not severely disrupted as a consequence of Persian and Byzantine influence and penetration. There is little mention in the sources of dissatisfaction with foreign domination. The question of whether the model of nativistic movements can be successfully applied to the case of Islam is thus left open to further research. It has to be acknowledged, however, that the evidence we have does not make this look like a promising line of investigation. If Crone is right about the lack of any particular social and economic malaise in Arabia and if the model of nativistic reaction seems not to fit too well we might be left with a theory of mere opportunism on the part of Muhammad. He was able to draw upon monotheistic ideas to forge an alliance and unity in the military and material interests of the Arabs in circumstances of exposure to foreign influences in terms of ideas and culture as well as in terms of military and economic power. It may not have been that foreign pressure sparked a nativistic Arab movement but that foreign influence facilitated an Arab nationalistic movement expressed in a new religious idiom.

The spread of Islam outside the Arabian peninsula, of course, was also very much associated with military conquest. Not that conversion of conquered populations was necessarily automatic or particularly rapid (Lapidus, 1988). The process was slow and uneven. The early converts were the members of the elites of the former Sassanian Empire. Conversion could secure retention of previous social position and privileges and a place in the new regime or social order. It was not common that whole groups or communities converted at this time. As time passed populations around the garrison towns converted while the mass of the people away from such centres retained their religious traditions.

Soon divisions arose within the Islamic community centred on distinctions between Muslim versus non-Muslim and Arab versus non-Arab. To a considerable extent such conflicts and divisions reflected the interests of different groups in Muslim society. The Yemenis, for example, were largely non-militarised Arabs many of whom were city dwellers and traders. They tended to favour full assimilation of non-Arab Muslims and were less interested in military expansion. The Qays in contrast tended to stress Arabic identity rather than Muslim. They represented those who were actively involved in the army and who depended for their incomes on further conquest and the tax revenues generated by it. These conflicts came to a head under Umar II (717–20) who realised that the Empire had to be a Muslim one and could not survive if it became too closely identified with Arabs. This meant conversion of all the peoples of the Empire to Islam. This took a long time to accomplish, however. It was not until the period of the tenth to the thirteenth centuries that most of the non-Arab population was converted. This was in part the consequence of the dissolution of the Abbasid empire, its replacement by foreign military rulers and the ruin of the landowning and administrative classes. In their place influence fell into the hands of Muslim religious leaders who actively converted and provided new leadership and forms of organisation to the masses who had been uprooted by events. A whole series of Sufi brotherhoods, Shi'ite sects and religious associations, frequently linked to the schools of law, grew up. They often became associated with particular communities, occupational and ethnic groups and either provided a new basis for community beyond kinship and tribal affiliations or gave a new Islamic identity to existing collectivities.

Beyond the Middle East, Islam spread in a wide variety of ways and conversion rested upon a wide variety of motives and processes. Lapidus (1988) summarises as follows:

> The expansion of Islam involved different forces. In North Africa, Anatolia, the Balkans, and India, Islam was carried by nomadic Arab or Turkish conquerors. In the Indian Ocean and West Africa it spread by peaceful contacts among merchants or through the preaching of missionaries. In some cases the diffusion of Islam depended upon its adoption by local ruling families; in others, it appealed to urban classes of the population or tribal communities. Sometimes its appeal was couched in terms of political and economic benefits; sometimes in terms of social status; sometimes in terms of a sophisticated culture and religion. (p. 242)

In accounting for the spread of Islam we must distinguish between different processes. The process of Islamisation of pastoral tribes must be distinguished from that of agricultural and state-type civilisations. The conversion of pagans must be distinguished form that of Jews, Christians, Zoroastrians and Buddhists.

Like Turner, Watt and Crone, Lapidus emphasises, in the case of conversion of nomadic Arab pastoralists, the attraction of a new political and economic framework of unity grounded in monotheistic conceptions on the lines of those of the Christians and Zoroastrians. The conversion of members of the elites of sedentary populations had more to do with the material and status advantages that conversion brought and consisted in exchanging a Byzantine or Sassanian political identity and a Jewish, Christian or Zoroastrian religious one for a Muslim identity. The eventual development of an urban and urbane literary culture on the one hand and popular Sufism on the other, which could be substituted for allegiance to the monotheistic religions of Judaism, Zoroastrianism and Christianity, facilitated the conversion of former adherents of these religions. Pagan conversion in many areas was closely associated with the winning over of local chiefs who saw in Islam a means of underpinning tribal coalitions and state formation. It was often adopted by pastoralist nomads to aid in the subordination of sedentary populations, the creation of long-distance trading arrangements or the forging of cohesive ethnic identities. The conversion of merchant groups in Malaya and Indonesia was bound up with the emergence of new small states based on trade and was in many respects a reaction to Dutch and Portuguese incursions and pressure to establish trading monopolies.

The adoption of Islam in Africa was often similarly bound up with trading interests. The pattern of spread and conversion in Africa was, however, highly selective. Horton (1971, 1975) attempts to understand this pattern in terms of intellectualist theory. Christianity and Islam in Africa, he argues, were catalysts for and accelerators of change that was already in the air. Concepts of supreme beings are linked to the existence and importance of social networks wider than the local microcosm. Lesser spirits and beings relate to these local microcosms. To the extent that involvement with the macrocosm of the wider world increases there will be an increased tendency to focus concern on supreme beings. The appearance of Christianity and Islam in Africa provided conceptions of supreme beings which were differentially attractive according to the degree to which a shift from microcosmic involvement to macrocosmic involvement was in process. Subsistence farmers in the stateless societies and rural peasants in the states remained confined within the boundaries of the local microcosms. Although exposed for many centuries to Islam they remained for long unaffected by it. Ruling groups and political office holders were divided in their concerns between microcosm and macrocosm. They were equally involved in the cults of communal and dynastic spirits on the one hand and cults of the supreme being, which drew selectively upon Islam, on the other. Merchants and traders mainly looked beyond the local microcosm and paid little heed to the cults of lesser spirits but were deeply involved in the Islamic forms of the cult of the supreme being. Pastoralist nomads again present a mixed picture while scholars and holy men adopted Islam in its purest and most exclusive form.

If there was any common factor in all the diversity in processes of conversion and adoption and expansion of Islam, Lapidus (1988) argues, it was the ability of Islam to generate a sense of identity in the creation of larger-scale communities and polities where previously rather fragmented societies had existed and where traditional social structures had been weakened for one reason or another.

But the result of these varied processes of conversion has, of course, been a diversity of types of Islam each taking on its distinctive character as a result of many factors in the local situation. An excellent illustration of this is the study of Geertz (1968) who deftly contrasts the character of Moroccan and Indonesian Islam relating each to the prevailing conditions in these two very different regions. In Morocco the dominant force shaping its version of Islam stemmed from the fierce individualism of a tribal and semi-nomadic population outside the settled areas. In Morocco Islam was introduced to virgin territory from the point of view of high culture and received a distinctive adaptation as a result. For the tribal peoples of the region the charismatic leader held great appeal. Replacing the old tribal chiefs, Sufi saints, the *marabouts*, became the focus for tribal Islam. The saints enjoyed a hereditary charisma claiming descent from members of the family of the prophet Muhammad and thus from a long line of charismatic leaders. Individualism and the tenuous control that the settled and urban groups exercised under the leadership of the monarchy over the tribal areas placed a great premium on unity and upon religious means of bolstering it. Moroccan Islam, at the same time as manifesting the ritualistic tendencies of the tribes, stressed orthodoxy and strict interpretation of the Sharia. The followers of the marabouts, despite marked deviation from orthodoxy, held it in high esteem and for both communities it served to express the value of unity.

Indonesian Islam was less focused upon doctrinal orthodoxy, purity and conformity but more upon personal fulfilment. It was eclectic, syncretistic and tolerant of diversity. Islam, in coming to Indonesia, came not to a tribal but to a largely peasant society which had long been under the domination of a Hindu–Buddhist Javanese state. In this more complex society different social strata and groupings interpreted and developed Islam in a variety of different ways, varying markedly in orthodoxy and purity and in degrees of syncretism. In Indonesia, in contrast to Morocco, prevailing social conditions fostered a role for Islam as a force for diversification rather than for consensus.

Each society, then, adopted a universalistic and ostensibly standard, fixed and unchangeable creed but in doing so adapted it to local circumstances. Islam in each case means very different things in terms of the values and styles of conduct it upholds; in Indonesia 'inwardness, imperturbability, patience, poise, sensibility, aestheticism, elitism and almost obsessive self-effacement' and in Morocco 'activism, fervor, impetuosity, nerve, toughness, moralism, populism, and almost obsessive self-assertion' (Geertz, 1968, p. 54).

Yet an overall pattern has been discerned in this variety in the bold analysis of Gellner (1981). Drawing upon the work or the medieval Arab scholar Ibn Khaldun, Gellner contrasts urban and tribal forms of Islam and builds a picture of the dynamics of historical Islamic societies based upon their interplay.

Khaldun's theory argued that there was in Middle Eastern society a cycle of emergence of regimes through conquest. Conquering groups were usually nomadic or semi-nomadic pastoralist tribes. These societies were highly mobile, used to warfare, tough and inured to hardship. They could often, as a consequence, subdue settled agricultural peoples and the urban centres. In this process lies the origins of the state, according to Khaldun. When one tribe or people subdues another by conquest it has to establish institutions of rule and government over the subject population. Previously, the homogeneity of the society had allowed it to function effectively along the lines of the traditional chiefship, but now the problems of maintaining control over a hostile and subject population require a new set of institutions. The centralised government was staffed by members of the dominant, conquering group and usually from the leading elite among this group. In this way a distinct ruling stratum is established which monopolises power. It taxes the subject population to finance the institutions of government and control and, of course, to maintain itself in a condition of luxury and privilege. It lays claim to the rulership of the tribal regions but its control over them is usually precarious and effective only when it is strong. Its privileged position eventually leads to it becoming weak and decadent and its taxation of the population arouses antagonism. Over time it loses its tribal solidarity. At this point it is ripe for overthrow from another tribal group sweeping in from the outlying regions. The conquering group now takes over the existing apparatus of rule from the ousted dynasty and the cycle repeats itself.

Broadly accepting this account, Gellner brings into the picture the factor of Islamic religion. The religion of the urban centres upheld by the ulama and the better-off sections of urban society is scriptural, legalistic and tends to Puritanism. It represents the high culture of Islamic civilisation, the 'great' tradition. It has little appeal for the urban poor, however, who seek in religion escape and release from a condition of hardship and alienation through ecstatic forms of practice and mystical or trance states. The religion of the tribesmen is centred upon charismatic saints and their cults and is often ritualistic and ecstatic. It is concerned with the social group, its identity, solidarity and boundaries, with seasons and the productive cycle, in short with Durkheimian themes. It represents the popular, local, 'little' tradition and as such, despite its divergence from the requirements of the urban tradition, holds the latter in great respect.[1]

The lifestyles and actions of the rulers frequently offend the pious upholders of Islamic law, the ulama, which considers itself to carry the obligation to ensure that the regime upholds Islamic principles. When the regime is weak it is not uncommon that an urban religious leader and preacher, backed by the ulama and the bourgeois strata, will call upon the tribes to overthrow a backsliding and decadent regime. Certain tribesmen, impressed as they are by the religious superiority of the urban preachers and attracted by the opportunity to seize power for themselves, will often seek to oblige and are sometimes successful.

Gellner's account has stimulated critical response from a number of scholars. Zubaida (1995) points out that it fails to recognise the diversity of Islamic societies. His model might be applied to some but not to all or even the majority. Gellner is aware that it does not apply universally. The Ottoman state, including Egypt, is exceptional according to Gellner. Here the state freed itself from both the ulama and the tribes by the establishment of the *devshirme* system by which the military and bureaucracy were staffed by slaves, the Janissaries, recruited as children from Christian communities and trained for their role by the state. It has often been observed that individuals in this situation, divorced from kin and community and therefore totally dependent upon the state, make very loyal servants. The state in turn can rely upon them and achieve a high degree of independence from traditional elites and other groups.

The problem with this argument, Zubaida argues, is that it excepts a very large part of the Islamic world from the model. Also, the question arises why other Islamic states did not use the same strategy. Gellner simply postulates the existence of alternative models of state organisation in the Islamic world, one of which was the Ottoman solution, but offers no explanation why it was used in this area and not in others. Finally, by the seventeenth century the Janissaries were recruited from the Muslim population and retained close links with their kin and communities. The system did not collapse as a consequence.

In many respects, Zubaida argues, Gellner's model oversimplifies and draws too stark a contrast between ulama and popular religiosity. The ulama were not all of a piece and there was considerable diversity, division and conflict within their body. They were by no means always as puritanical as Gellner supposes and were not always distinct from Sufism and the Sufi orders. Gellner's impression of the Puritanism of orthodox Muslims of the urban areas has been shaped, according to Zubaida, by modern reformist Muslims who have been concerned to combat stereotypes of Islam as backward, fatalistic, superstitious and sexually permissive. In this endeavour, these features of life in Islamic societies are attributed to decadent and corrupt elements which have deviated from true Islamic codes and principles. Theirs is a selective construction of tradition with a definite agenda behind it. Gellner has taken this construction, Zubaida accuses, and presents it a picture of the whole of urban Islam throughout its history.

The alliance between tribe and militant preacher that Gellner sees behind dynastic takeovers is a myth according to Zubaida. Such transformative movements may have existed in the Mahgreb but were not common elsewhere. What often or usually did happen was that contenders for power justified their actions in religious terms whatever their origin, tribal or otherwise, and their religious justifications were often of an heterodox or charismatic nature rather than orthodox. They would later consolidate their position by using the upholders of orthodoxy and guardians of the Sharia to ensure social control and social order. Lapidus (1988), on the other hand, confirms Gellner in this respect. There were many great tribal movements which led to formation of Islamic states, he observes in summarising this aspect of Islamic history, which 'were built upon Muslim religious leadership or the integration of Muslim religious and secular chieftainship' (ibid., p. 264).

The Islamic reformist movement which Zubaida believes was the source of Gellner's picture of urban bourgeois Islam was largely, according to Lapidus (1988), a reaction on the part of the ulama, in some places allied with Sufi groups, to the threat of European colonial pressure during the seventeenth and eighteenth centuries and the impact that this had on traditional Islamic social structures. It espoused a purified version of Islamic doctrine and practice founded upon the Koran, hadith and law interfused with Sufi asceticism. The ideal was imitation of the prophet in everyday life. It sought to eradicate veneration of saints as non-Islamic and was often inclined to interpret failures against the colonial powers and subordination to them as punishment by God for laxity in observance. The solution lay in an ethic of personal discipline and moral responsibility and the pursuit of what was seen as true Islamic justice.

This reformist Islam had considerable appeal, in various parts of the Islamic world, for village communities that had been disrupted. It was often able to restore unity and weld different groups together in opposition to rivals and to the regime. It lent itself to ideological use by conquering groups and later to anti-colonial movements of resistance. Lapidus identifies the Wahhabi movement as the earliest example of a reformist movement of this kind. A second constituency for reformism was that of agricultural and urban mercantile interests affected by European political and economic intervention and the new commercialism and urbanisation that resulted from it. Reformism has more recently become associated with the growth of national feeling and identity in many parts of the Muslim world. There has been a merging of religious and national identity and reformist Islam has increasingly been seen as an essential underpinning aspect of national identity.

It was this role of Islam that insulated Islamic society, Gellner (1992) argues, from the forces of secularisation. The social basis of the folk tradition has been extensively eroded while that of high Islam has strengthened as a result of modernisation. The close identification of reformist Islam with nationalism and internationalism transcending local, tribal and rural cultures facilitated its association with modernity. It was able to identify backwardness with popular traditions and contrast itself as rational, disciplined and systematic. For Gellner reformist Islam can thus be seen to be reminiscent of Weber's Protestant Ethic but Zubaida (1995) is highly critical of this idea claiming that there is much in Islamic practice which flies in the face of market rationality. Whether fundamentalist Islam can provide a stimulus for development and modernisation or whether it is fundamentally incompatible with these things is a complex issue over which there is much debate but the outcome is something that time is yet to reveal.

The political role of Islam in the modern world is, even more than its economic role, something which has attracted intense attention as a result of the rise of Islamic fundamentalism and particularly as a consequence of the Iranian revolution. Fundamentalism is not perhaps the best term to use since it has connotations which do not necessarily apply to the movements that have mushroomed in the Islamic world in the last few decades. The phenomenon is essentially one of the assertion of the relevance of Islamic values, in their 'puritan' interpretation, for politics in the contemporary situation (Halliday, 1994). Re-Islamicisation is perhaps a better term (Kepel, 1994). This re-Islamicisation has been attributed to the post-independence problems of Islamic nations. With the retreat of the colonial powers and the establishment of independent nations and regimes considerable optimism prevailed. The new regimes were on the whole modernist in outlook, concerned to develop their economies and take their countries along a path of Western influenced development. These economies were, however, weak. With a population explosion and mass migration from the rural areas severe economic and social dislocation resulted. The regimes themselves were often perceived as being corrupt and inefficient. Their failures were associated on the part of large sections of the population with their Western ethos. In many ways such successes as they had only contributed to their problems. Expansion of education helped to create an opposition among students and other articulate, educated sections of the population (Halliday, 1994). They were able to organise an opposition using all the techniques of modern culture aided by the concentration of numbers in the towns as a consequence of urbanisation and migration. In some ways, according to Turner (1991), Islamic fundamentalism is not wholly incompatible with aspects of modernism and with certain secularising trends of modernisation, for example in its anti-magical orthodoxy. It is the cultural aspects of modernity that it rejects. It is post-modernity and postmodernism more than modernity that faces Islamic fundamentalism with its most serious challenge, according to Turner, since post-modernism threatens to deconstruct all theological views of the world revealing their mythological nature. Islamic fundamentalism could thus be seen as to some degree a defence of modernity against postmodernism.

Criticism and opposition to the modernising regimes had come first from Marxist inspired quarters which labelled the regimes as imperialist puppets and ineffectual dependants of the Western capitalist powers. Later a re-Islamicisation movement developed which challenged and largely defeated the Marxists and the left in the battle to lead the opposition. In many respects this re-Islamicisation movement married the themes of anti-imperialism, critique of dependency, cultural nationalism, and third-worldism with Islamicism. As Gellner (1992) points out, the predominant answer of the Islamic world to the impact of the West has been not emulation of it nor a return to folk traditions but a reassertion of high Islam allied with nationalist sentiments. At first it sought to seize power and control of the state, Islamicisation from above, but was successful only in Iran. Since the late 1980s it has sought to build an Islamic society through the inculcation of Islamic values and principles throughout the society in such a way as to influence every aspect of daily life and conduct of affairs. The movements have sought to create Islamic organisations and structures of their own relating to many aspects of contemporary life, seeking often to provide a kind of alternative welfare system. From this base they are becoming increasing active in political life once again.

9 Conclusion

If religion is the search for meaningful understandings of reality it has taken an enormous diversity of forms. This should not, perhaps, surprise us too much since the range of possibilities is limited, as Stark and Bainbridge (1987) point out, only by the human imagination. The very diversity itself testifies to the problematic nature of this search. A not unreasonable conclusion to draw from this might well be that even after millennia of human endeavour in this respect, no satisfactory answers have yet been or are likely to be found. An equally reasonable conclusion, on the other hand, might be that many societies or social groups have found answers that work very well for them and with which they are satisfied. Religious beliefs, once established, can be remarkably resilient and resistant to change and modification; once established, a meaningful account of reality is not easily questioned or relinquished. To subject it to question is to pose too serious a threat to the sense that things hang together in a meaningful order. Religious answers, however, do change, develop and are sometimes supplanted by others. Such fluidity as religion manifests is undeniably closely bound up with social change. Religious beliefs are also highly exportable across social and cultural boundaries, although they generally undergo considerable change and reinterpretation in the process or become combined with indigenous beliefs in new syntheses or syncretistic fusions.

All this makes the task of identifying the nature of the links between religion and social patterns extremely difficult. If it is difficult to speak of a sociology of religion *per se*, it is equally difficult to speak of a sociology of Buddhism or of Islam, and so on, since these traditions are themselves so varied and diverse across the societies and historical time periods in which they can be found. The relationship between religion and society is a complex one. The fit is not necessarily close, yet is always apparent. Religion, also, is not only shaped by social forces and factors but is itself one of these forces and factors.

Even within a particular version of a particular tradition, espoused by a particular community at a particular period in time, it is not easy to bridge the gulf between the local particularities and the more general aspects of those 'great' traditions which span multiple communities and groups – the gulf, that is, between the micro and macro levels. Time and again we have met with the difficulty that scholars have encountered in dealing with the Buddhism or Islam or whatever of the village community they have studied when it is not quite like the Buddhism or Islam that one finds described in scripture or in text-books on the subject. Despite the fact that we think we know what Buddhism or Islam is, to say that this or that community is Buddhist or Islamic sometimes tells us little about what its members actually believe or do. While it is no wonder, then, that anthropologists con-centrate on small communities and sociologists have tended to be attracted by the small sect, anthropology cannot neglect the wider culture and sociology must endeavour to be more comparative.

Another major problem is the diversity of theoretical approaches that have been adopted which makes it very difficult to assess the contribution that sociology has made to the comparative study of religion. Until many more studies are undertaken in each of the major religious traditions utilising the range of theoretical perspectives on offer it is impossible to say which of them is the more fruitful in yielding better understanding. One could not get very far in this objective with, for example, one or two neo-Freudian accounts of Buddhism and Hinduism, a functionalist study of Confucianism and a Marxist approach to the Reformation.

Yet the body of work that has been carried out does begin to illuminate the social dimensions of these and other traditions as this book, hopefully, demonstrates. This body of work is best regarded as a small beginning in what is a very large endeavour. It would be rash, as a consequence, to attempt to draw too many conclusions at this stage of our knowledge, but the broad survey carried out here may, however, allow us to make, if tentatively, a number of observations relating to the larger comparative picture of religious diversity and development.

The religions of tribal and small-scale societies were contrasted in Chapter 2 with those which transcend local communities, and ethnic, cultural and linguistic divisions. The former lack the transcendental emphasis of the latter and their concern with wider questions of mean-ing and with salvation. The religions which emphasise these aspects, with some of which a large part of this book has been concerned, emerged at a time which has been termed the 'axial age' (Jaspers, 1949), namely the period of the first millennium BC. Certainly, between approximately 800 BC and the beginning of the Christian era religious, philosophical and ethical ideas emerged of a character quite unlike those which were prevalent in tribal societies or the earlier civilisations. The emergence of prophetic, monotheistic and later rabbinical Judaism, the rise of Upanishadic Hinduism and its inheritor Buddhism and the development of Confucianism and Taoism are features of this age. Christianity and Islam were later offsprings.

The emergence of these systems of thought and ideas in remotely separated areas of the globe in this relatively circumscribed period of time suggests that there may have been common factors at work. While the level of technological and economic development, degree of specialisation of labour and social differentiation and extent of political development and centralisation were not sufficient conditions for the rise of transcendental religious conceptions, these were clearly among the relevant background factors. In some of the centres of civilisation, for example Egypt, no such religious developments occurred, yet the spread of common cultural patterns and political rule over large geographical areas and populations with the rise of the larger states and empires played an important role in stimulating the emergence of the transcendental religions (Schwartz, 1975). Also important for the emergence of these systems of belief was the prior development of extensive communication systems, trading networks and wider political and military structures. Another crucial factor was the expansion of literacy. Complex messages such as those we are concerned with cannot be transmitted across extensive geographical and social space unless their form can be preserved in written texts not subject to the limitations and potential degradation of meaning that accompany oral communication (Mann, 1986).

Such preconditions, however, are only necessary and not sufficient to account for the rise of the transcendental religions. It has been suggested that the explanation of their emergence in only some places is in terms of particular crises that hit these regions to which the new religious ideas were a reaction and response but there is little by way of analysis of what sort of crises these may have been.

This survey of the sociological work on the world religions suggests to some extent what sort of conditions gave rise to the transcendental religions. We have seen that Upanishadic Hinduism and Buddhism arose at a time when the more egalitarian tribal republics were giving way to the centralised, bureaucratic and stratified larger states. Confucianism and Taoism were the response during the period of the warring states in China to the demise of the smaller state in a process of conquest and emergence of an imperial system. Judaism emerged from the oscillations in Palestine between domination on the part of one or other mighty bureaucratic neighbour on the one hand and autonomy on the other, circumstances that perennially led the people of the area, as Weber pointed out, to be astonished at the course of events. Christianity was in part the response to the undermining of community and local traditions and incorporation into the Roman Empire. Islam emerged in a situation of competing influence of large bureaucratic and centralised states over a tribal area undergoing in places a profound social and economic transformation which was undermining traditional patterns of relationship and obligation

In all these cases the religious messages developed by sages or prophets were intended to form the basis for a new social order. Both Christianity and Islam sought to replace increasingly inappropriate tribal, kinship and local loyalties with a new kind of community based in faith. In China the Confucians sought to found social order on new principles rather than those of the old feudal and militaristic elites. Buddhism sought to fill the vacuum of values left by the demise of the tribal republics and to combat a growing individualism. Over a long period of time in Palestine a degree of ethical rationalisation of life conduct was achieved in the face of the more usual peasant and proletarian magical and ritual style of religious life. In the process these religions often fused a new individualism with older virtues which were universalised and channelled in less particularistic directions. If individualism had previously been growing in an unregulated manner the new systems of belief sought to transform it into an ethically based, soteriological and eschatological individual responsibility.

A major consequence of the emergence of transcendental conceptions of the world was the perception of a tension between the transcendental and the mundane order and a concomitant problem of how the chasm between them could be bridged. Attempts to resolve these problems had a whole series of consequences for the way these societies developed. One such consequence was that already referred to, namely the emergence of identities based upon religion and culture rather than ethnicity or locality. Another was the emergence of a differentiation between the centre, the guardian of the new systems of belief, and the periphery where older local traditions continued to flourish (Eisenstadt, 1982).

Against the rise of more universalistic and transcendental belief systems we see in most cases a survival of local, 'little' or folk traditions alongside the 'great' traditions which spanned large areas giving rise to the interplay between them which is such a central feature of many of the studies reviewed here. We see, also, the emergence of great missionary traditions which have sought to carry, often successfully, more universalistic ideas and principles beyond the confines of the political units in which they originally emerged. These systems of belief and practice have also been spread by political, military and economic expansion over astonishingly wide areas, although, as previously noted, not without major alteration and adaptation in the process. Despite the commonalities of circumstance which gave rise to systems of belief sharing certain very broad features, the result was a set of divergences which played their part in establishing a number of distinct civilisations. The systems of ideas associated with these civilisations have often been in direct competition with one another while in other instances we observe a remarkable capacity for them to coexist alongside one another. Despite considerable local syncretism and coexistence, however, the world became broadly divided into the Hindu, Buddhist, Christian and Islamic spheres and to a considerable extent remains so even today. While we are witnessing an ever-increasing and accelerating process of globalisation this has not so far threatened this division. As theorists of globalisation who focus on religion have pointed out (for example, Robertson, 1985; Robertson and Chirico, 1985; Beyer, 1994) there has been a localising and particularising counter-reaction which centres on religious identity as much as upon any other and in many ways more so. The Christian world has witnessed a long-term process of marginalisation of religion which for some constitutes a deeply-rooted secularisation of society though the meanings given to this term and the extent and nature of this marginalisation are hotly debated. Whatever position one takes on this, however, and while patterns vary considerably from one place to another, it is clear that religion in much of the Christian world is not firmly at the centre of the concerns of the majority of the population nor prominent in public life and the conduct of affairs. Elsewhere religion is and seems set to remain for the foreseeable future, on the whole, an important aspect of social and political life and in the definition of personal, ethnic, national or cultural identity.

Notes

1 INTRODUCTION

1. Weber (1951, 1952, 1958, 1965).
2. For fuller discussions see Evans-Pritchard (1965) who provides one of the most succinct accounts, O'Toole (1984), Morris (1987), Preus (1987), Clarke and Byrne (1993), and Hamilton (1995).
3. Comte's *Positive Philosophy* was published between 1830 and 1842. Spencer published his *Principles of Sociology* between 1876 and 1896. Tylor published *Primitive Society* in 1871 and Frazer *The Golden Bough* in 1890.
4. See Horton (1993), in which his main contributions to the current debate are reprinted.
5. His *Threshold of Religion* was published in 1914.
6. For Malinowski's main works see Malinowski (1936, 1974).
7. For Freud's views see Freud (1928, 1938).
8. There is a useful collection of the writings of Marx and Engels on religion; see Marx and Engels (1957).
9. Durkheim's systematic treatment of religion, *The Elementary Forms of the Religious Life*, was published in 1889.
10. See Radcliffe-Brown (1952).
11. See Davis (1948), Yinger (1957, 1970) and O'Dea (1966).
12. In particular (1965, 1970b, 1970c).
13. For a discussion of Weber's concept of ideal interests see Kalberg (1985).
14. Berger (1973). See also Geertz (1966) and Luckmann (1967).

2 RELIGION IN TRIBAL SOCIETIES

71. Elsewhere I have discussed the themes of magical belief and behaviour, taboo and ritual avoidance and various types of ritual (Hamilton, 1995).
2. The Azande have three main forms of oracle or divination technique. The simplest and cheapest is the termite oracle which can be operated by anyone. Two sticks of equal length are inserted into a termite hill and left overnight. When pulled out one will invariably have been eaten shorter than the other. The oracle is asked, for example, to make a particular stick shorter if the answer to the question put is to be 'yes' and the other one shorter if it is 'no'. The rubbing board oracle consists of a smooth polished wooden base and a small wooden rubbing block and is operated by a specialist for a fee. The block is moved around on the base while the question is put. If it sticks the answer is 'yes' or 'no' as specified. The most reliable and expensive oracle, again operated by a specialist, is the chicken oracle. It is often used to check the results of one of the other types of oracle. A small amount of poison, known as *benge*, is wrapped in a piece of leaf and force fed to a young chicken and the question put with the specification that if the answer is 'yes' the chicken should fall dead or recover as stated.

3.   See Turner (1968) for an account of the process among the Ndembu and Marwick (1965a) on the Cewa.
4.   See the contributions to Bourguignon (1973).

3. HINDUISM

1.   Space does not permit a detailed account of the beliefs, practices and history of the world religions. In what follows and in subsequent chapters on the world religions knowledge of them will be assumed. those not familiar with them would do well to read Ling (1968) or Smart (1971). On occasions, however, brief mention of essential ideas and practices will be made in order to facilitate understanding of the argument.
2   The unfavourable ritual status of the Kshatriya compared to that of the Brahmin stemming from a caste dharma of life-taking may be offset to some extent by a sense of the relative purity of the warrior way of life. A warriour does not only take life by risks his life in the service of others. To undergo such risks shows a certain detachment and in this sense can be seen as related to the renunciatory ideal, especially when accompanied by the ideal of relinquishing all interest in the outcome. Such ideas also underlie the warriour ideal in Japan (see Tsunetomo, 1979). I am indebted to Christie Davies for these observations.

4 BUDDHISM

1.   Weber chracterised patrimonial rule or government as one in which the whole or a great part of land, territory and resources are regarded as the personal property or estate of the ruler and where administration was effectively an extension of the royal household, major positions within it evolving out of the domestic servants of the ruler and from court functionaries. Patrimonialism entailed a high degree of centralisation, at least in theory, compared, for example to feudal regimes.
2.   For similar instances in Sri Lankan Buddhism see Obeyesekere (1968); Gombrich (1971).

5 CHINESE RELIGIONS: CONFUCIANISM AND TAOISM

1.   Ethnicity as a basis for religious organisation has been giving way steadily, however, to locality in much of Taiwan (Weller, 1987).

6 JUDAISM

1.   Douglas has since added a further dimension to her work (Douglas, 1993) on the dietary laws as set out in Leviticus and Deuteronomy. Her earlier

interpretations, she acknowledges, did not account for why particular animals were chosen for avoidance. In this paper she is concerned to show how the dietary laws are not simply about purity and defilement but about moral values. The forbidden animals are symbolic of the victims of injustice and are chosen because they are appropriate to express this. This approach does not just add to her earlier work, then, but modifies it considerably since the rules no longer look like taboos of the kind found in many primitive societies. This is, perhaps, a rather curious reversal of Douglas's earlier readiness to apply anthropological insights learned from the study of tribal societies to more complex ones. The new emphasis on moral codes expressed through symbolic systems such as dietary rules echoes a long-persistent reluctance to treat ancient Judaism and its practices, the background from which Christianity emerged, on a par with the religious systems of tribal societies (Eilberg-Schwartz, 1990).

2.   For a discussion of the sociological approach to the understanding of millennialism see Hamilton (1995), Ch. 7.
3.   Contributions to the complex issue of the relationship between Jewish identity and religious observance include (Krausz, 1977; Lazerwitz, 1973; Katz, 1973).

7   CHRISTIANITY

1.   A similar view is taken by a much more recent scholar, S. G. F. Brandon (1968).
2.   For a critique of the idea of Jesus as a charismatic prophet see Malina (1984).
3.   See also Elliott (1986) on functionalism in Theissen.
4.   *The Peasant War in Germany; Ludwig Feuerbach and the End of Classical German Philosophy; Socialism: Utopian and Scientific.* (See Marx and Engels, 1957.)
5.   Weber's essay (1970) 'The Protestant sects and the spirit of capitalism', in Gerth and Mills (1970).
6.   Lowy (1989) disputes that Franklin's views derived from ascetic Protestant sources. They were, in Lowy's estimation, inspired by the quest purely and simply for wealth and status. Franklin did not consider industry to be a moral duty but principally a means to the end of acquiring wealth and status. In so far as the making of money did become for some, if not for Franklin, an end in itself such an ethos can be seen as deriving from capitalism rather than a factor in its emergence.

8   ISLAM

1.   For detailed ethnographic account of this type of Islamic religion see Gellner (1969) and Eickelman (1976).

Bibliography

Ahern, E. M. (1973) *The Cult of the Dead in a Chinese Village* (Stanford, Calif: Stanford University Press).

Ahern, E. M. (1981) *Chinese Ritual and Politics* (Cambridge: Cambridge University Press).

Albrektson, B. (1972) 'Prophecy and politics in the Old Testament', in H. Biezais (ed.), *The Myth of the State* (Stockholm: Almqvist and Wiksell).

Ames, M. (1964a) 'Buddha and the dancing goblins: a theory of magic and religion', *American Anthropologist*, 66, pp. 75–82.

Ames, M. (1964b) 'Sinhalese magical animism and Theravada Buddhism', in E. B. Harper (ed.), *Religion in South Asia* (Seattle: University of Washington Press).

Andreski, S. (1964) *Elements of Comparative Sociology* (London: Weidenfeld & Nicolson).

Arjomand, S. A. (1989) 'The emergence of Islamic political ideologies', in J. A. Beckford and T. Luckmann (eds), *The Changing Face of Religion* (London: Sage).

Aswad, B. (1970) 'Social and ecological aspects in the formation of Islam', in L. Sweet (ed.), *Peoples and Cultures of the Middle East* (Garden City, New York: Natural History Press).

Babb, L. A. (1975) *The Divine Hierarchy in Central India* (New York: Columbia University Press).

Babb, L. A. (1983) 'Destiny and responsibility: karma in popular Hinduism', in C. F. Keyes and E. V. Daniel (eds), *Karma: An Anthropological Inquiry* (Berkeley: University of California Press).

Baity, P. C. (1975) *Religion in a Chinese Town*. Taipei: Asian Folklore and Social Life Monographs, 64.

Barrett, D. B. (1968) *Schism and Renewal in Africa* (Nairobi: Oxford University Press).

Beckford, J. A. (1975) *The Trumpet of Prophecy* (Oxford: Blackwell).

Bellah, R. N. (1964) 'Religious evolution', *American Sociological Review*, 29, pp. 358–74.

Berger, P. L (1963) 'Charisma and religious innovation: the social location of Israelite prophecy', *American Sociological Review*, 28, 6, pp. 940–50.

Berger, P. L. (1973) *The Social Reality of Religion* (Harmondsworth: Penguin).

Berger, P. L. (1987) *The Capitalist Revolution: Fifty Propositions About Prosperity, Equality and Liberty* (Aldershot: Gower).

Berreman, G. D. (1966) 'Caste in cross cultural perspective', in G. De Vos and H. Wagatsuma (eds), *Japan's Invisible Race: Caste in Culture and Personality* (Berkeley: University of California Press).

Berreman, G. D. (1967) 'Caste as a social process', *Southwest Journal of Anthropology*, 23, pp. 351–70.

Best, E. (1984) 'The sociological study of the new testament: promise and peril of a discipline', *Scottish Journal of Theology*, 36, pp. 181–94.

Beyer, P. (1994) *Religion and Globalisation* (London: Sage).

Bokser, B. (1984) *The Origins of the Seder: The Passover Rite and Early Rabbinic Judaism* (Berkeley: University of California Press).

Bourguignon, E. (1966) 'World distribution and patterns of possession states', in R. Prince (ed.), *Trance and Possession States* (Montreal: R. M. Bucke Memorial Society).

Bourguignon, E. (1973) *Religion and Altered States of Consciousness* (Colombus, Ohio: Ohio State University Press).

Bourguignon, E. (1976) *Possession* (San Francisco: Chandler & Sharp).

Brain, J. (1973) 'Ancestors and elders in Africa – further thoughts', *Africa*, 43, 2, pp. 122–33.

Brandfon, F. R. (1981), 'Norman Gottwald on the Tribes of Yahwe', *Journal for the Study of the Old Testament*, 21, pp. 101–10.

Brandon, S. G. F. (1968) *The Trial of Jesus of Nazareth* (New York: Stein & Day).

Brown, P. (1981) *The Cult of the Saints* (London: SCM Press).

Bruce, S. (1990) *A House Divided: Protestantism, Schism and Secularisation* (London: Routledge).

Buchignani, N. L. (1976) 'The Weberian thesis in India', Archives de Sciences Sociales des Religions, 42, pp. 17–33.

Bulmer, R. (1967) 'Why the cassowary is not a bird: a problem of zoological taxonomy among the Karam of the New Guinea Highlands', *Man*, 2, pp. 5–25.

Burridge, K. (1960) *Mambu* (London: Methuen).

Burridge, K. (1969) *New Heaven, New Earth* (Oxford: Blackwell).

Buss, M. J. (1981) 'An anthropological perspective upon prophetic call narratives', *Semeia* 21, pp. 11–30.

Calhoun, C. J. (1980), 'Authority of ancestors: a sociological reconsideration of Fortes' Tallensi in response to Fortes' critics', *Man*, 15, pp. 304–19.

Carroll, M. P. (1978) 'One more time: Leviticus revisited', *Archives européennes de socologie* 19, pp. 339–46.

Carroll, M. P. (1986) *The Cult of the Virgin Mary: Psychological Origins* (Princeton: Princeton University Press).

Carroll, R. P. (1979) *When Prophecy Failed: Cognitive Dissonance in the Prophetic Traditions of the Old Testament* (New York: Seabury).

Carstairs, G. M. (1957) *The Twice Born* (London: Hogarth Press).

Causse, A. (1937) *Du groupe ethnique à la communauté religieuse: le problème sociologique de la religion d'Israel* (Paris: Alcan).

Chakravati, U. (1987) *The Social Dimensions of Early Buddhism* (Delhi: Oxford University Press).

Chang, H. (1980) 'Neo-Confucian moral thought and its modern legacy', *Journal of Asian Studies*, 39, 2, pp. 259–72.

Ch'ien, E. T. (1980) 'The trnasformation of neo-Confucianism as transfromative leverage', *Journal of Asian Studies, 39,2, pp. 255–58*.

Clarke, P. and Byrne, P. (1993) *Religion Defined and Explained* (Basingstoke: Macmillan).

Cohn, B. S. (1959) 'Changing traditions of a low caste', in M. Singer (ed.), *Traditional India: Structure and Change* (Philadelphia: American Folklore Society).

Cohn, N. (1970) *The Pursuit of the Millenium* (St Albans: Paladin).

Cooper, S. (1987) 'The laws of mixture: an anthropological study in Hala-khah', in H. Goldberg (ed.), *Judaism Viewed from Within and from Without* (Albany, New York: State University of New York Press).

Crone, P. (1987) *Meccan Trade and the Rise of Islam* (Princeton: Princeton University Press).

Daniel, S. B. (1983) 'The tool box approach of the Tamil to the issues of moral responsibility and human destiny', in C. F. Keyes and E. V. Daniel (eds), *Karma: An Anthropological Inquiry* (Berkeley: University of California Press).

Davis, K. (1948) *Human Society* (New York: Macmillan).

Davis, N. L. (1971) 'Missed connections: religion and regime', *Journal of Interdisciplinary History*, 1, pp. 381–94.

Dean, K. (1993) *Taoist Ritual and Popular Cults of South East China* (Princeton: Princeton University Press).

Douglas, M. (1963) *The Lele of Kasai* (London: Oxford University Press).

Douglas, M. (1966) *Purity and Danger* (London: Routledge).

Douglas, M. (1970) *Natural Symbols: Explorations in Cosmology* (London: Barrie and Rockliff, The Cresset Press).

Douglas, M. (1975) *Implicit Meanings* (London: Routledge).

Doulas, M. (1993) 'The forbidden animals in Leviticus', *Journal for the Study of the Old Testament*, 59, pp. 3–23.

Dumont, L. (1970a) *Homo Hierarchicus: The Caste System and its Implications* (London: Weidenfeld & Nicolson).

Dumont, L. (1970b) 'World renunciation in Indian religion', *Contributions to Indian Sociology* IV, pp. 33–62.

Durkheim, E. (1915) *The Elementary Forms of the Religious Life* (London: George Allen & Unwin).

Eickelman, D. F. (1967) 'Musaylima: an approach to the social anthropology of seventh century Arabia', *Journal of the Economic and Social History of the Orient*, 10, 1, pp. 17–52.

Eickelman, D. F. (1976) *Moroccan Islam* (Austin and London: University of Texas Press).

Eilberg-Schwartz, H. (1990) *The Savage in Judaism: An Anthropology of Israel-ite Religion and Ancient Judaism* (Bloomington: Indiana University Press).

Eisenstadt, S. N. (1982) 'The axial age: the emergence of transcendental visions and the rise of clerics', *European Journal of Sociology*, 23, pp. 294–314.

Eisenstadt, S. N. (1985) 'This worldly transcendentalism and the structuring of the world: Weber's "Religion of China" and the format of Chinese history and civilization', in A. S. Buss (ed.), *Max Weber in Asian Studies* (Leiden: E. J. Brill).

Eisenstadt, S. N. (1992) *Jewish Civilization: The Jewish Historical Experience in a Comparative Perspective* (Albany, New York: State University of New York Press).

Elliot, J. H. (1981) *A Home for the Homeless: A Sociological Exegesis of 1 Peter, Its Situation and Strategy* (Philadelphia: Fortress Press).

Elliott, J. H. (1986) 'Social scientific criticism of the New Testament and its social world', *Semeia*, 35, pp. 1–33.

Emmet, D. (1956) 'Prophets and their societies', *Journal of the Royal Anthro-pological Insitute*, 86, pp. 13–23.

Engels, F. (1965) *The Peasant War In Germany* (Moscow: Progress Publishers).
Esler, P. F. (1987) *Community and Gospel in Luke – Acts: The Social and Political Motivations of Lucan Theology* (Cambridge: Cambridge University Press).
Evans-Pritchard, E. E. (1937) *Withcraft, Oracles and Magic Among the Azande* (Oxford: Clarendon Press).
Evans-Pritchard, E. E. (1956) *Nuer Religion* (Oxford: Clarendon Press).
Evans-Pritchard, E. E. (1965) *Theories of Primitive Religion* (Oxford: Clarendon Press).
Evers, H. D. (1965) 'Magic and religion in Sinhalese society', *American Anthropologist*, 67, 1, pp. 97–9.
Festinger, L. (1956) *When Prophecy Fails* (New York and London: Harper & Row).
Feuchtwang, S. (1974) 'Domestic and communal worship in Taiwan', in A. P. Wolf (ed.), *Religion and Ritual in Chinese Society* (Stanford, Calif: Stanford University Press).
Feuchtwang, S. (1992) *The Imperial Metaphore: Popular Religion in China* (Routledge: London).
Fischoff, E. (1944) 'The protestant ethic and the spirit of capitalism', *Social Research*, 11, pp. 54–77.
Fortes, M. (1959) *Oedipus and Job in West African Religion* (Cambridge: Cambridge Unversity Press).
Fortes, M. (1961) 'Pietas in ancestor worship', *Journal of the Royal Anthropological Institute*, 91, pp. 166–91.
Fortes, M. (1965) 'Reflections on ancestor worship in Africa', in M. Fortes and G. Dieterlen (eds), *African Systems of Thought* (London: Oxford University Press for International African Institute).
Fortes, M. (1987) 'Custom and conscience', in Idem., *Religion, Morality and the Person* (Cambridge: Cambridge University Press).
Freedman, M. (1967) 'Ancestor worship: two facets of the Chinese case', in M. Freedman (ed.), *Social Organisation: Essays Presented to Raymond Firth* (Chicago: Aldine).
Freedman, M. (1974) 'On the sociological study of Chinese religion', in A. P. Wolf (ed.), *Religion and Ritual in Chinese Society* (Stanford, Calif: Stanford University Press).
Freedman, R. G. (1981) *The Passover Seder: Afikoman in Exile* (Philadelphia: University of Pennsylvania Press).
Freud, S. (1928) *The Future of an Illusion* (London: Hogarth Press).
Freud, S. (1938) *Totem and Tabu* (Harmondsworth: Penguin).
Fulbrook, M. (1978) 'Max Weber's interpretative sociology: A comparison of conception and practice', *British Journal of Sociology*, 29, pp. 71–82.
Fuller, C. J. (1992) *The Camphor Flame* (Princeton: Princeton University Press).
Gager, J. G. (1975) *Kingdom and Community: The Social World of Early Christianity* (Englewood Cliffs, NJ: Prentice Hall).
Garrett, W. R. (1990) 'Reinterpreting the Reformation: a Weberian alternative', in W. H. Swatos (ed.), *Time, Place and Circumstance* (Westport, Conneticut: Greenwood Press).
Garrett, W. R. (1992) 'The ascetic conundrum: The Confucian ethic and Taoism', in W. H. Swatos (ed.), *Twentieth-Century World Religious Movements in Neo-Weberian Perspective* (New York: Edwin Mellen Press).

Geertz, C. (1966) 'Religion as a Cultural System', in M. Banton (ed.), *Anthropological Approaches to the Study of Religion*, ASA Monographs No. 3 (London: Tavistock).

Geertz, C. (1968) *Islam Observed: Religious Development in Morocco and Indonesia* (New Haven, Conn.: Yale University Press).

Gellner, D. (1992) *Monk, Householder and Tantric Priest* (Cambridge: Cambridge University Press).

Gellner, E. (1969) 'A pendulum swing theory of Islam', in R. Robertson (ed.), *Sociology of Religion* (Harmondsworth: Penguin).

Gellner, E. (1981) *Muslim Society* (Cambridge: Cambridge University Press).

Gellner, E. (1992) *Postmodernism, Reason and Religion* (London: Routledge).

George, K. and George, C. H. (1953–5) 'Roman Catholic sainthood and social status', *Journal of Religion*, 5, pp. 33–5.

Gluckman, M. (1972) 'The allocation of responsibility', in idem. (ed.), *Moral Crises: The Allocation of Responsibility* (Manchester: Manchester University Press).

Gold, A. G. (1988) *Fruitful Journeys: The Ways of Rajasthan Pilgrims* (Berkeley: University of California Press).

Goldstein, S. and Goldscheider, C. (1968) *Jewish Americans: Three Generations in a Jewish Community* (Englewood Cliffs, NJ: Prentice Hall).

Gombrich, R. F. (1971) *Precept and Practice* (Oxford: Clarendon Press).

Gombrich, R. F. (1972) 'Buddhsim and society', *Modern Asian Studies*, 6, 3, pp. 483–96.

Gombrich, R. F. (1989) *Theravada Buddhism* (London: Routledge).

Gomm, R. (1975) 'Bargaining from weakness', *Man*, New Series, 10, 4, pp. 530–43.

Gottwald, N. K. (1979) *The Tribes of Yahwe: A Sociology of Liberated Israel 1250–1000 BC* (Maryknoll, NY: Orbis).

Gough, E. K. (1960) 'Caste in a Tanjore village', in E. R. Leach (ed.), *Aspects of Caste in South India, Ceylon and NW Pakistan* (Cambridge: Cambridge University Press).

Grabbe, L. L. (1989) 'The social setting of early Apocalypticism', *Journal for the Study of the Pseudepigrapha*, 4, pp. 27–47.

Greenbaum, L. (1973) 'Societal correlates of possession trance in sub-Saharan Africa', in E. Bouguignon (ed.), *Religion, Altered States of Consciouness and Social Change* (Columbus, Ohio: Ohio State University Press).

Greyerz, K. von (1993) 'Biographical evidence on predestination, covenant and special providence', in H. Lehmann and G. Roth (eds), *Weber's Protestant Ethic: Origins, Evidence, Contexts* (Cambridge: Cambridge University Press).

Hahn, H. F. (1970) *Old Testament in Modern Research* (Philadelphia: Fortress Press).

Halliday, F. (1994) 'The politics of Islamic fundamentalism: Iran, Tunisia and the challenge of the secular state', in A. S. Ahmed and D. Hastings (eds), *Islam, Globalisation and Post-Modernity* (London: Routledge).

Hamilton, M. B. (1995) *The Sociology of Religion: Theoretical and Comparative Perspectives* (London: Routledge).

Hanson, P. (1975) *The Dawn of Apocalyptic* (Philadelphia: Fortress Press).

Harootunian, H. D. (1980) 'Metzger's predicament', *Journal of Asian Studies*, 39, 2, pp. 245–54.

Harper, E. B. (1959) 'A Hindu village pantheon', *South West Journal of Anthropology*, 15, 3, pp. 227–34.

Harper, E. B. (ed.) (1964) *Religion in South Asia* (Seattle: University of Washington Press).

Hepworth, W. and Turner, B. S. (1982) *Confession: Studies in Deviance and Religion* (London: Routledge).

Hill, C. (1961), 'Protestantism and the rise of capitalism', in F. J. Fisher (ed.), *Essays in the Economic and Social History of Tudor and Stuart England in Honour of R. H. Tawney* (Cambridge: Cambridge University Press).

Hill, C. (1963) *The Century of Revolution 1603–1714* (Edinburgh: Nelson).

Hill, C. (1966) *Society and Puritanism in Pre-Revolutionary England* (London: Secker & Warburg).

Holmberg, B. (1990) *Sociology and the New Testament: An Appraisal* (Minneapolis: Fortress Press).

Horsley, R. A. (1987) *Jesus and the Spiral of Violence: Popular Jewish Resistance in Roman Palestine* (San Francisco: Harper & Row).

Horsley, R. A. (1989) *Sociology and the Jesus Movement* (New York: Crossroad Press).

Horton, R. (1971) 'African conversion', *Africa*, 41, 2, pp. 85–108.

Horton, R. (1975) 'On the rationality of conversion', *Africa* 43, 3, pp. 373–99 and 219–35.

Horton, R. (1993) *Patterns of Thought in Africa and the West: Essays on Magic, Religion and Science* (Cambridge: Cambridge University Press).

Houtart, F. (1977) 'Theravada Buddhism and political power: construction and destruction of its ideological function', *Social Compass*, 24, 2/3, pp. 207–46.

Hsu, F. L. K. (1949) *Under the Ancestors' Shadow* (London: Routledge).

Hsu, F. L. K. (1963) *Clan, Caste and Club* (Princeton, NJ: Princeton University Press).

Jackson, M. (1975) 'The resurrection belief of the earliest church: a response to the failure of prophecy', *Journal of Religion*, 55, pp. 415–25.

Jacobson, D. (1982) *The Story of the Stories: The Chosen People and its God* (London: Secker and Warburg).

Janelli, R. L. and Janelli, D. Y. (1982) *Ancestor Worship and Korean Society* (Stanford, Calif.: Stanford University Press).

Jaspers, K. (1949) *Vom Ursprung und Zeit der Geschichte* (Munich: R. Piper).

Jones, R. L. (1976) 'Spirit possession in Nepal', in J. T. Hitchcock and R. L. Jones (eds), *Spirit Possession in the Nepal Himalayas* (Warminster: Aris & Phillips).

Jordan, D. K. (1972) *Gods, Ghosts and Ancestors* (Berkeley: University of California Press).

Judge, E. A. (1960) *The Social Pattern of the Christian Groups in the First Century* (London: Tyndale Press).

Judge, E. A. (1960–61) 'The early Christians as a scholastic community', *Journal of Religious History*, 1, pp. 4–15 and 125–37.

Kakar, S. (1978) *The Inner World: A Psycho-analytic study of Childhood and Society in India* (Delhi: Oxford University Press).

Kalberg, S. (1985) 'The role of ideal interests in Max Weber's comparative historical sociology', in R. J. Antonio and R. M. Glassman (eds), *A Max Weber Dialogue* (Lawrence: University Press of Kansas).

Katz, E. (1973) 'Culture and communication in Israel: the transformation of tradition', *The Jewish Journal of Sociology* 15, 1, pp. 5–21.

Kautsky, K. (1925) *The Foundations of Christianity* (London: Orbach and Chambers).

Kautsky, K. (1988) *The Materialist Conception of History*, abridged and translated by R. Meyer and J. H. Kautsky (New Haven, Conn.: Yale University Press).

Kepel, G. (1994) *The Revenge of God* (Oxford: Polity).

Kerner, K. (1976) 'The malevolent ancestor: ancestral influence in a Japanese religious sect', in W. H. Newell (ed.), *Ancestors* (The Hague: Mouton).

Keyes, C. F. (1983) 'Merit transference in the Kammic theory of popular Theravada Buddhism' in C. F. Keyes and E. V. Daniel (eds), *Karma: An Anthropological Inquiry* (Berkeley: University of California Press).

Kimbrough S. T. Jr. (1969) 'Une conception sociologique de la religion d'Israel', *Revue d'Histoire et de Philosophie Religieuses*, 49, pp. 313–30.

Kimbrough S. T. Jr. (1972) 'A non-Weberian sociological approach to Israelite religion', *Journal of Near Eastern Studies*, 31, pp. 195–202.

Kimbrough, S. T. Jr. (1978) *Israelite Religion in Sociological Perspective* (Wiesbaden: Harrassowitz).

Kolenda, P. M. (1964) 'Religious anxiety and Hindu fate', in E. B. Harper (ed.), *Religion in South Asia* (Seattle: University of Washington Press).

Kopytoff, I. (1971) 'Ancestors as elders in Africa', *Africa*, 41, 2, pp. 129–42.

Kosambi, D. D. (1965) *The Culture and Civilisation of Ancient India in Historical Outline* (Routledge: London).

Krausz, E. (1977) 'The religious factors in Jewish identity', *International Social Science Journal*, 29, pp. 250–60.

Lang, B. (1983) *Monotheism and the Prophetic Minority: An Essay in Biblical History and Sociology* (Sheffield: Almond Press).

Lapidus, I. M. (1988) *A History of Islamic Societies* (Cambridge: Cambridge University Press).

Lazerwitz, B. (1973) 'Religious identification and its ethnic correlates: a multivariate model', *Social Forces* 52, pp. 204–22.

Lemche, N. P. (1985) *Early Israel: Anthropological and Historical Studies on the Early Israelite Society before the Monarchy Supplements to Vitus Testamentum.*

Lessnoff, M. H. (1994) *The Spirit of Capitalism and the Protestant Ethic: An Enquiry into the Weber thesis* (Aldershot: Edward Elgar).

Lewis, I. M. (1971) *Ecstatic Religion* (Harmondsworth: Penguin).

Ling, T. (1968) *A History of Religion East and West* (London: Macmillan).

Ling, T. (1976) *The Buddha* (Harmondsworth: Penguin).

Lofland, J. (1977) ' "Becoming a world saver" revisited', in J. T. Richardson (ed.), *Conversion Careers: In and Out of the New Religions* (London: Sage).

Long, B. O. (1981) 'Social dimensions of prophetic conflict', *Semeia*, 21, pp. 31–53.

Lowy, M. (1989) 'Weber against Marx: the polemic with historical materialism in the Protestant ethic', *Science and Society* 53, pp. 71–83.

Luckmann, T. (1967) *The Invisible Religion* (New York: Macmillan).

Luethy, H. (1964) 'Once again, Calvinism and capitalism', *Encounter*, 22, pp. 26–38.

MacDonald, M. Y. (1988) *The Pauline Churches: A Socio-Historical Study of Institutionalization in the Pauline and Deutero-Pauline Writings* (Cambridge: Cambridge University Press).

Macfarlane, A. (1970) *Witchcraft in Tudor and Stuart England* (London: Routledge).

Mack, B. L. (1988) *A Myth of Innocence: Mark and Christian Origins* (Philadelphia: Fortress Press).

MacKinnon, M. H. (1988a) 'Part 1: Calvinism and the infallible assurance of grace: the Weber thesis reconsidered', *British Journal of Sociology*, 39, 2, pp. 143–77.

MacKinnon, M. H. (1988b) 'Part 2: Weber's exploration of Calvinism: the undiscovered provenance of capitalism', *British Journal of Sociology*, 39, 2, pp. 178–210.

MacKinnon, M. H. (1993) 'The longevity of the thesis: a critique of the critics', in H. Lehmann and G. Roth (eds), *Weber's Protestant Ethic: Origins, Evidence, Contexts* (Cambridge: Cambridge University Press).

Macklin, J. (1977) 'A Connecticut Yankee in Summer Land', in V. Crapanzano and V. Garrison (eds), *Case Studies in Spirit Possession* (New York: John Wiley).

Malherbe, A. (1977) *Social Aspects of Early Christianity* (Baton Rouge: Louisiana State University Press).

Malina, B.J. (1984) 'Jesus as Charismatic leader', *Biblical Theology Bulletin*, 14, pp. 55–62.

Malinowski, B. (1936) *The Foundation of Faith and Morals* (London: Oxford University Press).

Malinowski, B. (1974) *Magic, Science and Religion* (London: Souvenir Press).

Maloney, C. (1975) 'Religious beliefs and social hierarchy in Tamil Nadu, India', *American Ethnologist*, 2, pp. 169–91.

Mandelbaum, D. (1966) 'Transcendental and pragmatic aspects of religion', *American Anthropologist*, 68, pp. 1174–91.

Mann, M. (1986) *The Sources of Social Power: A History of Power from the Beginning to A. D. 1760* (Cambridge: Cambridge University Press).

Marett, R. R. (1914) *The Threshold of Religion* (London: Methuen).

Marriott, M. (1955) 'Little communities in an indigenous civilization', in M. Marriott (ed.), *Village India* (Chicago and London: University of Chicago Press).

Marshall, G. (1980) *Presbyteries and Profits: Calvinism and the Development of Capitalism in Scotland, 1560–1707* (Oxford: Clarendon Press).

Marshall, G. (1982) *In Search of the Spirit of Capitalism* (London: Hutchinson).

Marwick, M. G. (1965a) 'Some problems in the sociology of sorcery and witchcraft', in M. Fortes and G. Dieterlen (eds), *African Systems of Thought* (London: Oxford University Press for International African Institute).

Marwick, M. G. (1965b) *Sorcery in its Social Setting* (Manchester: Manchester University Press).

Marx, K. and Engels, F. (1957) *On Religion* (Moscow: Progress Publishers).

McKnight, J. D. (1967) 'Extra-descent group ancestor cults in African societies', *Africa*, 37, pp. 1–21.

Meeks, W. A. (1982) 'The social context of Pauline theology', *Interpretation*, 36, pp. 266–77.

260 *Bibliography*

Meeks, W. A. (1983) *The First Urban Christians: A Social Description of Pauline Christianity* (New Haven, Conn.: Yale University Press).

Meeks, W. A. (1987) *The Moral World of the First Christians* (London: SPCK).

Mendelson, E. M. (1975) *Sangha and State in Burma* (Ithaca: Cornell University Press).

Mendonsa, E. L. (1976) 'Elders, office-holders and ancestors among the Sisala of Northern Ghana', *Africa*, 46, 1, pp. 56–65.

Metzger, T. A. (1977) *Escape from Predicament: Neo-Confucianism and China's Evolving Political Culture* (New York: Columbia University Press).

Middleton, J. F. M. (1960) *Lugbara Religion: Ritual and Authority Among an East African People* (London: Oxford University Press).

Middleton, J. F. M. and Winter, E. J. (eds) (1963) *Witchcraft and Sorcery in East Africa* (London: Routledge).

Mitchell, J. C. (1956) *The Yao Village* (Manchester: Manchester University Press).

Milner, M. (1994) *Status and Sacredness: A General Theory of Status Relations and an Analysis of Indian Culture* (New York: Oxford University Press).

Moaddel, M. (1989) 'State autonomy and class conflict in the Reformation (Comment on Wuthnow)', *American Sociological Review*, 54, pp. 472–4.

Moffatt, M. (1979) 'Harijan religion: consensus at the bottom of caste', *American Ethnologist*, 6, pp. 244–60.

Molloy, S. (1980) 'Max Weber and the religions of China', *British Journal of Sociology*, 31, 3, pp. 377–400.

Morris, B. (1987) *Anthropological Studies of Religion* (Cambridge: Cambridge University Press).

Morton, A. (1977) 'Davrit: competition and integration in an Ethiopian waqabi cult group', in V. Crapanzano and V. Garrison (eds), *Case Studies in Spirit Possession* (New York: John Wiley).

Nadel, S. F. (1954) *Nupe Religion* (London: Routledge).

Nevaskar, B. (1971) *Capitalists Without Capitalism* (Westport, Conn.: Greenwood Press).

Newell, W. H. (ed.) (1976) *Ancestors* (The Hague: Mouton).

Nielsen, D. A. (1990) 'Max Weber and the sociology of early Christianity', in W. H. Swatos (ed.), *Time, Place and Circumstance* (Westport, Conn.: Greenwood Press).

Obeyesekere, G. (1963) 'The Great Tradition and the Little Tradition in the perspective of Sinhalese Buddhism', *Journal of Asian Studies*, 22, 2, pp. 139–53.

Obeyesekere, G. (1966) 'The Buddhist pantheon in Ceylon and its extensions', in M. Nash (ed.), *Anthropological Studies in Theravada Buddhism* (Yale University South-East Asia Studies. Cultural Report Series No. 13).

Obeyesekere, G. (1968) 'Theodicy, sin and salvation in a sociology of Buddhism', in E. Leach (ed.), *Dialectic in Practical Religion* (Cambridge: Cambridge University Press).

Obeyesekere, G. (1977) 'Psychological exegesis of a case of spirit possession in Sri Lanka', in V. Crapanzano and V. Garrison (eds), *Case Studies in Spirit Possession* (New York: John Wiley).

Obeyesekere, G. (1980) 'Rebirth eschatology and its transformations', in W. O'Flaherty (ed.), *Karma and Rebirth in Classical Indian Traditions* (Berkeley: University of California Press).

Obeyesekere, G. (1984) *The Cult of the Goddess Pattini* (Chicago: Chicago University Press).

O'Dea T. (1966) *The Sociology of Religion* (Englewood Cliffs, NJ: Prentice Hall).

O'Toole, R. (1984) *Religion: Classic Sociological Approaches* (Toronto: McGraw-Hill Ryerson).

Ozment, S. E. (1975) *The Reformation in the Cities: The Appeal of Protestantism to Sixteenth-Century Germany and Switzerland* (New Haven, Conn.: Yale University Press).

Parsons, T. (1949) *The Structure of Social Action* (New York: Free Press).

Parsons, T. (1965) 'Introduction', in M. Weber, *The Sociology of Religon* (London: Methuen).

Petersen D. L. (1979) 'Max Weber and the sociological study of ancient Israel', in H. M. Johnson (ed.), *Religious Change and Continuity* (San Francisco: Jossey Bass).

Pressel, E. (1973) 'Umbanda in São Paulo: religious innovation in a developing society', in E. Bourguignon (ed.), *Altered States of Consciousness and Social Change* (Columbus, Ohio: Ohio State University Press).

Preus, J. S. (1987) *Explaining Religion: Criticism and Theory from Bodin to Freud* (New Haven: Yale University Press).

Radcliffe-Brown, A. R. (1952) 'Religion and Society', in idem, *Structure and Function in Primitive Society* (London: Cohen & West).

Redfield, R. and Singer M. B. (1954) 'The cultural role of cities', *Economic Development and Cultural Change*, 3, pp. 53–73.

Redfield, R. (1956) *Peasant Society and Culture* (Chicago: University of Chicago Press).

Richter, P. J. (1984) 'Recent sociological approaches to the study of the New Testament', *Religion*, 14, pp. 77–90.

Robertson, R. (1970) *The Sociological Interpretation of Religion* (Oxford: Blackwell).

Robertson, R. (1985) 'The sacred and the world system.' in P. E. Hammond, (ed.), *The Sacred in a Secular Age* (Berkeley: University of California Press).

Robertson, R. and Chirico, J. (1985) 'Humanity, globalisation and worldwide religious resurgence: a theoretical explanation', *Sociological Analysis*, 46, 3, pp. 219–42.

Rogerson, J. W. (1990) 'Anthropology and the Old Testament', in R. E. Clements (ed.), *The World of Ancient Israel: Social, Anthropological and Political Perspectives* (Cambridge: Cambridge University Press).

Rohrbaugh, R.L. (1984) 'Methodological considerations in the debate over the social class status of early Christians', *Journal of the American Academy of Religion*, 52, pp. 519–46.

Rohrbaugh, R. L. (1987) 'Social location of thought as a heuristic construct in the New Testament study', *Journal for the Study of the New Testament*, 30, pp. 103–19.

Rowland, C. (1985) 'Reading the New Testament sociologically', *Theology* 88, pp. 358–64.

Ryan, B. (1958) *Sinhalese Village* (Coral Gables, Fl.: University of Miami Press).

Samuelsson, K. (1961) *Religion and Economic Action* (Stockholm: Scandinavian University Books).

Sangren, P. S. (1983) 'Female gender in Chinese religious symbols: Kuan Yin, Ma Tsu and the Eternal Mother', *Signs*, 9, pp. 4–25.

Sangren, P. S. (1984) 'Great traditions and little traditions reconsidered: the question of cultural integration in China', *Journal of Chinese Studies*, 1, pp. 1–24.

Sangren, P. S. (1987) *History and Magical Power in a Chinese Community* (Stanford, Calif.: Stanford University Press).

Saunders, L. W. (1977) 'Variants in Zar experience in an Egyptian village', in V. Crapanzano and V. Garrison (eds), *Case Studies in Spirit Possession* (New York: John Wiley).

Schwartz, B. I. (1975) 'The age of transcendence.' *Deadalus*, Spring, pp. 1–7.

Schonfield, H. J. (1974) *The Pentecost Revolution: The Story of the Jesus Party in Israel, A.D. 36–66* (London: MacDonald).

Scroggs, R. (1975) 'The earliest Christian communities as sectarian movements', in *Christianity, Judaism and other Greco-Roman Cults: Studies for Morton Smith at Sixty*, vol 2. (Leiden: E. J. Brill).

Scroggs, R. (1980) 'The sociological interpretation of the new testament: the present state of research', *New Testament Studies*, 26, pp. 164–79.

Sharma, R. S. (1983) *Material Culture and Social Formation in Ancient India* (Delhi: Macmillan).

Sharma, U. M. (1970) 'The problem of village Hinduism: fragmentation and integration', *Contributions to Indian Sociology*, New Series, 4, pp. 1–21.

Sharma, U. M. (1973) 'Theodicy and the doctrine of Karma', *Man*, 8, pp. 347–64.

Sharot, S. (1976) *Judaism: A Sociology* (New York: Holmes & Meier).

Sharot, S. (1982) *Messianism, Mysticism and Magic: A Sociological Analysis of Jewish Religious Movements* (Chapel Hill: University of North Carolina Press).

Sharot, S. (1991) 'Judaism and the secularisation debate', *Sociological Analysis*, 52, pp. 255–75.

Shmueli, E. (1960) 'The novelties of the Bible and the problem of theodicy in Max Weber's Ancient Judaism', *Jewish Quarterly Review*, 60, pp. 172–82.

Shmueli, E. (1968) 'The "pariah people" and its "charismatic leadership": a re-evaluation of Max Weber's "Ancient Judaism"', *Proceedings of the Academy for Jewish Research*, 36, pp. 167–247.

Sklare, M. (1971) *America's Jews* (New York: Random House).

Smart, N. (1971) *The Religious Experience of Mankind* (London: Fontana).

Smith, D. H. (1974) *Confucius* (St Albans: Paladin).

Smith, D. L. (1989) *The Religion of the Landless: the Social Context of the Babylonian Exile* (Bloomington, Indiana: Meyer Stone Books).

Smith, H. (1970) 'Transcendence in traditional China', in J. T. C. Liu and W. Tu (eds), *Traditional China* (Englewood Cliffs: Prentice Hall).

Smith, J. Z. (1978) 'Too much Kingdom, too little community', *Zygon*, 13, pp. 123–30.

Smith, M. (1971) *Palestinian Parties and Politics that Shaped the Old Testament* (New York: Columbia University Press).

Smith, R. H. (1983) 'Were the early Christians middle class? A sociological analysis of the New Testament', in N. K. Gottwald (ed.), *The Bible and Liberation: Political and Social Hermenentics* (London: Society for the Promulgation of Christian Knowledge).

Smith, R. J. (1974) *Ancestor Worship in Contemporary Japan* (Stanford, Calif.: Stanford University Press).

Snow, D. A. and Machalek, R. (1982) 'On the presumed fragility of unconventional beliefs', *Journal for the Scientific Study of Religion*, 21, 1, pp. 15–26.

Southwold, M. (1983) *Buddhism in Life: The Anthropological Study of Religion and the Sinhalese Practice of Buddhism* (Manchester: Manchester University Press).

Spiro, M. E. (1965) 'Religious systems as culturally constituted defence mechanisms', in M. Spiro (ed.), *Context and Meaning in Cultural Anthropology* (Glencoe: Free Press).

Spiro, M. E. (1971) *Buddhism and Society* (London: Allen and Unwin).

Spiro, M. E. (1978) *Burmese Supernaturalism* (Philadelphia: Institute for the Study of Human Issues).

Srinivas, M. N. (1952) *Religion and Society Among the Coorgs of South India* (London: Oxford University Press).

Stark, R. (1986) 'Jewish conversion and the rise of Christianity: rethinking the received wisdom', *Society of Biblical Literature Seminar Papers*, pp. 314–29. (Atlanta: Scholars Press).

Stark, R. and Bainbridge, W. S. (1980) 'Towards a theory of religion: religious committment', *Journal for the Scientific Study of Religion*, 19, 2, pp. 114–28.

Stark, R. and Bainbridge, W. S. (1987) *A Theory of Religion* (New York: Lang).

Steinberg, S. (1975) 'The anatomy of Jewish identification: a historical and theoretical view', *Review of Religious Research*, 7, 1, pp. 1–9.

Stowers, S. (1985) 'The social sciences and the study of early Christianity' in W. S. Green (ed.), *Approaches to Ancient Judaism*, Vol 5, Studies in Judaism in its Greco-Roman Context (Atlanta: Scholars Press for Brown University).

Swanson, G. (1967) *Religion and Regime* (Ann Arbor: University of Michigan Press).

Talmon, Y. (1962) 'The pursuit of the millenium: the relation between religion and social change', *Archives Européennes de Sociologie*, 3, pp. 125–48.

Talmon, Y. (1966) 'Millenial movements', *Archives Européennes de Sociologie*, 7, pp. 159–200.

Tambiah, S. J. (1968) 'The ideology of merit and the social correlates of Buddhism in a Thai village', in E. Leach (ed.), *Dialectic in Practical Religion* (Cambridge: Cambridge Universiy Press).

Tambiah, S. J. (1969) 'Animals are good to think and good to prohibit', *Ethnology*, 7, pp. 423–59.

Tambiah, S. J. (1970) *Buddhism and the Spirit Cults of North East Thailand* (Cambridge: Cambridge University Press).

Tambiah, S. J. (1976) *World Conqueror, World Renouncer* (Cambridge: Cambridge University Press).

Tawney, R. H. (1938) *Religion and the Rise of Capitalism* (Harmondsworth: Penguin).

Tenbruck, F. (1980) 'The problem of thematic unity in the works of Max Weber', *British Journal of Sociology*, 31, 3, pp. 316–51.

Tentler, T. N. (1974) 'The *summa* for confessors as an instrument for social control', in C. Trinkaus and H. A. Oberman (eds), *The Pursuit of Holiness in Late Medieval and Renaissance Religion* (Leiden: E. J. Brill).

Theissen, G. (1975) 'The sociological interpretation of religious traditions: its methodological problems as exemplified in early Christianity', in N. K. Gottwald, *The Bible and Liberation* (London: Society for the Promulgation of Christian Knowledge).

Theissen, G. (1978) *The First Followers of Jesus: A Sociological Analysis of the Earliest Christianity* (London: SCM Press).

Theissen, G. (1982) *The Social Setting of Pauline Christianity* (Edinburgh: T. and T. Clark).

Theissen, G. (1992) *Social Reality and the Early Christians: Theology, Ethics and the World of the New Testament* (Minneapolis: Fortress Press).

Thomas, K. (1973) *Religion and the Decline of Magic* (Harmondsworth: Penguin).

Tidball, D. (1985) *The Social Context of the New Testament* (Grand Rapids: Zondervan).

Trevor-Roper, H. (1967) *Religion, the Reformation and Social Change*, 2nd edn. (London: Macmillan).

Tsunetomo, Y. (1979) *Hagakure* (Tokyo: Kadansha International).

Turner, B. S. (1974) *Weber and Islam* (London: Routledge).

Turner, B. S. (1976) 'Origins and traditions in Islam and Christianity', *Religion*, 6, pp. 13–30.

Turner, B. S. (1977) 'Confession and social structure', *Annual Review of the Social Sciences of Religion*, 1, pp. 2–58.

Turner, B. S. (1991) 'Politics and culture in Islamic globalism', in W. Garrett and R. Robertson (eds), *Religion and the Global Search for Order* (New York: Paragon).

Turner, V. W. (1964) 'Withcraft and sorcery: taxonomy versus dynamics', *Africa*, 34, 4, pp. 314–25.

Turner, V. W. (1965) 'Ritual symbolism among the Ndembu', in M. Fortes and G. Dieterlen (eds), *African Systems of Thought* (Oxford: Oxford University Press for International African Institute).

Turner, V. W. (1968) *The Drums of Afflication* (Oxford: Clarendon Press and International African Institute).

Van der Veer, P. (1988) *Gods on Earth: The Management of Religious Experience and Identity in a North Indian Pilgrimage Centre* (London: Athlone).

Wadley, S. S. (1975) *Shakti: Power in the Conceptual Structure of Karimpur Religion* (Chicago: University of Chicago, Department of Anthropology).

Wadley, S. S. and Derr, B. W. (1989) 'Eating sins in Karimpur', *Contributions to Indian Sociology*, New Series, 23, pp. 131–48.

Walker, S. S. (1972) *Ceremonial Spirit Possession in Africa and Afro-America* (Leiden: E. J. Brill).

Wallace, A. F. C. (1966) *Religion: An Anthroplogical View* (New York: Random House).

Walzer, M. (1963) 'Puritanism as a revolutionary ideology', *History and Theory*, 3, pp. 59–90.

Warner, R. S. (1970) 'The role of religious ideas and the use of models in Max Weber's comparative studies of non-capitalist societies', *Journal of Economic History*, 30, pp. 74–99.

Watson, F. (1986) *Paul, Judaism and the Gentiles* (Cambridge: Cambridge University Press).

Watson, J. L. (1976) 'Anthropological analyses of Chinese religion', *The China Quarterly*, 66, June, pp. 355–64.

Watt, W. M. (1961) *Islam and the Integration of Society* (London: Routledge).

Weber, M. (1930) *The Protestant Ethic and the Spirit of Capitalism* (London: Allen & Unwin).

Weber, M. (1951) *The Religion of China* (New York: Free Press).

Weber, M. (1952) *Ancient Judaism* (New York: Free Press).

Weber, M. (1958) *The Religions of India* (New York: Free Press).

Weber, M. (1961) *General Economic History* (New York: Collier).

Weber, M. (1965) *The Sociology of Religion* (London: Methuen).

Weber, M. (1968) *Economy and Society: An Outline of Interpretive Sociology*, ed. G. Roth and C. Wittich (New York: Bedminster Press).

Weber, M. (1970a) 'The protestant sects and the spirit of capitalism', in H. Gerth and C. W. Mills (eds), *From Max Weber: Essays in Social Theory* (London: Routledge).

Weber M. (1970b) 'Religious rejections of the world and their directions', in H. Gerth and C. W. Mills (eds), *From Max Weber: Essays in Social Theory* (London: Routledge).

Weber, M. (1970c) 'The social psychology of the world religions', in H. Gerth and C. W. Mills (eds), *From Max Weber: Essays in Social Theory* (London: Routledge).

Weller, R. (1987) *Unities and Diversities in Chinese Religion: Aspects of Chinese Sectarianism in Taiwan* (London: Macmillan).

Williams, J. (1987) *Conceptual Change and Religious Practice* (Aldershot: Avebury).

Williams, J. G. (1969) 'The social location of Israelite prophecy', *Journal of the American Academy of Religion*, 37, pp. 153–65.

Wilson, B. (1961) *Sects and Society* (London: Heinemann).

Wilson, B. (1967) *Patterns of Sectarianism* (London: Heinemann).

Wilson, B. (1970) *Religious Sects* (London: Weidenfeld Nicolson).

Wilson, B. (1975) *Magic and the Millenium* (St Albans: Paladin).

Wilson, B. (1976) *Contemporary Transformations of Religion* (London: Oxford University Press).

Wilson, B. (1990) *The Social Sources of Sectarianism* (Oxford: Clarendon Press).

Wilson, M. (1951) *Good Company* (London: Oxford University Press).

Wilson, P. (1967) 'Status ambiguity and spirit possession', *Man*, 2, 3, pp. 366–78.

Wilson, R. (1980) *Prophecy and Society in Ancient Israel* (Philadelphia: Fortress Press).

Wolf, A. P. (1974a) 'Introduction', in Idem. (ed.), *Religion and Ritual in Chinese Society* (Stanford, Calif: Stanford University Press).

Wolf, A. P. (1974b) 'Gods, ghosts and ancestors', in A. P. Wolf (ed.), *Ritual and Religion in Chinese Society* (Stanford, Calif: Stanford University Press).

Wolf, E. (1951) 'The social organisation of Mecca and the origins of Islam', *Southwestern Journal of Anthropology*, 7, 4, pp. 329–56.

Worsley, P. (1970) *The Trumpet Shall Sound* (St Albans: Paladin).

Wuthnow, R. (1985) 'State structures and ideological outcomes', *American Sociological Review*, 50, pp. 799–821.

Yang, C. K. (1951) 'Introduction', in M. Weber, *The Religions of China* (New York: Free Press).

Yang, C. K. (1957) 'The functional relationship between Confucian thought and Chinese religion', in J. K. Fairbank (ed.), *Chinese Thought and Institutions* (Chicago: University of Chicago Press).

Yang, C. K. (1961) *Relgion in Chinese Society* (Berkeley: University of California Press).

Yinger, J. M. (1957) *Religion, Society and the Individual* (New York: Macmillan).

Yinger, J. M. (1970) *The Scientific Study of Religion* (London: Routledge).

Yonemura, S. (1976) 'Dozuku and ancestor worship in Japan', in W. H. Newell (ed.), *Ancestors* (The Hague and Paris: Mouton).

Zaret, D. (1993) 'The use and abuse of textual data', in H. Lehmann and G. Roth (eds), *Weber's Protestant Ethic: Origins, Evidence, Contexts* (Cambridge: Cambridge University Press).

Zeitlin, I. M. (1988) *Jesus and the Judism of his Time* (Cambridge: Polity).

Zubaida, S. (1972) 'Economic and political activism in Islam', *Economy and Society*, 1, pp. 308–38.

Zubaida, S. (1995) 'Is there a Muslim society?: Ernest Gellner's sociology of Islam', *Economy and Society*, 24, 2, pp. 151–88.

Zuckerman-Bareli, C. (1975) 'The religious factor in opinion formation among Israeli youth', in S. Poll and E. Krausz (eds), *On Ethnic and Religious Diversity in Israel* (Ramat-Gan Institute for the Study of Ethnic and Religious Groups. Bar Han University).

Index